D0593654

"Scott Shay has written an engaging personal account of Jewish history, connecting his and his father's experiences into a larger narrative which starts millennia ago. This book should be required reading for any high school or college student interested in Jewish heritage who is looking for insight into how the Jewish journey relates to some of the most hot button issues of today."

— Simone Friedman, Head of Philanthropy and Impact Investment, EJF Philanthropies

"Scott Shay has once again written a well-researched and compelling book on a scourge of our time: the conspiracy theory. He defines what such theories are, demonstrates their ugly reach, and describes their stubborn persistence in his own search for an abiding truth."

— Dr. Erica Brown, Director of the Mayberg Center for Jewish Education and Leadership, The George Washington University

"This book is a wake-up call to anyone, in the US or the UK, who cares about the state of higher education. The book is painstakingly researched and documents anti-Semitic conspiracy theories from both the far right and the far left. It's not an easy read but is sadly an important one. Shay has written a tough love letter to Northwestern University and to all of academia."

— Rabbi Shoshana Boyd Gelfand, London, UK

"The education of the next generation is vital in the fight against anti-Semitism, for history teaches us that the Jewish people have always been the 'canary in the coal mine,' whose mistreatment inevitably indicates broader societal danger coming to other minorities. Scott Shay takes a courageous look at what is being taught in our universities today and its dangerous consequences. Shay brilliantly explains what we can do to change the narrative now. With it all, Shay has written a love letter to Northwestern University, but make no mistake, *Conspiracy U* has some tough love."

— Bishop Robert Stearns, Executive Director, Eagles' Wings

"Though the assault on truth and the proliferation of conspiracy theories are not new in the long course of history, the unique issues on today's college campuses require thoughtful analysis. Scott Shay's new book *Conspiracy U* provides that and more, offering prescriptions for tackling this challenge that speaks to who we are as a people and who we will be as today's students become tomorrow's leaders."

— Rabbi Rick Jacobs, President, Union for Reform Judaism

"This is a thoughtful book which I recommend, while noting my disagreement with some of its conclusions. Scott Shay presents extensive evidence of increasing anti-Semitic attacks in America. While I believe that the overall situation is less ominous than he does—I strongly differ from his discussion of Jews and 'whiteness'—those committed to combating prejudice in America will benefit from understanding why he, as a Jew who has worked hard to promote mutual respect among all sectors of our society, has come to feel as he does."

— Former Congressman Barney Frank, D-MA

"*Conspiracy U* is an urgent book that appears just in time. Full of facts and history, the book argues unironically that, without facts and history, a theory quickly becomes a conspiracy theory—and that conspiracy theories about the Jews have devastating consequences, not just for the Jews. Shay's argument is unimpeachable, and readers will be armed with a complex understanding of Jewish history and Zionism, conspiracy theories and their political positioning, and the illiberal and dangerous trajectory of the American academy. This is a fight that liberals and progressives must take on ourselves, and *Conspiracy U* will be instructive for all of us."

— Amanda Berman, Founder and Executive Director of the
   Zioness Movement

"Scott Shay has written a book that is compelling and telling. Shay is a much-needed referee calling fouls on professors who aren't playing by the rules."

— Walt "Clyde" Frazier, NBA Legend and Basketball Hall of
   Fame Member

"Conspiracy theories threaten our society and civil discourse as they undermine logic and reason. In this persuasive book, Shay builds a case against the foundational conspiracy theories underlying anti-Semitism and anti-Zionism. He unfolds their arguments to first understand and then discredit this dysfunction and evil. Written as a love story for an alma mater not living up to its motto, the author meticulously dissects the key arguments of the loudest anti-Semites in the United States, some of whom, are, sadly, tenured at that same institution. Written for a general audience, this book unmasks the spurious claims of anti-Semites in academia. As Shay's father put it, 'crazy, worthless, stupid, made-up tales bring out the demons in susceptible, unthinking people.' After reading this book, you'd be *meshuganah* not to think about the dangerous nature of anti-Semitism and why it is a threat to all of us."

— Congressman Patrick McHenry, North Carolina, 10th District

"Scott Shay has written a courageous and compelling critique of the ways that anti-Semitic conspiracy theories have taken root in parts of academia. While focusing on Northwestern University—the beloved alma mater of us both—he could just as well have written about any major American campus. The liberal spirit, indispensable to the modern Jewish success story, is under sustained assault from right and left. This book is a powerful guide to helping us push back."
— Yossi Klein Halevi, Senior Fellow, Shalom Hartman Institute, Author of *Letters to My Palestinian Neighbor*

"This book is a wake-up call to all of us, whether we are Jewish or not. The author methodically lays out the threat of Conspiracy Theories. We should all learn the lessons from this book. In today's world, too much distortion of facts has been done, with Conspiracy Theories as the weapon of choice. Hopefully the Golden Rule of 'Do unto others as you would have them do unto you' will be the shining light and overcome the darkness."
— Fred Teng, President, America China Public Affairs Institute

"Conspiracy U is at once moving and maddening while inviting thinking and motivating action. Shay carefully dissects the anti-Zionist antisemitism of the far left and far right, finding frightening points of convergence and demonstrating that much of anti-Israelism is just plain anti-Semitism. This is a must-read not just for those interested in Israel but for anyone trying to understand the broad cross currents that are buffeting society."
— Mark Mellman, President and CEO, Democratic Majority for Israel

"Conspiracy U is a devastating and clear-minded deep dive into the phenomenon of conspiracy theories. In doing so, the author identifies two prominent professors who have engaged in perpetuating anti-Zionist conspiracy theories. It's a Masterclass in identifying and weeding out conspiracy theories wherever they exist."
— John Kelly, *Detroit Free Press*

"I found this book extremely thought-provoking, and my eyes were truly opened to the politics of the far right and far left in their anti-Jewish, anti-Semitic, and anti-Zionist conspiracy theories…. I also fully comprehend the complete depth of harm conspiracy theories can cause in all aspects of society. This heartfelt, and well-researched book makes fascinating and enlightening reading. Highly recommended."
— Susan Keefe, Midwest Book Review

Also by Scott A. Shay

In Good Faith: Questioning Religion and Atheism
Getting Our Groove Back: How to Energize American Jewry

CONSPIRACY U

A CASE STUDY

SCOTT A. SHAY

A WICKED SON BOOK
An Imprint of Post Hill Press
ISBN: 978-1-63758-092-9
ISBN (eBook): 978-1-63758-093-6

Conspiracy U:
A Case Study
© 2021 by Scott A. Shay
All Rights Reserved

Cover Design by Tiffani Shea

No part of this book may be reproduced, stored in a retrieval system, or transmitted by any means without the written permission of the author and publisher.

Post Hill Press
New York • Nashville
posthillpress.com

Published in the United States of America
1 2 3 4 5 6 7 8 9 10

George Shay z"l (1928–2001)
– His memory is a blessing.

CONTENTS

INTRODUCTION

Northwestern University, my beloved alma mater and a jewel of American academia, has enabled some of its professors to openly promote conspiracy theories. These conspiracy theories are the direct descendants of far-left (communist/Soviet) and far-right (fascist/Nazi) conspiracy theories that should have been discredited long ago for the absurdity of their claims and their murderous legacies. Sadly, many academics can no longer even identify conspiracy theories. Professorial proponents insist that far from being conspiracy theorists, they are brave truth tellers. More accurately, this phenomenon points to a sweeping degradation of academic standards in the humanities and social sciences which Northwestern claims to uphold. This book is a wake-up call not just about Northwestern but of academia writ large. I will explain the societal implications of this breakdown and why it urgently needs fixing.

A conspiracy theory has key features that place it outside the realm of legitimate academic theory. While there are certainly genuine conspiracies and valid academic theories based on facts and logic, a conspiracy theory is different. It is improbable, often baseless, or based on half-truths, and it demonstrates a simplistic and a Manichean (all good or all bad) worldview. Conspiracy theories are tightly linked to political propaganda and totalitarian ideologies and usually demonize certain groups. They differ from harsh or unbalanced criticism even if this too can and should meet disapproval by those committed to academic standards. The first part of the book will expand on the definition and history of conspiracy theories as a necessary background to show how they are being peddled at Northwestern, an institution that in principle is committed to the highest academic standards. Conspiracy theories are a betrayal of the essence of Northwestern, whose very motto appropriately expresses the foundation of academic standards.

In my day at Northwestern, the motto of the university was conspicuously present, and my experience there was so valuable because most of my professors lived up to its ideals.

The motto reads as follows:

> Finally, brethren, whatsoever things are true, whatsoever things are honest, whatsoever things are just, whatsoever things are pure, whatsoever things are lovely, whatsoever things are of good report; if there be any virtue, and if there be any praise, think on these things.

> —Philippians 4:8

This adage comes from Paul's Epistle to the Philippians and though a religious text, it nonetheless emphasizes universal philosophical axioms. Indeed, it includes both an intellectual and ethical dimension. Its intellectual dimension underlines the importance of striving for truth. The motto implies that through curiosity, open-mindedness, observation, and inquiry, facts can be recognized and discovered. Other views should be considered fairly with a sympathetic reading for their validity ("if there be any praise"). Further, the motto makes explicit that based on the accurate description ("good report") of evidence, new concepts and theories can be developed and we should "think on these things."

The earliest public explanation of the motto at Northwestern came from Charles William Pearson, who was largely educated at Northwestern and later became a professor and chair of the English Department. He elucidated, "The purpose of the university is to perpetuate and diffuse knowledge and to advance it by research and discovery."[1] Pearson cautions that scholarship should be careful, with "no reckless spirit of innovation." He writes, "Be sure you are right and then go ahead." He also quotes the verse of James Russell Lowell, a storied abolitionist and poet who wrote, "They must upward still and onward who would keep abreast of Truth." Pearson refers, as well, to the Hebrew prophet Jeremiah and to Jesus to testify to the imperative of truth, no matter the consequences.[2]

The motto's ethical dimension describes the existence of the common humanity, "brethren," and common values: "honesty, justice, purity, beauty, and goodness." The message comes from the Christian Scriptures, yet these same values can be found in an ethical framework with echoes across global cultures, namely the Golden Rule. The Rule is articulated as follows: "Do unto others as you would have them do unto you." Major world religions and moral philosophies ascribe to the Golden Rule and doubtlessly would endorse Northwestern's choice of motto for scholarship.[3] To be clear—this does not just mean the monotheistic faiths but the philosophical traditions of China, India, and Tibet, as well as the traditional wisdom of many Native American and African cultures.[4]

Personally, I am partial to the most modest Golden Rule formulation coined by the ancient Jewish sage Hillel, who put it this way: "What is hateful to you don't do to your fellow." In other words, says Hillel, "Don't treat others in a way you wouldn't want to be treated yourself." This very minimal approach requires acceptance of a common humanity and leads to a common adherence to various principles that are universally understood by all. I don't want someone to steal my double-parked Honda Civic while I pick up my takeout food, and I won't steal your Chevrolet Cruze while you are parked in the lot at the mall, and thus stealing will be societally forbidden.

Northwestern's motto encourages us to learn about the world and to seek out the best in other peoples and cultures with humility. Geniuses at self-justification, as we mortals are, the motto challenges us to be sympathetic in the way we understand the motives, intentions, and actions of others. The motto's universal appeal invites us to think of scholarship in universal terms. We are asked to explore our observations about the world in relation to other philosophical and ethical traditions from the vantage point of those others.

While we are far from a global approach to knowledge, examples are everywhere. Consider *guanxi*, a Confucian term about social networks used in sociology and organizational behavior studies. *Vipassana*, a Tibetan Buddhist term for mindfulness and meditation used in psychology and religious studies, has become a point of reference, even in the academy. The motto is thus more than an affirmation of the possibility of legitimate scientific inquiry; it opens up the possibility of recognizing a plurality of perspectives without nihilism or relativism. At the same time, it asks us to recognize falsehoods, made-up stuff, and lies.

This book begins with a case study of two very smart and accomplished scholars at Northwestern, Arthur Butz and Steven Thrasher, as a springboard to examine the proliferation of anti-Zionist conspiracy theories more generally. Though they teach in vastly different fields, they both can boast of well-deserved accolades while promoting anti-Zionist conspiracy theories in their online communications, publications, public pronouncements, and interviews. I believe and will explain why both have betrayed the school's motto by choosing to describe Zionism, the national liberation movement of the Jewish people, as a malignant conspiracy intended to harm other peoples through the use of covert, dishonest, manipulative, and/or violent means.

The comparison of these two professors will surprise many. Arthur Butz's writings—particularly his book *The Hoax of the Twentieth Century*[5]—promote neo-Nazi Holocaust denial. Yes, he is a Holocaust denier, and a peddler of anti-Jewish tropes, but we will find that he is at heart an anti-Zionist conspiracy theorist. In contrast, while Thrasher and many of his colleagues openly and proudly oppose the Jewish state, whether in their teachings or on social media, he is unlikely to be identified as a conspiracy theorist. Thrasher does not claim to be a scholar of the Middle East, but rather his writings serve as a prime example of how anti-Zionist conspiracy theories have become *de rigueur* in academia, so much so that they are repeated without all the footnotes and painstaking attention Butz dedicated to them. I will show that both

Thrasher and Butz share a pernicious view of Zionism differing only in their primary victims: for Butz, Europeans and white Americans, and for Thrasher, all people of color. Further, I will demonstrate that Thrasher and Butz articulate classic far-left and far-right anti-Zionist conspiracy theories respectively with a direct genealogy to their Soviet/New Left and Nazi/far-right origins, though in updated form. Alarmingly, these ideologies are making a significant comeback today in the academy, political organizations, and on the web.

One could ask, though: Why should it matter if certain scholars have such distorted views of one area of human knowledge, especially when it is not their specialty, while they demonstrate excellence in other areas? It matters because this gets to the heart of two of the greatest challenges societies face today: what to do with such grave inconsistencies, and how to handle the impact of these inconsistencies on scholarly standards more generally.

Regarding the first issue, great minds of the past, whatever their geographical origin, have evidenced severe character flaws, blind spots, biases, prejudices, and bold-faced contradictions that don't square with the brilliance and accomplishments for which history recognizes them. The Enlightenment German philosopher Kant was both a masterful philosopher and a bigoted slanderer of non-Europeans.[6] The ancient Chinese philosopher Confucius, still famed for his wisdom, also expressed Chinese superiority.[7] Kocc Barma Fall, a seventeenth-century West African philosopher celebrated for his proverbs, expressed misogynistic views about women.[8] James Watson, co-discoverer of DNA for which he won the Nobel Prize in medicine, has made repeated racist and sexist comments. It is not only men who are inconsistent. Alice Paul, who led the national suffragette movement in the United States, did not let Black women participate.[9] Other famous women leaders of the suffragette movement have been criticized for insensitive and prejudiced language and positions toward Blacks.

The list is long, indeed, of respected scholars, journalists, artists, and scientists whose writings are of immense value within their disciplines but who at the same time have showed the shoddiest attention to basic scholarly or ethical standards on others. Still, we have to ask ourselves, would we want to "cancel" Thrasher and Butz on account of their views on one topic if that meant we would lose their valuable insights and work on important topics within their fields of expertise? In practice, we do live with these sorts of inconsistencies in our daily lives and as part of society.

However, regarding the second issue, the impact on scholarly standards more generally, we can't let false views from accredited faculty go unchallenged. While one should not cancel either of these scholars, academics have a professional responsibility to uphold academic standards, and peer review, the tenure process, and university codes of conduct are supposed to achieve this goal. When these processes fail, challenges must come from elsewhere, be it citizens at large, students, and think tanks. It is also important to understand why the university's own mechanism for upholding standards has failed. We shall explore why this happened in the case of Thrasher and Butz, as well as why Zionism seems to be a particular target. And although this book is focused on the academy, no institution or industry is immune to a corruption of standards. Indeed, I will describe how a parallel with my own industry, banking, can shed light on what is happening in the academy.

In writing this book, I join a growing number of people both within and outside academia who are concerned with academic standards on any number of issues in the humanities, social sciences, and physical sciences.[10] The measure I will use for identifying the corruption will be Northwestern's motto. It will also serve as a critique of these two scholars' writings on Zionism, though this method could be used for other topics. I want to emphasize that although I focused on Professors Butz and Thrasher as a case study, my urgent contention is that they are part of a much larger phenomenon that extends beyond both them and Northwestern and even the academy. In fact, they could have been replaced by others with the same effect, and to this point we will consider some other professors at Northwestern as well as faculty in other universities who also promulgate anti-Zionist conspiracy theories.

This book is divided into five parts. In each, Northwestern's motto will map our path of investigating the conspiracy theories that make up this case study.

Part I describes what conspiracy theories are. It begins by recounting how I first encountered far-right and far-left conspiracies on campus. It then covers the defining features, history, and functions of conspiracy theories and also describes how conspiracy theories differ from theories about genuine conspiracies and criticism of given individuals and groups. We then analyze the distinction between judging groups to be genuinely evil according to the Golden Rule and falsely demonizing them. It outlines how these theories are inimical to Northwestern's motto and the Golden Rule. We will conclude this section with a review of Thrasher's and Butz's conspiracy theories about Zionism.

Part II breaks down how Butz's and Thrasher's views of Zionism demonstrate all the classic features of conspiracy theories. It looks at their use (or lack) of evidence, the probabilities within their theories, and their portrayal of the alleged conspirators, in this case the Zionists. It also looks at how their claims to intellectual and moral standards, as well as their use of Jewish witnesses to bolster their claims to truth and objectivity, form a gloss over their demonization of Zionists. The section ends with a discussion of basic undisputable facts about Zionism and Zionists (whatever solution one prefers for the Israeli-Palestinian/regional conflict) that make these conspiracy theories so improbable and so obviously a betrayal of Northwestern's motto.

Part III outlines the intellectual and political lineages of these theories. I describe how these theories have been central to far-right and far-left discourse during the twentieth century and even today. I show the role of intellectuals in disseminating these theories. The section also discusses the place of anti-Zionist conspiracy theories among the far right and far left in the postwar period, claiming that both extremes have been consistently anti-Zionist—even conspiratorially so. It will also analyze the pro-Zionism of some alt-right parties. Finally, it will discuss how conspiracy theories are absent in the moderate right and left, which remain closer to the Golden Rule.

In Part IV, I show how conspiracy theories relate to highly influential contemporary academic theories like decolonialism, as well as current far-left and far-right ideologies. The section examines how both these theories and ideologies betray (though to differing extents and in very different ways) the intellectual and moral aspects of the Golden Rule and often lead to conspiracy theories. Finally, it claims that Jews and Zionism are central to conspiracy theories today because both defy the neat Manichean categories and simplifying logic that extreme ideologies, and increasingly many academic theories, are built upon.

Part V considers the mechanisms that enabled conspiracy theories to gain so much ground in the American academy (both inside and outside the classroom) and suggests some tentative solutions. To do so, it compares motives and methods that lead to the gradual corruption of the academy to an unrelated industry, banking, specifically the pre-financial crisis mortgage market. It also shows the real-time corrosive impact of these theories on campus organizations and policies and on the minds of a generation. Finally, it considers how the Golden Rule can be restored as the ideal at Northwestern and across the United States.

To achieve these objectives, this book brings together research on a variety of topics. It looks at writings on conspiracy theories, on the history of far-left and far-right political ideologies and their relation to Zionism, on Middle Eastern history, and on various academic theories, as well as more philosophical considerations about academic standards and theories of knowledge generally. It also includes a close reading of the writings of Butz and Thrasher and a discussion of developments in the university as well as in other industries.

Along with this material, readers might be surprised to note some biblical references in this book. The reasons are severalfold. First, the Northwestern motto is from the Christian Scriptures, and Professor Pearson and other interpreters understood it in its biblical context. More specifically, I will use several references from the Book of Jeremiah, which Professor Pearson highlights, as well as the Book of Kings. What these two biblical texts have in common is that they were both written in exile by author/s trying to figure out what went wrong with the wonderful institution they admired, namely the Davidic kingship that commenced with many flaws, but also with promise and glory, and ended in corruption and devastation. Whatever the author/s' identity, the sense of the writing of both books portrays the author/s as sad and angry but not bewildered by what happened. Perhaps for this reason, Jewish tradition has it that Jeremiah, who highly valued truth even when it hurt, authored both books.

These lessons from an ancient text also speak to a broader argument in this book—that of the universality of wisdom and truth across time and space, as well as the perennial nature of some basic human ethical and intellectual problems. Had I been a Chinese American, I might have offered quotations from Chinese classics as references, or an Indian American the Upanishads, and so on, but as a Jew, I turn to the moral and intellectual tradition of my forbearers, which is also the one I am most familiar with.

One other important point for understanding this book is that it is not a critique or defense of particular Israeli policies with respect to the Palestinians or vice versa, of particular Palestinian policies towards Israel. Nor is it a discussion of the peace process or of the respective suffering of either people over the course of the conflict. Rather, this book will deal with the core view the far right and far left share about Israel (and not about Palestine), namely that it is evil and should not exist. It will also examine the ways that they buttress this view.

This is not a book I planned on writing, nor am I pleased to have to write it. As I did research, Isabel Allende's words partially inspired me: "Write down what should not be forgotten."

The well-known phrase "I say this in sadness, not in anger" more often than not is a code for *schadenfreude* tinged with feigned sadness and long-cultivated anger. But at the risk of sounding clichéd, for me it is accurate and true.

My feeling of sadness is genuine. As I said, Northwestern University is my alma mater. I owe much to Northwestern and have much gratitude to the institution. I am keen to offer the reasons for my gratitude.

I was the first person on either side of my family to attend university, and my heart was set on Northwestern. (I had applied to one other school, just in case.) I cobbled together the funds to pay for Northwestern with a combination of an Illinois state scholarship, a Teamsters local union scholarship (of which my mother was a member), a student loan program, wages from various jobs, Northwestern financial aid, and, last but not least, my father's reparations check from Germany of between eighty to ninety dollars each month, depending on the deutschmark/US dollar exchange. Plus, my parents chipped in what they could to close the gap. I cashed a check for twenty dollars each Monday in the bursar's office that had to cover twelve meals plus any incidental expenses beyond books. Luckily, many student events even then had free food. If I ran out of money, well, I had to make do.

I loved the learning ecosystem at Northwestern and felt so lucky to be there. The classes, the extracurriculars, and the fellow students I met were all great. I made friendships my freshman year that I still have today. I got to learn microeconomics from Hugo Sonnenschein (who revolutionized our understanding of the demand curve) and macroeconomics from Robert Gordon (who pioneered rational expectations in economics). David Campbell took it upon himself to reteach me how to write in my mother tongue of English, despite being a French literature professor. I could gladly sing the praises of most of the professors I met.

I also loved that my teachers fostered lively debates about big ideas and the issues of the day. While most discussions weren't political per se, the discipline of intellectual rigor was such that if we strayed into politics, it would be hard to know on which side a professor stood from the give and take alone. A case in point was Bari Watkins, who was involved in starting up the Women's Studies program at Northwestern.

No one doubted that she was a staunch feminist and extremely pro-gressive, but heaven help you if you made a pro-feminist assertion without the evidence ready at hand to rebut her surprisingly persuasive counterargument. Dr. Watkins took an interest in each and every stu-dent and invited groups of students to her apartment on occasion. It would be hard to imagine anyone in my day being afraid of expressing a political opinion quite contrary to her views inside or outside the classroom. Actually, I suspect she might have rounded their grade *up* for *not* kowtowing to her.

It was these sorts of professors who inspired me always to consider the question motivated by the motto: What if the other person is right? Of course, that would raise the shocking possibility that I am wrong. Not only that, but if the other person's reasoning is superior to mine, then why am I stubbornly sticking to my claim? What are my hidden assumptions? What of value can I learn from the other person's argu-ment even if I disagree with their point of view? Most importantly, I learned that the only way to have any confidence in my views was to deeply understand the other person's outlook and reasoning. I learned to engage with people of vastly differing worldviews and approaches to issues and even entire disciplines. I even loved those post-midnight dorm debates in the halls of Willard, where we all fancied ourselves as the cerebral equals of Jean-Paul Sartre and Simone de Beauvoir. Intellectual jostling was a joy, and we covered more categories than a season's worth of *Jeopardy*. No idea would go uncontested. I thank Northwestern for that.

Early in my sophomore year, my father's small carpenter contract-ing business took some severe hits. The economy went south, and his biggest customer defaulted. This quickly drove my father to become bankrupt, even though he would refuse to declare so in a legal manner. My parents now needed the reparation check, so that the key pipe-line to finance my education went dry. I couldn't make ends meet. The twenty-dollar check would have bounced if I wrote it. I feared hav-ing to withdraw from Northwestern in the winter quarter. Desperate and distraught, I went to the financial aid office, where to my great relief they found $400 to award me that filled the immediate gap and allowed me to remain enrolled. Later, a close friend I'd met my first day on campus personally lent me funds, which bought me a bit more breathing room.

My time at Northwestern University inspired me to become a lifelong learner, and my graduate studies at the business school gave me the skills to compete in the banking and investment world. I feel so very indebted to Northwestern that I am overwhelmed by a sense of gratitude. I gave my first donation to Northwestern the very year I graduated and have done so every year since. But now I am wondering what has happened to intellectual integrity at my alma mater and to academia writ large. The struggle for answers led me to write this book.

We are at a moment of our history when we as Americans as well as other people across the world are continuing on the path of progress with the intention of righting or at least mitigating some historical wrongs. But our efforts risk being compromised by the resurgence of extreme ideologies that should have been placed in history's dumpster. Although far-right viewpoints are today formally excluded from the university, many of the most prominent anti-Zionist conspiracy theorists on this side of the spectrum have held or continue to hold university positions. Further, their writings are gaining ground on the dark web as the credentialed dissident viewpoint. A survey of US adults under forty found that 11 percent believe that the Jews were responsible for the Holocaust, 15 percent agree with Butz that the Holocaust is a myth or very exaggerated, and 20 percent think that too much attention is paid to the Holocaust. About 50 percent had seen Holocaust denial literature online.[11] As we shall see, Holocaust deniers today universally blame Zionists for a Holocaust hoax.

Far-left viewpoints, by contrast, are increasingly ascendant if not hegemonic in American universities, particularly in social sciences and humanities departments. Thrasher's views on a wide range of topics are consistent with radical perspectives in his field, and few of the views he promulgates when it comes to Zionism originate with him. The latter are for all intents and purposes taken for granted by his peers and students. Dr. Thrasher made front page news when he jettisoned his prepared speech at the May 2019 New York University Doctoral Convocation to declare, "I am so proud, so proud...of my colleagues... for supporting the Boycott, Divestment, and Sanctions (BDS) movement against the apartheid state government in Israel—because that is what we are called to do." The boisterous whoops and cheers he received confirmed that he was only stating the obvious to many of his fellow doctoral graduates. His position on Zionism is nowhere near unique. It circulates in popular view and is taught in courses across America as broadly accepted fact. Many inside and outside academia believe they know for sure that the self-determination of Jewish people is very, very bad.

This book started as an article to commemorate my father's liberation from the Nazi concentration camps, so the reader will note my father's experiences make instructive appearances in the text. As I kept thinking about my father's life in conjunction with the writings of Professors Butz and Thrasher, I came to appreciate with apprehension the larger consequences of their writings and ideologies. Dr. Arthur Butz, electrical engineer, and Dr. Steven Thrasher, journalist, may seem as dissimilar as purple and white except for their positions as Northwestern faculty members and their passion for anti-Zionism. The far right and far left may have excelled in anti-Jewish and later anti-Zionist conspiracy theories, but they lied about many other groups as well. We have witnessed in the twentieth century a catalog of murderous outcomes from totalitarian ideologies and of their many different victims, from Georgian nationalists to Cambodian peasants, from the Chinese bourgeoisie to Orthodox Christian priests, from Sinti and Roma to Slavs, from the differently abled to political opponents, all in the name of a brighter future based on ideological certainty.

I hope this book will open the eyes of those who aspire for universities to enlighten and raise up our fellow members of humanity rather than subvert and falsely demonize them. Most importantly, I hope it will remind us that there is a wide tent between the far left and far right that offers plenty of perspectives and effective solutions to the troubles of the world that risk being dismissed by the extremes. So, I write this book in sadness but not in despair. My father taught me never to despair.

PART I

FINALLY

ANTI-ZIONIST CONSPIRACY THEORIES IN THE 1970S: EVIL IDEAS HAVE CONSEQUENCES

The word "finally" often means a new beginning. Paul certainly meant his charge to the Philippians as setting them out on a new path. Universities call their final ceremony of graduation and departure a commencement. My father started his new life on May 1, 1945, when he finally departed from Dachau, the Nazi concentration camp located about ten miles from Munich in scenic Bavaria. At his liberation, he was brought to an American field hospital weighing less than seventy pounds. It would take a year for him to regain his health, a physical recovery made all the more difficult by the haunted loneliness of having lost his father, his brothers, his aunts, uncles, and most of his cousins to the Nazi regime and at the hands of complicit civilian neighbors. (His mother died during childbirth prior to the war.) When the Arab League declared war against the nascent state of Israel, my father was still living in a displaced persons (DP) camp.

It might seem that my father's ordeal began in late June of 1941. Summer was just beginning when the Nazis entered his small hometown of Sveksna, Lithuania, but none of this could have happened without the propaganda and intellectual preparation that began years earlier. There was a straight line from the careful dissemination of lies to an environment that was indifferent to concentration camps. In 1922, the Jews of Sveksna were victims of a blood libel that triggered four days of violent pogroms, which devastated the *shtetel* and left many Jews battered, bruised, and impoverished. A blood libel is the centuries-old slander that Jews murder Christian children to use their blood in the baking of matzah for Passover. It is hard to believe that this discredited notion lost none of its potency in the modern age.

Born six years later, my father vividly recalled another blood libel promulgated against the Jews when he was a young boy in the 1930s, in which tragedy was averted when the alleged victim showed up in good health. During most of the 1930s, there were organized (nonviolent) economic boycotts against Jewish merchants as well. Shop signs were smeared with hot black tar to indicate the boycott. The anti-Jewish text *The Protocols of the Elders of Zion* was widely available in Europe in the interwar period and widely believed. Indeed, my father lived through a time when libels against Jews and anti-Jewish conspiracy theories were as common as Indo-European languages across the continent.

I found this all incomprehensible until I was a young college student in the late 1970s, when I noticed the emerging trend to characterize Zionism as an evil conspiracy. But before I describe my experiences, it is essential to define Zionism and its place in Jewish life. Zionism is simply the expression of the Jewish people's right to national self-determination in their ancestral homeland. In this respect, Zionism is part of a larger global anti-imperialist movement, whose moral foundations are well established. Indeed, the Jews are one of many peoples who have regained their sovereignty in their indigenous/historical homeland in the nineteenth and twentieth centuries after having been conquered by various empires. Others include European peoples like the Greeks, the Balkan (Serb, Croat, Macedonian, Romanian, and Bulgarian) peoples and Baltic (Finnish, Estonian, Lithuanian, and Latvian) peoples, and certain central European peoples, like the Slovaks or Slovenes who were conquered by the Ottoman, Russian, and Austro-Hungarian

Empires respectively. Or the many African and Asian peoples who acquired independence from the British, Belgian, French, Portuguese, and Dutch Empires after World War II. All of these peoples and the countries they established further have in common the fact that they sought sovereignty in their homelands and their homelands only, which is why they are understood as national liberation movements—unlike the empires that conquered them who emerged from their homelands (Russia, Turkey, and Austria) and ruled over the homelands of others, which are understood as imperial powers. Many of these reclaimed states have become successful economically, socially, and politically. Many also continue to include minorities composed of descendants of the imperial peoples, like the Russian minorities in the Baltic countries, or Hungarians in Slovakia.

Israel nevertheless stands out among this large group of liberated nations due to certain particular historical features. First, with the Babylonian, Persian, Greek, and Roman imperial conquests of antiquity, the Jews—who had constituted a people in the area since c. 1200 BCE and had a kingdom from c. 1000 BCE—lost their sovereignty and were variously expelled and/or forced to leave their homeland due to oppressive policies. This created the Jewish Diaspora as well as settler colonies of imperial peoples in the historic land of Israel. After their conquest, the Romans further renamed the land of Israel Palestine and severely repressed the remaining Jews, who according to some scholars were gradually outnumbered by pagan and Christian Greek and Syrian speakers by the fourth century. In the view of others, though, Jews were a majority of the population until the Arab conquest in the seventh century.[1] Either way, the descendants of the colonizing Arabs gradually (over the course of a few hundred years) outnumbered Jews and Christians through imperial policies favoring Arab settlement and oppressing Jewish and Christian communities. These policies as well as the deprivations from numerous wars all led to non-Muslim emigration. Thus, Jews not only lost their sovereignty but ceased to be a majority in their homeland from the time of the Crusades until the modern period, though Jewish communities persisted.

This is a situation Jews shared only with the Armenian people. Like the Jews, the Armenians became a people in the Bronze Age. They had their ethnogenesis as tribes in the Armenian Highlands around 1200 BCE and a sovereign state with the Kingdom of Armenia from 321 BCE. Likewise, they were also conquered by multiple empires, leading to expulsions, flight, and thereby, an important diaspora. Yet, during periods without sovereignty, they remained a majority in all of their historic homelands until the Safavid Persian conquest in the early seventeenth century. They were then forcibly displaced by their imperial masters. The Safavids subsequently repopulated the area with Persians, Kurds, and Turkic peoples who became a majority there, leading to a situation where Armenians were no longer a majority in Eastern Armenia, which was the core of their historic homeland, nor did they have sovereignty in the Western part. It is also worth noting that in the twentieth century, when neither people had sovereignty, both Armenians and Jews in the Diaspora would be subjected to genocidal mass murder by other imperial states (the Ottoman/Turkish state and Nazi Germany) as well as repression under the Soviet regime.

Yet Jewish and Armenian history is not identical. Both Armenians and Jews developed a national liberation movement in the modern period, and both movements sought help from imperial powers to reestablish a demographic presence and eventually political power in their homeland. Yet, for Armenia, this led to a complete demographic reversal and only later a state. When the Russian Empire conquered Eastern Armenia during the Russo-Persian wars in the early nineteenth century, it encouraged Armenians to move back to Eastern Armenia, which they did in the hope of autonomy. It also caused the Persians, Kurds, and Turkic peoples to flee to their homelands or other regions of the Persian and Ottoman Empires. This made Eastern Armenia once again an Armenian majority area, though Armenians would not gain independence from their new imperial master Russia until 1991.

In contrast, while the Jews sought the help of first the Ottomans and then the British to populate their historic homeland, neither empire was as unequivocally favorable to the Jewish side demographically as the Russians were to the Armenians. Both the Ottomans and later the British limited Jewish immigration and land purchase. Further, far from forcing the Palestinian Arabs to flee or controlling the territory, they offered them, along with the Jews, an independent state. Their partition plans for a Jewish and Palestinian state were confirmed by the international community in 1947. The Palestinian Arab leadership declined this offer and joined the war alongside the Arab League countries when the Jews declared a state based on the UN partition plan in 1948. The Arabs tried to recapture the territory in 1967 and 1973, while also expelling their domestic Jewish populations. Finally, since the Oslo Peace Process, which reaffirmed the idea of partition, Palestinian leaders have turned down offers of state sovereignty in exchange for peace with Israel in 2000, 2001, and 2008. Today, some Palestinians have self-rule after Israel's unilateral withdrawal from Gaza. The Islamist organization Hamas took power in Gaza in 2007, which caused both Israel and Egypt to respond with a military blockade, with devastating consequences.

Israel is the story of a successful national liberation movement, yet its unique history has led to many challenges. On the one hand, it is a strong state with a robust economy and powerful military. In this respect, it is like other independent nations such as Finland and Poland. However, as described above, unlike most post-colonial nations, it is still in conflict with a significant percentage of the descendants of former colonizers, who unlike the Russians in Estonia or the Turks in Bulgaria have neither accepted becoming a minority within Israel as a Jewish democratic state; relinquished their claims on all of the territory of the land of Israel/Palestine—hence the slogan "from the River to the Sea Palestine will be Free"; nor been naturalized in the neighboring countries who fought alongside them and expelled their Jewish minorities. The fact that Israel is strong militarily and the Palestinians relatively weak (though they have the backing of strong regional powers like Qatar and Iran) does not change the reality that Israel is a nation-state whose territorial ambitions are limited to its historic homeland like Estonia, Slovakia, or Armenia, not an imperial one like Turkey, Iran, or Russia, while Palestinians belong to a larger Arab people with an imperial history.

Those people and academics in particular who espouse anti-Zionist conspiracy theories are therefore not critics of how Israel handles its ongoing conflict with the Palestinians and its neighbors, but rather people who demonize Zionism and the notion that Jews should be allowed national sovereignty. Those who accept Jewish national self-determination while criticizing specific Israeli policies, whether its system of checkpoints, the settlements, its rejection of the Iran deal, its treatment of Palestinian-Arab citizens, or its positions on Jerusalem or the Jordan Valley during peace negotiations, have nothing to do with anti-Zionist conspiracy theorists. All of these policies can and should be debated. This book does not take a stand on particular Israeli policies or on how to resolve the Israel-Palestinian or Iranian-Israel, Syrian-Israel, or other regional conflicts. Rather, it addresses academics and others who single out the national liberation movement of the Jews called Zionism as uniquely malevolent, inherently mendacious, racist, violent, and imperial, and who see Israel as a global force of evil conspiring to oppress other peoples, physically, economically, and culturally. These conspiracy theorists are never consistently against national self-determination per se nor against the liberation of other specific peoples (indeed they are all fervent Palestinian nationalists), nor do they view other states (even imperial ones such as Iran, Turkey, or China) in such demonic terms despite their bad track records of oppression. As a result, these conspiracy theorists are focused on and obsessed with the need to dismantle or destroy Israel and only Israel, by distorting or fabricating Jewish history.

It is important to note that there has always been a portion of Jews in the Diaspora who chose/choose to assimilate to the majority culture and who do not feel an affinity to Jews or to Judaism, let alone Israel. There are also those Jews who may have enjoyed/enjoy being Jewish but felt/feel a strong affinity and indeed preference to the culture of the Diaspora in which they live and perhaps no affinity to the land of Israel or the state of Israel. This is true with other national diasporas as well. This book does not judge these preferences or the choices of any individual. However, the reality of the flip side should not be dismissed either, that since late antiquity there has always been a substantial portion of Jews who identified both religiously and ethnically as Jews and who wished to regain/retain their sovereignty in their historic homeland, the land of Israel. It is fair to have one or the other preference. It is not, however, fair (for anyone, Jewish or not) to on the one hand affirm the need for Palestinian national determination and on the other to describe those Jews who desire national self-determination as illegitimate or join anti-Zionist conspiracy theorists in demonizing Zionists and Israel. Yet in the 1970s this is what happened at an increasing rate.

The 1970s produced a rush of accusations against the movement for Jewish national determination, otherwise known as Zionism, as a uniquely manipulative and predatory conspiracy. In 1976, when I was a sophomore at Northwestern, an up-and-coming tenured associate professor of engineering published a book, *The Hoax of the Twentieth Century: The Case Against the Presumed Extermination of European Jewry.* The book has seen four editions and had been easy to obtain online at Amazon until it was removed in 2017. (It is still readily available elsewhere.) While its many footnotes, appendices, and bibliographic references abet the book's disguise as an academic treatise, the work is usually described as a Holocaust denial. In fact, it is more accurately a screed against Zionism. Butz himself would agree. In his first interview with the *Daily Northwestern*[2] after the publication of his book, he asserted that the "legend" of the extermination camps "is a concoction of the Zionist movement…They use it very often in support of Israel."[3] His statement mirrors the Nazis' opposition to Zionism—as Hitler wrote in *Mein Kampf*, "For while the Zionists try to make the rest of the world believe that the national consciousness of the Jew finds its satisfaction in the creation of a Palestinian state, the Jews again slyly dupe the dumb Goyim. It doesn't even enter their heads to build up a Jewish state in Palestine for the purpose of living there; all they want is a central organization for their international world swindle, endowed with its own sovereign rights and removed from the intervention of other states: a haven for convicted scoundrels and a university for budding crooks."[4] Butz begins by "noting the obvious ways in which this legend [the Holocaust] is exploited in contemporary politics, notably in connection with the completely illogical support the U.S. extends Israel I had long had lingering doubts about it."[5] Butz tells us of "unspeakable criminal acts: in the sense in which that term is used in the Luxembourg treaty [German reparations agreement], are largely a hoax, specifically a Zionist hoax."[6] Butz believes that Zionism was the motive for the "legend" of the Holocaust, which in his view was a trumped-up typhus outbreak during which a modest number of Jews died.

In the antediluvian era before 24/7 breaking news cycles, internet search engines, and social media, Butz's book was scarcely known. The early few who did see it were understandably outraged, and Northwestern's tepid response was to release a banal statement noting Butz's right to publish whatever he wanted as a private citizen and as a professor protected by tenure. Only after the *Chicago Sun-Times* reported on the controversy, which generated more heat for the university, did Northwestern issue a somewhat stronger statement. It was put out not in the name of the university or the president but relegated to the provost.

As a student, I closely followed the controversy and wrote a letter to the editor of the *Daily Northwestern*[7] critical of the administration's handling of the Butz situation. My letter questioned Northwestern's first instinct to try to minimize the issue and argued that the statement "has no moral grounding and is therefore worthless."[8] My argument was that the provost's statement was not based on principle but was intended to simply mitigate public criticism. In response, I received a deluge of Nazi propaganda literature to my dorm mailbox via the inter-office mail of Northwestern. The content was disturbing, but equally unsettling was the other message that the sender was someone within the school who had access to the university's internal mail system.

I reported the matter to the vice president for student affairs, Dr. Jim Carleton, expecting it would not be that difficult to determine the source of the hate mail. At a minimum, the general origination mail drop could be traced, particularly since I received multiple packages and they were somewhat strangely addressed. In those days, the sorting of interoffice mail was done by hand. The vice president's response to me was that the university would not pursue this. It occurred to me at the time that during the first part of his career at Northwestern (in the 1960s), there had been a de facto quota on admitting Jewish students, which had only been lifted in practice in 1970 (it had been lifted on paper in the mid-1960s, but it was only in 1970 that Jewish admissions increased meaningfully).

After sustained public criticism, the Northwestern administration's response was to fly in a few high-profile scholars in Holocaust history to deliver well-publicized lectures. The hate mail to my dorm room eventually stopped, yet I had learned a lesson I would not forget. The university at the time was very concerned about its own PR but less so in protecting an individual student targeted by a neo-Nazi within the university. At around this same time, I began to follow closely the attempts by members of the National Socialist (Nazi) Party of America to march in Skokie, a Chicago suburb where some of my father's Holocaust survivor friends happened to live. My father was somber but surprised by none of this.

At Northwestern, I also began to observe radical critiques of Jewish national self-determination as a predatory, manipulative, and murderous conspiracy from the political left. Already as a senior in high school, I was glued to the TV set as Yasser Arafat (the leader of the Palestinian Liberation Organization from 1969 to 2004) delivered his 1974 address to the United Nations, in which he described Zionism as a criminal and murderous offshoot of European imperialism and likened Israel to apartheid South Africa. He also claimed Zionists were conspiring to harm other national liberation movements across the globe. At the conclusion of the speech, Arafat received a thunderous standing ovation and beamed with satisfaction as he waved his clasped hands high.

Yasser Arafat was an innovative early promulgater of what today would be called decolonial theory. I was a freshman one year later when, as a consequence of Arafat's speech, the UN passed a resolution equating Zionism with racism (Resolution 3379). Arafat succeeded in coupling pan-Arabism/pan-Islamism—which considered territory conquered by Muslim Arabs forever Muslim Arab—with Soviet anti-Zionism (a fact one can now read about with the disclosure of Soviet-era documents on this topic),[9] both of which accused Zionism of being racist and aligned with European and American imperialism. Somehow it fell in the comfort zone of the UN to declare that the nefarious goals of world Zionists were to destroy Islam, socialism, and national liberation movements across the globe in no particular order.

I still shudder as I remember sitting with my parents watching on television as Arafat entered the UN General Assembly packing a gun in his holster. But his speech shocked us more. He defined Jews in a twisted way that none of us recognized. We didn't have the vocabulary at the time, but he re-appropriated our entire Jewish past and cancelled it. Essentially, he called the Hebrew and Christian Scriptures a pack of lies and, for good measure, branded classic Roman historians liars for affirming any Jewish connection with the land of Israel. His "imperialist" characterization of the "Zionist entity"—as though it rivaled Queen Victoria's empire upon which the sun never set—was so ludicrous it would have been funny if it weren't so tragic. Keep in mind that the state of Israel is smaller in size than either New Hampshire or Vermont. I thought of my father's horrified face during Yom Kippur in 1973 when the rabbi interrupted services to tell us of the surprise attack against Israel from all directions. My father's immediate concerns were of Israel's challenge in procuring arms and of the Israelis who would die in the coming days—mainly descendants of refugees from persecuted Diaspora communities in Europe, North Africa, and the Middle East.

I was still studying on campus in 1980 as a grad student when a group of Puerto Rican separatists known by the organizational name of FALN were arrested, tried, found guilty, and later sentenced to lengthy prison terms for thwarted terrorist activities. These FALN members were dressed as joggers when they were arrested, which hit home since in those days I used to jog around campus on a route circling the Bahá'í Temple a few miles north of campus. The FALN arrests bothered me deeply—totally unrelated to Puerto Rican nationalism, which I could appreciate—because the group's materials connected its struggle for Puerto Rican independence with the struggle to end Jewish self-determination. It was only then that I truly understood the depth of left-wing conspiracy theories about Zionism. Although the route I jogged was largely a matter of convenience, I included the Bahá'í Temple on purpose. The ayatollahs who seized power with the Iranian revolution of 1979 were soon subjecting the Bahá'í people in Iran to pogroms, leading to a mini genocide. Ayatollah Khomeini declared adherents of the Bahá'í faith to be heretics and without the right to religious freedom or to life. The Wilmette Bahá'í Temple was a sanctuary space for a few of those who escaped.

The seeds of fanatical opposition to Zionism that were planted in the 1970s on American college campuses not only remained viable but are now in full bloom. Professor Arthur Butz still inhabits an office on the north side of campus and is still teaching undergraduates a required course in electrical engineering. As we shall see, far-right anti-Zionists have continued to tout Butz's views on Zionism for decades, and occasional pieces by Butz have appeared in the *Daily Northwestern*. Butz's book is now considered a classic work by the far right.

Over on the south side of campus, Professor Steven Thrasher, a more recent hire, occupies the prestigious new position of the Daniel H. Renberg Chair of Social Justice Reporting. He has promulgated the far-left anti-Zionist views expressed in Arafat's speech and by FALN despite the conflict being removed from his geographical and thematic area of expertise—race, gender, and public health in America.

Yet my assessment that Butz and Thrasher are two sides of the same coin has not been much considered. Indeed, most people within the university would dismiss Butz's writings on Holocaust denial as not worthy of any consideration. Nor are most academics troubled by the fact that a significant percentage of millennials agree with Butz.[10] Further, very few would be aware that he claims not to oppose Jews but Zionism. In Thrasher's case, though many academics embrace his negative view of Zionism, they would reject the claim that by agreeing with him on Zionism they were also embracing a conspiracy theory. They would certainly reject any notion that Thrasher's views resembled the views of someone like Butz. Yet a closer examination of these Northwestern professors' writings on Zionism reveals that both share classic commonalities of conspiracy theories, and so it is to this topic we now turn.

WHATSOEVER THINGS ARE LOVELY 1

CONSPIRACY THEORIES: WHAT THEY ARE AND WHY THEY ARE BAD

To say something is a conspiracy theory should not be some general rhetorical charge. Rather, conspiracy theories have definable parameters. They claim to be explanations of political or social phenomena that are the result of a covert conspiracy by powerful and frequently, though not always, secret actors. Scholars have traditionally taken pains to distinguish between a theory about an actual conspiracy and a conspiracy theory.[1] Actual conspiracies have existed throughout history, and many of them can be documented for certain or argued within a high degree of probability. A good phrase for this would be a "theory about a conspiracy."[2]

A conspiracy is simply the agreement between two or more parties to commit a crime. We know that the Nazi leadership conspired—famously at the Wannsee Conference—to murder the Jews. Likewise, it is a fact that the Nazi leadership had a plan for a thousand-year Reich founded on a racial division of the Lebensraum (living space) leading to the conspiracy to conquer Eastern Europe. We similarly know that the Hutu Power movement planned the mass murder of Tutsis and even of moderate Hutus, and that the Turkish Committee of Union and Progress incited hatred against Armenians; called them spies, vermin, and infidels; and advocated the cleansing of Turkey by removal of all non-Muslims by any means. The American government conspired to relocate Native Americans westward to barren terrain, dispossessing, impoverishing, and killing countless multitudes. Many American states passed Jim Crow laws as early as the 1870s, which were enforced until 1965. Selective and highly punitive drug laws caused the mass incarceration of Blacks for many decades. All of these are sadly known conspiracies of political parties or governments with known political power and are attested to through various eyewitnesses or documents with a high degree of probability.

Conspiracy theories, in contrast to conspiracies, are dubious and improbable hypotheses in some cases and intentional lies in others about powerful and sinister groups conspiring to harm good people, often via a secret cabal. Conspiracy theories thus differ from actual conspiracies in their relationship to facts, evidence, and logic. To make the distinction between theories about conspiracies and conspiracy theories clear, from now on I will capitalize Conspiracy Theories.[3]

Famous Conspiracy Theories include the new world order theory that a group of elites controls the world. The identity of the elites varies by case, but included among others are the Federal Reserve System, the Council on Foreign Relations, the European Union, the United Nations, and the World Bank. QAnon is a recently evolved Conspiracy Theory that has grown with frightening speed and even has two adherents in Congress. There are numerous Conspiracy Theories about George Soros that claim he controls a large portion of the world's wealth and governments. Similar theories are made against the Freemasons, who are accused of controlling large parts of the judiciary across the world. A number of Conspiracy Theories on the far left and far right, as we shall see, incorporate and update the well-known Conspiracy Theory of *The Protocols of the Elders of Zion*, which falsely depicts the existence of a Jewish plan for world domination by subverting gentile morals and controlling the press and the world economies.

None of these Conspiracy Theories are probable or based on the facts. Conspiracy Theories have two additional intellectual elements that distance them not only from evidence but from logic: they tend to have one overarching idea or cause for an otherwise complex situation, which makes them a simplified, easy-to-understand view of reality. Indeed, most events don't have a single cause, but Conspiracy Theories tend to be reductionist—The Jews! The Freemasons! The UN!—when multiple causes are far more probable.[4] Further, for Conspiracy Theorists, their theories are unfalsifiable since any evidence to the contrary is simply proof of a cover-up.[5]

Conspiracy Theories are defined by other features. As scholars Jovan Byford and Quassim Cassam, authors of *Conspiracy Theories: A Critical Introduction*[6] and *Conspiracy Theories*[7] respectively, explain, in addition to the improbable and unaccounted-for nature of Conspiracy Theories, there are other dimensions. Cassam builds on Byford's explanation that Conspiracy Theories are essentially a form of political propaganda that has the purpose of persuading people to adopt a particular political agenda.[8] Here, political agenda does not necessarily refer to a specific party but rather to a general political or even cultural outlook or even a position on a specific policy. Cassam gives the example of the Conspiracy Theory of Holocaust denial as promoting the view that Jews are evil, or the example of the Sandy Hook Conspiracy Theory—that the shootings never happened but rather were a staged false flag operation—with the alleged objective of opposing gun control.[9] Those who communicate these theories may or may not believe them, but either way they are committed to the political agenda the theory communicates. In other words, those who propagate the Conspiracy Theories range from true believers to conscious manipulators.[10] On occasion there are Conspiracy Theories that are not political, like the theory that "Paul McCartney is dead" or, as Cassam mentions, that "Elvis is alive."[11] For the most part, though, Conspiracy Theories are political in nature and no more believable than thinking Elvis is getting ready to reappear at Graceland.

Conspiracy Theories must be distinguished from unwarranted criticism or even unfair/prejudiced perspectives toward a certain group. Unwarranted criticism or unfair/prejudiced perspectives share with Conspiracy Theories a lack of evidence, a distortion of evidence, or even in some cases a failure of logic, but they don't claim any secret cabals, covert machinations, or powerful manipulations by political parties, ethnic groups, or states. These prejudicial or unwarranted criticisms come in many forms, including libels or false accusations, like the claim that Jews eat matzah with Christian blood, or persistent myths about the negative characteristics of a group, like the idea that all Jews are cheap, all Africans are lazy, or all Roma are dishonest. They may even take on more sophisticated forms, like attributing malice or evil intentions to certain historical actors that they did not have—for example, many non-Nazi Germans after World War I accused the Allies of wanting to totally ruin Germany—or conversely blaming victims for an ill befallen on them, such as primarily blaming consumers willing to sign up for the exotic mortgages that some unscrupulous brokers pushed prior to the 2008 financial crisis. In both cases, there is a distortion rather than a total lie that alters the true narrative. These negative views manifest themselves in tabloids, talk radio, folk sayings, and these days on social media. But they are a step away from Conspiracy Theories because they are still falsifiable in the minds of their adherents. The distinctive feature of Conspiracy Theories is the power and success attributed to the imagined conspirators in addition to their evil intentions to harm others. Thus, the view that all Jews are greedy is a baseless accusation that is a step toward the view that the Jews are secretly plotting to make the citizens of the world into their slaves. The existence of widespread prejudices about a given group make people more susceptible to believing Conspiracy Theories targeting that group.

According to Byford, Conspiracy Theories have a definite structure.[12] Specifically, the identity of both the alleged conspirators or theorists of Conspiracy Theories are a pivotal part of the story. Byford explains that Conspiracy Theories have a clear conspiratorial group.

The conspirators in Conspiracy Theories can be very specific people like John F. Kennedy's would-be assassins (in addition to or other than Lee Harvey Oswald) or political actors, or they can be larger groups such as all communists, Jews, or, in our case, Zionists. These groups are typically portrayed as unequivocally evil, with a clear goal and a willingness to stop at nothing to achieve it. Conspiracy Theories typically view the world in Manichean terms—the conspirators are totally evil and the victims totally good. The theorists themselves can be individuals working as lone amateur researchers producing books to uncover the conspiracy, or they can be governments, as was the case with the Turkish government's promotion of anti-Armenian Conspiracy Theories or both the Nazi and Czarist promotion of *The Protocols of the Elders of Zion*.[3] Conspiracy Theories are not monopolized by the political right or left.[14] The Nazis promoted Conspiracy Theories about the Jews as we mentioned, but so did the Soviets and other communist governments about various groups. Byford demonstrates that extreme political ideologies are far more closely linked with Conspiracy Theories than moderate political parties.[15]

Finally, there is a certain naivety about Conspiracy Theories. They depend on a stunning amount of uniformity of belief and coordination of action without contingencies that is more like a perfectly executed Hollywood movie thriller than a possibility in real life, though this rarely matters for their promoters who advance them.[16] They ignore the fact that it is very hard to keep a secret among more than a few people and that governments do a particularly bad job of keeping secrets these days.

The political nature of Conspiracy Theories is particularly clear in the modern period. Modern Conspiracy Theorists have tried to explain important political changes and events by hidden forces—in other words, to show that things are not as they seem. Byford says that this type of Conspiracy Theory dates from the French Revolution, where we have the first theories denying that the people had risen up and insisting that there was a covert group manipulating the entire event.[17]

This is the origin of the Illuminati Conspiracy Theory, which alleged that this secret group, the Illuminati, had orchestrated the French Revolution to their own benefit. Byford further shows that one of the groups most often accused of being behind a major political event, be it the French Revolution, the Bolshevik Revolution, the German loss during World War I, or the Stock Market Crash of 1929, are Jews.[18] Part of this has to do with the long history of European anti-Jewish prejudice and, related especially with regard to twentieth-century Conspiracy Theories, the shameful popularity of *The Protocols of the Elders of Zion*, which gained wide currency throughout the Western world since its publication in 1903. This is not to say that Jews have been blamed for everything; other groups have been targeted as well. However, anti-Jewish Conspiracy Theories comprise a disproportionate share of Western and even non-Western Conspiracy Theories. The more extreme the ideology, the more this share rises.

Both Cassam and Byford highlight the centrality of Jews and Zionism in Nazi and communist Conspiracy Theories.[19] The conspiratorial nature of Nazi views of the Jews is well known. In *Mein Kampf*, Hitler describes his perspective that the Jews seek to survive at the expense of the Germans in a racial struggle to the death. Nazis saw the Jews as a cancer seeking to destroy Germany. Thus, Jews were blamed for Germany's defeat in World War I, Jewish capitalists were exploiting German workers, Jewish intellectuals were destroying German culture, and Jewish communists were attacking the German state. Hitler was well acquainted with the Conspiracy Theory of *The Protocols of the Elders of Zion*, one of the most important sources for Nazi anti-Jewish propaganda. The Nazis disseminated these theories in newspapers like *Der Stürmer*, in images, and of course in the many broadcast speeches Hitler gave. As we shall describe in greater detail later, the Nazi anti-Jewish propaganda became anti-Zionist in the postwar period. On the far right, prewar terms like "international Jewry" have increasingly been replaced with terms like "Zionist Occupied Government (ZOG)," which like the former term claims a Jewish/Zionist conspiracy to control all banks and Western governments, leading these entities to fight wars and serve the interests of the state of Israel and world Jewry against the interests of Western people.

But Nazis were not the only ones to put forward propaganda focusing on Conspiracy Theories about Jews. Soviet anti-Zionist propaganda sponsored by the department of propaganda and the KGB, which started in the 1950s and escalated in the 1960s, under the euphemism of Zionology (the academic study of Zionism), was unequivocally conspiratorial. The entry on Zionism for the *Great Soviet Encyclopedia* includes the following:

- "the main posits of modern Zionism are militant chauvinism, racism, anti-Communism and anti-Sovietism"

- "the anti-human reactionary essence of Zionism" is an "overt and covert fight against freedom movements and against the USSR"

- "International Zionist Organization owns major financial funds, partly through Jewish monopolists and partly collected by Jewish mandatory charities," it also "influences or controls significant parts of media agencies and outlets in the West"

- "serving as the front squad of colonialism and neo-colonialism, international Zionism actively participates in the fight against national liberation movements of the peoples of Africa, Asia and Latin America."

The Soviets also widely disseminated this Conspiracy Theory in the form of propaganda leaflets and lectures. Scholars have shown how Soviet anti-Zionist classics like Yuri Ivanov's *Beware: Zionism* were essentially updated versions of *The Protocols of the Elders of Zion*.

Another feature of postwar anti-Zionist Conspiracy Theories on both the far left and the far right is the perceived power of the so-called Israel lobby.[20] That there are Jewish groups lobbying for Israel and that the Israeli government promotes its interests to other governments is natural and beyond dispute. This is true of all diaspora groups and states. The heart of many anti-Zionist Conspiracy Theories is that the Israel lobby is a monolithic and powerful organization that succeeds in manipulating and orchestrating other governments and organizations to do Israel's bidding against their own interests. While the imagined power of the Israel lobby is central to Conspiracy Theories on both the far left and far right, it operates differently. On the far left, all Zionists, not just lobby members, are included in the Conspiracy Theory. On the far right, all Jews must be part of the lobby even if they are card-carrying members of an anti-Zionist Jewish group like Jewish Voice for Peace.

Conspiracy Theories have a deadly history. The proliferation of Conspiracy Theories commonly precedes mass murder and genocide. This was true in Turkey prior to the Armenian genocide, in Germany prior to the Jewish genocide, and in Rwanda prior to the genocide of the Tutsis and moderate Hutus, to name a few. Conspiracy Theories have found fertile ground for fetid abundance in both fascist and communist dictatorships. In the former USSR and in China, Conspiracy Theories about minorities have proliferated. Prior to the massive anti-Uyghur campaign, the Chinese populace was prepared with propaganda about Uyghur separatism and terrorism. Conspiracy Theories also often accompany atrocity denial. For example, those who deny the mass murders by the Khmer Rouge in Cambodia often attribute these as lies clandestinely originated by the CIA. Why people believe or promote these theories has been the topic of much scholarly debate, and we will discuss this question in relation to the Conspiracy Theories promoted by faculty at Northwestern.

While theories about conspiracies that actually occurred are compatible with Northwestern's motto and the Golden Rule, Conspiracy Theories are not. Despite the academic veneer that Conspiracy Theorists give to their theories, often with considerable efforts and reams of footnotes, Conspiracy Theories have little concern for evaluating evidence

according to accepted standards of logic and truthfulness.[21] The consideration of evidence is selective, distorted, blatantly untrue, uncorroborated, and/or illogical. For this reason, most Conspiracy Theories have been refuted. Conspiracy Theories are also immoral in that they demonize the conspirators based on nonexistent, distorted, or false evidence. ·
Thus, scholars following the Northwestern motto and the Golden Rule could certainly claim that the Nazis were conspiring to kills Jews and Roma and that their behavior—which included theft, murder, torture, and genocide—was evil. All of this is documented. Therefore, the key difference is the evidence and how it is evaluated. Reliable historians, journalists, lawyers, and citizens must first approach the question of the cause or the identity of the perpetrators and victims of an event or process with an open mind, not prejudiced to either party, and then evaluate the evidence.

Despite these many features that compromise the intellectual and moral standards of Conspiracy Theories, Conspiracy Theorists usually rigorously deny their limitations. That being said, Conspiracy Theories come in different forms. Some are short and dubious, like *The Protocols of the Elders of Zion*, with little effort made to provide supporting evidence. In other cases, Conspiracy Theorists have written long, drawn-out descriptions of details that make their theories appear flawlessly documented and proven. In still other cases, the Conspiracy Theories appeal to the moral authority of specific authors or groups. In any case, Conspiracy Theorists are notoriously convinced of their theories and indeed rarely change their minds when presented with contrary evidence. As Cassam argues, the point in addressing Conspiracy Theories is not necessarily to change the minds of the Conspiracy Theorists themselves but rather the minds of those susceptible to getting caught up by the theories.[22]

In my freshman writing class with David Campbell, I learned that Aristotle had set forth more than two millennia ago that there are three types of persuasion, and each of these relates to a part of our personhood. Aristotle famously called them, *logos*, *ethos*, and *pathos*. These are the three ways to persuade us to take an action, the three aspects to our agency, and the three parts of us that together make us human actors—in other words, persons.[23] *Logos* means trying to convince someone using facts, evidence, or math. *Ethos* means persuading someone based on ethical considerations or by citing a purportedly reliable source—as a professor, for example, I say X and you can just trust me based on my credentials. Finally, *pathos* is resorting to pure emotion— if you don't leave you will be among fools, or if you don't do X you don't have a heart. Conspiracy Theories are so successful because they deprive us of what makes us reasoning persons able to evaluate the world by using false or made-up evidence and having us rely on unreliable sources. We are left with only *pathos*, our most easily exploitable motivator. We become beings that can be deftly manipulated by anger, fear, or other emotions. Believing in Conspiracy Theories deprives us of our human capacities, which is what leads us to crazy actions. No wonder that exploiters of people have figured out that getting their followers to believe in Conspiracy Theories is the best hack to get them to do whatever the leaders want.

While Conspiracy Theories have made their comeback in the modern world, especially as political propaganda and in the service of totalitarian ideologies, the earliest example of them—to my knowledge— can be drawn from the Bible. I was listening to a lecture from one of my most influential teachers, Rabbi David Silber, on the Book of 2 Kings, in which he mentioned in an offhand way that the narrative in chapter 7 was an early description of a Conspiracy Theory. By way of background, the chapter describes the mighty Aramean army as laying siege to the capital of the Northern Kingdom in Samaria. The Israelites are at the brink of starvation and destruction. The author then tells us that God caused the Arameans to hear loud noises that they took for the sound of an attacking army. "They said to one another, 'The King of Israel must have hired the kings of the Hittites or the kings of Egypt to attack us!' So, they scurried and fled in the twilight, abandoning their tents and horses and asses. They left the whole camp just as it was because they fled for their lives." (2 Kings 7:5–7)

Silber pointed out that the Arameans heard loud noises and they assumed the worst of the worst, but the story they told themselves made no sense. The Hittites and the Egyptians had no reason to help the Israelites (actually the obverse was true), and the Israelites had no money or other resources to pay anyone. Israel was suffering from a seven-year famine and was at the brink of starvation. Silber asked how the Arameans could have believed such a crazy idea. The answer he gave comes from a previous episode in 2 Samuel, chapter 10, in which the Ammonites declare war on King David's United Kingdom of Israel and hire the Arameans as mercenaries to double their forces. The strategy almost worked, but the healthy, well-fed, united Israelites of that story managed to thwart their combined enemies on the battlefield.

In short, the explanation is that since the Arameans themselves were willing to be mercenaries, they could certainly imagine other forces being hired as mercenaries. All that needed to happen was for them to hear a threatening sound and their own demons came back to haunt them. There was no need for a splitting of the Reed Sea[24] or other major miracle. At that point, I stopped listening to the lecture and was reminded of a conversation with my father that I hadn't thought of for decades. Just before I moved to New York, as I was cleaning out my room at home, I came upon the neo-Nazi hate mail I had received at my Northwestern dorm and I threw it out. I then mentioned the mail to my father and a small bit of its Conspiracy Theory contents, which I very much sanitized in my recounting because I did not want to upset him too much. I recall his response as, "*Meshuganah gornisht bolbe* brings out the *dybbuks* in *nuchshleppers*." Translated as to how I think my father intended, "Crazy, worthless, stupid, made-up tales bring out the demons in susceptible, unthinking people."

Conspiracy Theories are the exact opposite of the Golden Rule. People's demons cause them to do terrible things to others, and since they can imagine what they are capable of doing, they fear other people doing those very same things to them. Everyone has demons, and to the degree that they don't control them, they become susceptible to

Conspiracy Theories. Unfortunately, evil leaders well understand that they can harness these demons for political purposes, or worse.

The mighty Aramean army should have known better. Armies are in the business of rationally judging facts. Opponents are always attempting decoys, feints, gambits, pincers, ambushes, false flags, and the like. Armies deploy scouts to discern facts and intelligence officers to analyze the facts. The facts were clear: the Israelites were starving, many had perished from starvation and disease, and they had only a few horses remaining that could be used in battle. (2 Kings 7:13) The Aramean scouts must have said that they saw no attacking army. The only people in sight were four lepers. (2 Kings 7:8) The proper discerning response from the leaders of the Aramean army would have been that the sounds were a decoy or noise, not a signal based on all the facts. Yet that is not what happened. Certainly, all the scouts and intelligence officers must have given their recounting and analysis of the actual evidence, but the Conspiracy Theory that took hold became the only compelling theory of the situation. The scouts and intelligence officers must have been astounded that no one cared about the facts or their plausible explanations. Anything they said regarding actual facts must have been rebuffed with a torrent of fearful rhetoric that shut down rational discourse. The Arameans became so overwhelmed with *pathos* that they saw no alternative but to flee on foot immediately.

There is no doubt about their sincere belief in their Conspiracy Theory. They left behind not only all of their animals, armaments, and supplies, but all of their food, gold, silver, and clothes. (2 Kings 7:8) Even the scouts and intelligence officers fled along with the rest of the troops, as they must have feared being trampled by their comrades or perhaps they began to doubt their own sanity. In terms of effect, this Conspiracy Theory was like a self-inflicted neutron bomb. Today there are scholars in our universities who, like the Aramean army, are convinced of Conspiracy Theories, including one that Zionists are conspiring to harm all good people.

BRETHREN

BUTZ AND THRASHER: CONSPIRACY THEORISTS

Arthur Butz and Steven Thrasher are two experts in their respective fields who also happen to believe Zionists are conspiring to harm vast swaths of people. Butz and Thrasher are both acknowledged scholars. Professor Butz was not just any researcher when he wrote *The Hoax of the Twentieth Century*; he was hot. He had solved the Hilbert's space-filling curve problem with an algorithm that considerably advanced computational power. His algorithm was so novel that it was named after him. It was probably an easy decision by Northwestern to grant him tenure two years prior to the publication of his Holocaust denial book.

Even more can be said of Professor Thrasher. He is not just any professor of journalism; he is a rock star. Thrasher was named one of the one hundred most influential and impactful LGBTQ+ people of 2019 by *Out* magazine. He frequently appears on television on Al Jazeera, PBS, CNN, and the show *Democracy Now!* and has received many awards and accolades. He is a gifted writer who had already published hundreds of articles in top Western newspapers, from *The Guardian* to the *New York Times*, before getting his PhD. His articles have made major contributions to the field of public health, especially addressing the AIDS crisis among people of color and the intersection between health, criminal justice, and race.

Despite their credentials, both scholars' writings on Zionists have all of the classic features of Conspiracy Theories. It is worth taking a moment to consider the specific conspiracies these scholars are describing, as well as the claims they are making against the conspirators, in this case the Zionists.

Butz's book and articles emphasize Zionism as a sinister political movement aimed at despoiling Arabs but primarily at duping and robbing the world—especially Germans. He writes, "The consequences of World War II did not create Zionism as an effective political movement; they merely gave Zionism the world political victory it needed for the final stage of takeover of Palestine."[1] Butz claimed that Zionists won this victory through various treacheries. The first was that Zionists conspired to create "the hoax" that six million Jews died in the Holocaust to force the Allies to grant them Palestine. Butz makes his view glaringly clear: "The thesis of this book is that the story of the Jewish extermination in WWII is a propaganda hoax."[22] According to Butz, Hitler simply meant to end Jewish influence and power in Germany, never to murder Jews. He writes, "A Hitler reference to 'die Vernichtung des Judentums' if lifted out of context and interpreted in a purely literal way, can be interpreted as meaning the killing of all Jews, but it can also mean the destruction of Jewish influence and power, which is what the politician Hitler actually meant by such a remark, although it is true he could have chosen his words more carefully."[3] For Butz, Jews did not die en masse but rather immigrated to the United States and British Mandatory Palestine.[4]

Butz argues that Zionists used two main strategies to perpetuate this hoax. During the war, they conspired to disseminate the hoax through the US Treasury and World Jewish Congress, which pressured Washington, the *New York Times*, which publicized the murders, and the War Refugee Board, which sought to help the make-believe refugees. He devotes the first chapter of his book to outline this thesis.[5]

Secondly, after the war, the Zionists conspired to take over the war crimes tribunals, using them to prove the "hoax." Butz calls the post-war war crimes trials a "frame-up."[6] His evidence is that Jews such as Samuel Rosenman, Murray Bernays, Myron Cramer, and Mickey Marcus, as well as Jewish organizations such as the International Auschwitz Committee, conspired to choose the prosecution and defense lawyers, manipulate witnesses, and use "irregular methods" to forward the hoax of the Holocaust.[7] He writes about Marcus: "The filling of the war crimes branch with a fanatical Zionist, 'the first soldier since biblical times to hold the rank of general in the army of Israel,' is not only significant in terms of what the Zionist might do in the position, but also significant in revealing, in a simple way, the nature of the overall political forces operating in the trials."[8] Additionally, he asserts, the Zionists conspired in manipulating the American government to do their bidding in Palestine with the myth of the six million. In particular, Butz claims that "the Zionist Lobbying" led to the appointment of John Hilldring to the position of assistant secretary of state in charge of occupied areas (including Germany) and then special advisor on Palestine of the US delegation to the UN, stating that Hilldring (an American of Swedish descent) "frequently conversed with Zionist strategists."[9] According to Butz, Zionists succeeded in co-opting important Christian American leaders like Eisenhower, exaggerating claims of anti-Semitism in Europe to flee the continent and using their influence to turn the DP camps and therefore American resources into "military training camps for the invasion of Palestine."[10]

His next allegation is that the Zionists conspired to make the German government beholden to them and to rob Germans of money with their slander. Butz alludes to this conspiracy by mentioning that the German chancellor Willy Brandt's press aid upon his postwar reentry into German politics was a Jew, Hans Hirschfeld.[11] He later writes, "The Bonn government has undertaken additional programs of indemnification that have been similarly motivated."[12] Because this has shown that the "unspeakable criminal acts, in the sense in which that term is used in the Luxembourg [reparations] Treaty, are largely a hoax, specifically a Zionist hoax," he then argues that Israel owes Germany a lot of money.[13] Finally, Butz claims throughout his book that Zionists conspired to silence opponents.

Unlike Butz, Thrasher did not write a book on Zionism and only wrote one entire article related to Israel. Instead, like many academics today, he seems to take the evilness of Zionism as beyond any doubt and has included conspiratorial texts, like Angela Davis's *Freedom Is a Constant Struggle: Ferguson, Palestine, and the Foundations of a Movement*,[14] in his NYU classes on race in America. Thrasher's anti-Zionism is indeed laced into the many other topics he writes about. We will be parsing his public pronouncements, journalistic writings, and tweets carefully, as they merit close inspection. Like Butz, Thrasher considers Zionism to be an illegitimate and murderous political movement that has manipulated and used Americans, though he focuses on his assertions that it oppresses and murders Palestinians while providing a model for harming other people of color.

His first conspiratorial claim is that Zionists are imperialists who collude to commit genocide against Palestinians. He repeats these views on Twitter, and I only cite tweets that he has not deleted as of the time of this writing. An example is a June 11, 2018, tweet: "Peak white cultural New York liberalism is when a musical from Israel wins a Tony & no one mentions the genocide of Israel occupied Palestine & a play nominally about AIDS wins & no one mentions the ongoing genocide of HIV/AIDS." In a May 15 tweet the same year he wrote, "The US backed Israeli slaughter of Gazans makes me think: if the million Black ppl in the US locked up in prisons peacefully walked up to the fences which cage them in like Gazans, would they, too, be shot? Likely. Colonial states (US, Israel, apartheid SA) control similarly."

The second claim is that Zionists conspire to inspire and/or assist murdering other people of color as well. On May 15, 2018, he tweeted, "Disinterested parties in the slaughter in Gaza should pay attention for its horror but also out of self-interest: Israel used drones to gas people. Colonial powers (US, Apartheid SA, Israel) test weapons of war on colonial subjects before bringing them home to the metropole." On March 5, 2018, he made the same accusations: "Angela Davis teaches us how connected the policing is from Ferguson to Baltimore—and how the tactics of control and intimidation circulate across the U.S. border, as the U.S. sends our police to train in Israel." Later, on April 5, 2018, he tweeted that Israel's policies would affect Central Americans: "I am *pretty* sure he [Trump] did this bc he was watching TV & saw Israel go batshit on Palestinians approaching peacefully and he was like, 'I wanna do the same when the CARAVAN approaches.' This is scary."

The third claim is that Zionists conspire to force "the establishment" in America to provide automatic support to Israel. Here he retweets Chanda Prescod-Weinstein, a professor of physics at the University of New Hampshire and an African American and Jewish critic of Israel, March 4, 2019: "What happens to Ilhan Omar of course matters deeply but no matter what comes next in her political career, she has done a magnificent job of putting the establishment's stance on compulsory allegiance to Israel on full display. The more they deny it, the more it shows."

Finally, the fourth claim is that Israel and Zionists conspire to defame and silence their opponents like himself. In a series of tweets in March 2018, Thrasher contends that the Israeli consulate sought to get him fired from the *Village Voice*. Elsewhere he alludes to Israeli conspiracies against other public figures and academics: "The past couple of days, I have been thinking about the price Marc Lamont Hill, Steven Salaita, Angela Davis, Emily Henochowicz, Razan al-Najar, Rachel Corrie & others have paid to speak & act against violence." In June of the same year he writes, "The goal of the police in Selma and of the IDF was the same: physically destroy the rebellion, no matter how peaceful. Israel is going a step further: kill the medics helping the wounded and the journos covering on site, to squash all future dissent, aid & coverage."

Butz and Thrasher's claims ultimately demonize Zionists and Jews who agree with Zionists in several ways. The first is through the prism of race or the Jewish essence. Both agree Zionism is racism. (Butz cites the UN.) For Thrasher, the Arabs are joined by all people of color as victims of Zionist racism; for Butz, they are joined by white people such as Germans and Americans. For Thrasher, Zionists strengthen white power; for Butz, they undermine it. In other words, Jews are a category of deviant whites rather than people on their own terms. For both, Jews pollute what should be their appropriate categories.

For Thrasher, Zionist Jews are deviant whites by being, what I term, "hyper white." They are not only the new Nazis but conduct a graduate school for white supremacists (white Americans and other colonial powers) on how to harm people of color in new and ever more cunning ways. In this imagined view, the labors of the far left are being undermined by the hyper-white Zionists who are embedded in some sort of colonialist stealth guerrilla battalion. Zionist Jews don't just infiltrate European society; they co-opt and magnify its racism in a common ideological cause. So, for Thrasher, they influence the police, the military, the security apparatus, and foreign policy, all the while hiding their agenda by claiming to be victims of the very people of color they victimize. The cry of anti-Semitism is used to cover up Zionist crimes. Zionism is thus white supremacy in Thrasher's view and in that of members of Jewish Voice for Peace (JVP) such as Chanda Prescod-Weinstein. They support this accusation against all Jews and non-Jews who support Zionism, approving only of "enlightened" Jews who agree with them.

For Butz, Jews are deviant whites by being "fake white." They use their American, German, and other European citizenships together with their fake white faces to infiltrate and control various agencies to do their will against the interests of real whites. In this way of thinking, Jews undermine white attempts to put people of color in their place. Butz asserts Zionists controlled the press and influenced leaders like Roosevelt and Eisenhower in the US and Brandt in Germany. Alas, even associating with Jews creates a taint for the hapless non-Jew. Butz lauds some Germans and Americans of European descent with a "clearheaded view" as people who called out the Zionists and refused to be bamboozled. Further, according to Butz, Jews craftily and unfairly accuse these Europeans of anti-Semitism for refusing to be used for Zionist political interests.

For both intellectuals, Jews can only escape their warped whiteness and become worthy of being loved by disavowing any independent political identity. So, for Butz, the Jews should be satisfied with living in a "host society," keeping themselves subordinate to real whites and stopping their lies and blackmail. As Kevin MacDonald, a California State University professor, puts it, "What I would want to see the Jewish community do is change their position on these things. Realize that what they're doing is not fair to the white community, and that the world may not be very nice to them, either."[15] For Thrasher, Jews can be grateful they live privileged lives and help people of color to dismantle white supremacy and become vocal allies in opposing Israel. In either case, Butz and Thrasher instruct Jews that they must comply with their respective political doctrines in relation to whiteness. If not, they must be dealt with. MacDonald puts it succinctly: "Can we make alliances with the Jews? The answer is, provisionally yes…as long as they really subscribe to our interests."[16]

Thrasher and Butz's Conspiracy Theories about Zionists also demonize Zionists as rootless bandits. Butz reported: "When in November 1975, an overwhelming majority of the United Nations, in a burst of intellectual clarity rare for the organization, endorsed a resolution declaring Zionism to be a form of racism, a truth as inescapable as 2+2 = 4, the US representative Daniel Patrick Moynihan, an otherwise impressive intellect, was reduced in astonishingly short order to hysterical yapping about the six million."[17] Butz does not view Israel's fundamental sin as colonialism but rather parasitism; he claims that everywhere the Jews go they take from what belongs to others and seize important levers of control. Therefore, in the US and Germany they take over. Where the Zionists ought to live for Butz is unclear—they ought perhaps not to live at all.

Thrasher, like Butz, takes the UN's view of Israel as a colonizer for granted. He dismisses any notion that Jews have a tie to the land. Like Butz, he does not really elaborate on the rightful home of the Jews—perhaps America, perhaps Europe, but certainly not Palestine. In either case, Jews are unlike other peoples who clearly have a right to national self-determination in their historic homeland.

Butz and Thrasher's commonality is evident in their attitude toward Iran. In 2006, Butz praised former president of Iran Mahmoud Ahmadinejad for his Holocaust denial. Ahmadinejad was not an aberration but representative of Iranian attitudes. The Supreme Leader Ali Khamenei has stated in a Quds (Jerusalem) Day speech, in May 2020: "The Zionist regime is a deadly and harmful appendage for this region, and it will certainly be eradicated."[18] (A collection of Khamenei's statements on Israel is available in his 2011 book, *Palestine*.[19]) Thrasher's support for Iran is less direct but no less disturbing. In an August 2015 tweet he implicitly absolves Iran: "What is this obsession with Iran and ISIS (who hurt no one) but scant mention of white supremacy & police killing endless Americans?"

To buttress their points about Zionism and Zionists, both Butz and Thrasher are fond of referring to Jews who agree with them. Butz refers positively to Josef Ginsburg, who under the pseudonym of J. G. Burg published several books describing Zionist conspiracies to harm and expropriate Germans by exaggerating the Holocaust. Butz writes: "After the war Burg took his family to Israel, but he eventually became very anti-Zionist and moved back to Europe, eventually setting up a book bindery in Munich. While he believes that many Jews perished as a result of the combined effects of Nazi policies and wartime conditions, he denies that the German government ever contemplated the extermination of the Jews of Europe, and he is particularly scornful of the six million figure."[20] According to Butz, for his efforts to get to the truth, "Ginsburg, a small man and not young, was beaten up by Jewish thugs while visiting his wife's grave in the 'Israelite' cemetery in Munich."[21] As mentioned above, Thrasher cites Chanda Prescod-Weinstein (again, who is of Black and Jewish descent), who has written of anti-Zionist Conspiracy Theories that she claims harm people of color and control the establishment.

PART II

WHATSOEVER THINGS ARE TRUE 1

WHY BUTZ AND THRASHER'S CONSPIRACY THEORIES ARE WORTHLESS (OR AS MY FATHER WOULD SAY, *GORNISHT*)

One may legitimately ask, what if Butz and Thrasher are right? As I already mentioned, conspiracies do exist and so do malevolent powers. However, Butz and Thrasher's views of Zionists have all the classic features of Conspiracy Theories. They are not only improbable, they are demonstrably untrue, relying on specific types of parallel falsehoods characteristic of conspiratorial thinking. I will examine these features for both in turn.

Let's start with Butz. His first falsehood is simply dismissing evidence. For example, his primary conspiratorial claim—that the Holocaust is a Zionist hoax—requires him to dismiss or scorn vast amounts of evidence by survivors, Allied forces, and even the perpetrators themselves. This includes all testimony and eyewitness accounts, which he dismisses as lies committed by Zionists and their collaborators. This is particularly difficult for me, having lost my grandfather, my aunts, my uncles, and many other relatives to the Nazi murders. Butz also has to imagine that refugees from all over Europe coordinated these falsehoods and, more to the point, managed to convince all the soldiers who had liberated the camps of a massive set of lies. It also requires a false interpretation of Nazi writings as mentioned above, as well as gargantuan and easily falsifiable deliberate misrepresentations and fabrications. For example, he claims that the many German perpetrators who confessed and provided details of massacres of Jews were lying. Mass graves that have been unearthed just sort of happened. Non-perpetrators who weren't Jewish but swore to witnessing the mass murders are also dismissed by Butz, all under varying theories of being gaslighted by Zionists. Any anomaly is just proof of how good the Zionists are at lying, scheming, and covering up.

Butz also makes the outlandish claim that most of the missing European Jews simply immigrated to the United States, despite the great difficulty they faced both before and after the war to do so. He bases these claims on some minor inconsistencies in various demographic tables relating to the number of Jews in various places. None of these discrepancies are large or unusual for any sort of similar demographic data. America had closed its doors to the Jews in 1924, and almost no other countries were willing to accept any Jewish refugees. The Bermuda Conference of 1943 convened to find some refuge for Jews was a complete failure. Canada as an example had a policy on Jewish immigration that was reflected in an oft-cited quote from an immigration official that "none is too many."[1] Governments across the world had essentially the same rule.

With respect to the United States, sadly, the story has become clear since World War II documents have been declassified. There were many tens of thousands of annual unused immigration quotas before and during the war. In Rafael Medoff's meticulously researched book *The Jews Should Keep Quiet: Franklin D. Roosevelt, Rabbi Stephen S. Wise, and the Holocaust*,[2] he demonstrates that Roosevelt simply did not want more Jews in the US. In documented interviews found by Medoff, Roosevelt tells of his views that Jews alienated their German and Polish neighbors and as such the Jews were responsible for the hatred against them. Roosevelt's labor secretary, Frances Perkins, prepared an executable plan in 1934 to bring substantial numbers of Jews to the US, but the president quashed the plan. While Roosevelt later argued there were no ships to carry Jewish refugees to the US, at the same time American ships bringing troops and materiel to Europe were returning empty and desperately seeking ballast so they could safely make the return journey. Allied ships provided the transportation for twenty thousand visitors from Egypt to Arabia for the Hajj in 1944. About 425,000 German prisoners of war were moved to the US by ship as well. All at the peak of the German slaughter of Jews.

Even after the war, my father, who wanted to come to the United States, faced major difficulties being able to immigrate. A quiet hero by the name of Dr. Julius Meyer began the process of bringing my father to the US in 1946. It took over three years until my father could arrive on these shores. Dr. Meyer signed an indemnification to the US government that my father would not be a financial burden on the country. To prove that he could perform under the indemnification, Dr. Meyer had to provide his income tax return, his personal balance sheet, his life insurance policy, and his living expenses. The US was not taking any chances when it came to accepting Jews emigrating from Europe.

Butz's view of the role of the *New York Times* and Nuremberg trials in disseminating this "hoax" also relies on perversions and falsifications. For example, as Laurel Leff described in her book *Buried by The Times*,[3] between 1939 and 1945 very few stories about the Jewish victims of the war made the front pages, and of those that did, only six mentioned Jews specifically. Another problem was that far from being pro-Zionist, a number of the European correspondents were openly pro-fascist Jew haters. As to the Nuremberg trials, the Allies sought to punish Germany for its war crimes, of which the genocide of the Jews was just one example of the subcategory, and none of the judges or main prosecutors were Jews.

As to his second conspiracy, that Zionists manipulated Americans into doing their bidding, Butz uses omission and gross exaggeration. He makes it sound like anyone who spoke to or had any association with a Jew was compromised and/or brainwashed into doing the Zionists' bidding. Clearly, Butz does not think it is safe to be around Jews. He omits the instances when America did not support Israel—for example refusing military support in the Arab-Israeli wars of 1948 and 1967 and subsequently giving military support with the condition that it had to be entirely spent on US products and that each purchase had to be agreed to by the Defense Department.

Likewise, his third conspiracy—that Zionists conspired to make the German government beholden to them and to rob Germans of money by defaming them—also depends on gross omission and exaggeration. He fails to mention that Germans first paid retribution (via cash, the transfer of industrial assets, and forced labor) to the Allied powers and not to Holocaust victims. Butz also doesn't note that Israel's Knesset authorized the negotiations with Germany with only 61 of 120 votes in favor. Many Israelis passionately opposed accepting any money from Germany. (My father too was deeply conflicted over whether to accept the German reparations checks that began to come to him around 1970. He decided to do so in part because he hoped I would go to college. He really wanted me to become a medical doctor like his sponsor, Dr. Meyer.) Butz also omits that West Germany did not have diplomatic relations with Israel until 1965. Also, during the 1973 Yom Kippur War, West German chancellor Willy Brandt did not allow American armed forces to use German military bases to refuel for missions supplying Israel with weapons due to his policy of neutrality. He kept to this policy even as the survival of Israel hung in the balance. Hardly a country blindly doing Israel's bidding.

Butz also alleges that Jews and their lackeys among the Allies conspired to victimize Germans in the concentration camps. He informs us that Jews mistreated German guards at Dachau[4] and that "British liberators deliberately exposed SS women to contagious diseases" by ordering them to prepare graves for the dead Jews.[5] Butz's allegations as to the Nuremberg trials also require actual history to be jettisoned to a parallel universe. The main trials were judged and staffed by a consortium of Soviet, French, British, and American participants.[6] The Soviets were neither wallflowers to the proceedings nor pawns of Butz's imagined Jewish cabal. The Nuremberg trials were also not specifically focused on the genocide against the Jews but on crimes against broad segments of humanity.[7]

Like Butz's theories, Thrasher's conspiracies also depend on certain patterns of demonstrable lies. To buttress his accusation of conspiracy to genocide, he must invent atrocities through deliberate distortions. His May 2018 tweet is again, "Disinterested parties in the slaughter in Gaza should pay attention for its horror but also out of self-interest: Israel used drones to gas people." This is part of Thrasher's repetition of the charge of genocide. That would be really evil if it were true as Thrasher insinuates it to be. By using the words "gas people," he is using Holocaust imagery that totally distorts reality. The gas in the drones that he refers to in his tweet was nonlethal tear gas, not Zycklon B used by the Nazis to murder Jews in gas chambers or the mustard gas and nerve agents Saddam Hussein used to murder Kurds in the al-Anfal campaign. Instead, tear gas was used to deter Gazan militants from crossing the international boundary fence at the 1967 border and unleashing weapons designed to kill Israelis. No UN agency has made the assertion that drones were launched into Gaza to unleash lethal gas. Further, tear gas is used by most governments to disperse demonstrations (including the Venezuelan, French, Nigerian, and Canadian governments, to name some examples from around the world), yet you would not know this from Thrasher's tweet.

The reason for Israel's measures, then and now, is border protection (often provided with armed guards), a universally accepted concept. No UN member country allows militants to unilaterally decide to cross their international border.[8] Indeed, this concept is so accepted that it is entirely legal under international law for government to use tear gas, and other law enforcement measures including rubber bullets, to disperse riots at their border. In the event that border activities are part of a military operation, or an invasion carried out by civilians, it is legal to use lethal force.[9] While scholars have debated whether Israel should or should not have used lethal force during the March of Return, anti-Zionist Conspiracy Theorists have had little to say about the Egyptian guards, for example, who have shot to kill many Gazans who approached the Rafah Border Crossing and other parts of their border with Gaza, including at sea. Moreover, given that Gaza's government is controlled entirely by Hamas, which receives funds from Israel's enemies such as Qatar and Iran, builds invasion tunnels, launches missiles, and floats kites over the border designed to burn forests, it is hard to assert that Israel controls or occupies Gaza, let alone that it is committing genocide against Gazans.[10] In fact, it is Gaza's belligerence since Israeli withdrawal that has led to the Israeli blockade. The Gazans' rage against Israel is such that after the Israeli disengagement from Gaza in 2005, they destroyed assets such as greenhouses, houses, and agricultural equipment that Israel left behind for the new government's benefit.[11] Egypt's blockade is much more complete, despite being a fellow Arab and Muslim country and not being the target of constant Gazan rocket or terrorist attacks.[12]

A second tactic is rhetorical: as above, he frequently compares Israel to Nazi Germany. For example, in a May 15, 2018 tweet, he writes, "As the Nazis did on Jews, homosexuals & the disabled...As enslavers did to Africans...and as U.S. police departments have on Black urban neighborhoods US backed Israel is testing the limits of what it can get away with in controlling humans in Gaza. Will the world care?" Israel blockades Gaza militarily, a legitimate measure against a hostile military enemy under international law. Civilian supplies regularly pass through to Gaza. It is hard to equate these actions with an experiment in controlling humans. The previous quote also serves to support his accusation of a conspiracy to oppress people of color globally by claiming that Israel serves as a testing ground for evil. Indeed, for his second conspiracy, he uses insinuation and prediction as fact. This is the rhetorical effect of the rest of the tweet: "Colonial powers (US, Apartheid SA, Israel) test weapons of war on colonial subjects before bringing them home to the metropole." Or in another instance: "Watch how

(US backed) Israel is using them on Palestinians: drones will be used on rebellious PoC [people of color] in the US soon enough." Thrasher does not even bother to support these wild accusations with any evidence, but the point is clear: Israel—which has a long history of technological and social cooperation with many countries in the global south—is paradoxically a testing ground for global oppression. Thrasher, for example, nowhere writes of how Israel shares its water technologies with African countries.[13]

Yet another tactic to promote the accusation of conspiracy to global oppression is to make bogus comparisons. Following Angela Davis, Thrasher claims that Ferguson, Missouri, is Gaza. Showing a picture of the cover of Davis's *Freedom is a Constant Struggle*, he tweets on March 5, 2019: "Angela Davis teaches us how connected the policing is from Ferguson to Baltimore—and how the tactics of control and intimidation circulate across the U.S. border, as the U.S. sends our police to train in Israel." Or as Davis herself puts it in her book, "The militarization of the police leads us to think about Israel and the militarization of the police there—if only the images of the police and not the demonstrators had been shown, one might have assumed that Ferguson was Gaza."

Davis's constant affirmations of the similarities she sees between the events in Ferguson and in Gaza[14] are so enormously wrong that one can only conflate them if one abandons reality. For starters, the demonstrators in Ferguson were unarmed and unorganized and seeking primarily to protest against police violence against their community. In contrast, protesters in Gaza have launched thousands of rockets aimed at neighboring communities, continued to divert humanitarian aid to build tunnels to infiltrate bordering towns so they could kill residents there, and continued to vow to reclaim every inch of land of the surrounding communities and put the present residents "to the sword" or "into the sea." I saw one unexploded rocket that was aimed at an Israeli school near the Gaza border at the beginning of the school year. Of the Hebrew and Arabic written on the fuselage, I could read the Hebrew (*baruch haba kita aleph*), which roughly translates into "Welcome, First Graders." Most recently during the so-called peaceful March of Return, protesters flew kites designed to burn forests and buildings and harm Israel (thousands of acres of forest and farmland in the south of Israel were destroyed). The forthright goal of the March of Return was the destruction of the state of Israel.[15]

As to his final conspiracy, Thrasher does not even bother to explain how the Zionists are able to strong-arm the establishment. Rather, his African-American and American/Palestinian comparisons are intended to make two points: (1) Zionism is racist, and (2) just as the establishment is racist against Blacks, it is likewise racist against Palestinians. In a series of tweets about the March of Return on June 2, 2018, Thrasher makes these comparisons explicit: "Imagine that instead of sicking dogs & fire hoses on Black marchers at Selma, Bull Connor had snipers shoot them, the medics helping & the journos covering. THAT's what Israel's doing." And "The goal of the police in Selma and of the IDF was the same: physically destroy the rebellion, no matter how peaceful. Israel is going a step further: kill the medics helping the wounded and the journos covering on site, to squash all future dissent, aid & coverage." In actual fact, there is no one American "establishment"—different forces within the US government have backed Israelis or Palestinians for all kinds of reasons, as they do with other states as well.[16] Hamas routinely uses hospitals and other medical facilities to store weapons and launch missiles, which risks making them targets. Actually, it would be difficult for Ferguson and Gaza to have less to do with each other in terms of underlying issues. Simply asserting a comparison does not make it a credible one, as any scholar should know.

There are, however, two main dissimilarities in the two Conspiracy Theories: the first is the victims. For Butz, they are the Germans, especially the Nazis and the Americans smart enough not to be duped by the

Jews. For Thrasher, they are people of color. Indeed, the Zionists seem to be the archenemy of the very people that Butz and Thrasher uphold as their moral and political community. Despite these differences, it is significant that the website of the Institute for Historical Review (IHR), which focuses on far-right anti-Zionist Conspiracy Theories, consistently publishes far-left anti-Zionist Conspiracy Theorists and material from anti-Zionist websites like Mondoweiss and Electronic Intifada. The opposite is not the case.

The second is the Holocaust: both the far right and the far left claim Jews use the Holocaust illegitimately for Zionist ends; however, unlike the far right, the far left rarely denies the Holocaust occurred. For many people, this difference is the end of the story. But the reality is more nuanced. Given its focus on decolonialism, the far left is not interested in rehabilitating German Europeans by questioning that they could commit immense evil. Nevertheless, both extremes do unite in accusing Jews of maliciously abusing the notion of their suffering. Deborah Lipstadt has called this accusation "playing the Holocaust card."[17] In the case of the far left, as Steven Salaita contends, "The problem with remembrance...of the Nazi Holocaust is that it happens in isolation from relevant historical events and, worse from their ongoing consequences.... It's not very useful at all if a corresponding genocide is taking place, as with the Palestinians at the hands of Israel."[18]

Yet this accusation of misusing the Holocaust is bunk for several reasons. First, even if the Jewish community did "use" the Holocaust in order to justify any policy towards Palestinians, the Holocaust is not relevant to the central claim of the anti-Zionism Conspiracy Theorists that Zionism is inherently evil and illegitimate. Indeed, the Jewish right to national self-determination in the land of Israel is not based on the Holocaust but precedes it. Amazingly, Salaita tries to deal with this obvious point by conflating them and suggesting causation. "The Nazi Holocaust in Europe seems a direct antecedent to Israel's founding... there were plans from the outset of Zionism to rid the Promised Land of its indigenous population."[19] This sleight of hand however does not have the slightest truth. Salaita conjures a multi-generational geo-political conspiracy from "the outset," somehow including a cabal of evil Europeans involved in the "Nazi Holocaust in Europe" and "Zionists" ridding the "Promised Land of its indigenous population," in other words a genocide. All based on the proof that, it "seems." A perfect, non-falsifiable Conspiracy Theory.

Like any movement for self-determination, Zionism is based on the right to have one's own state, not on attempting to take from other peoples as empires often seek to do. Further, the demonization of Zionism precedes the creation of the state of Israel and the Holocaust, as the Soviet contentions make clear and as Hitler's view of Zionism demonstrates. Second, the claim of "playing the Holocaust card" is similar to the claim of Zionists compulsorily silencing their critics. It flies in the face of reality. Anti-Zionists and anti-Zionist Conspiracy Theorists have vocally expressed their perspectives since the creation of the State of Israel. Indeed, the entire Soviet and Arab orbit did so. In other words, even if there was an attempt to "play the Holocaust card," it has been remarkably ineffective. Third, the same is true for policy, including in the West, where Jews have supposedly been the most successful in "abusing" the Holocaust. The Holocaust card did not prevent Willy Brandt from refusing to let American planes land in Germany to help Israel when its survival was on the line, or stop Germany from doing business with Iran, which has made repeated existential threats against Israel. In fact, there is little evidence that the Holocaust, however much it is mentioned, is particularly relevant to the policy decisions of Israel's allies or enemies in practice. Rather, these are based on cold economic and national interest considerations.

WHATSOEVER THINGS ARE LOVELY 2

WHY BUTZ AND THRASHER'S DEMONIZATION OF ZIONISTS IS CRAZY (OR WHAT MY FATHER WOULD CALL *MESHUGANAH*)

Butz and Thrasher's demonization of their alleged Zionist conspirators is not only demonstrably false but also contains two classic features typically imbedded in politically motivated Conspiracy Theories.

Butz and Thrasher's Conspiracy Theories are similar and have adjacent narratives. Both see the Zionists as intentionally malevolent actors whose primary purpose is to hurt their victims. The Zionists are excised from the most basic norms of human behavior, where groups are composed of good and bad actors who adopt multiple strategies to defend their perceived interests, and transported into the world of the satanic, where they are all bad and where they are interested only in harming others. Let's switch the actors for a second to reinforce this point. Imagine if you read about African Americans as a mono-lithic group out to harm all white people in the world. Or of white Americans covertly pulling the strings of every major state, including China, Iran, and India, to their destruction, and doing it so cunningly that the citizens of China, Iran, and India don't even know it. Sound far-fetched? It is.

Jews are imagined as having power out of any sense of context and proportion. The Jews of Europe were, all told, a relatively small population of about nine million in relation to the total European population of four hundred million, excluding the former USSR. Even more disproportionately, Israel is a country of 8.5 million in a world of 7.5 billion. Yet despite being a small group, Israel is not alone. The Armenians total just three million in Armenia proper, yet are the subject of dubious conspiracies that they harm their far more numerous neighbors.

Both authors believe that there is fantastic unity and unlimited power among Zionists, yet people who believe in the Jewish right to national self-determination are a motley group to say the least, with political, social, and religious views spanning a wide spectrum. All one has to do is read the Israeli or Jewish newspapers to find that out. There is no doubt that Zionists and Israel are organized politically.[1] Then so are the Palestinians.[2] There is nothing more normal than lobbying and politics with regard to any advocacy, including supporting Israel. And there are many instances when Israel failed to achieve international alliances or goals, such as when it became quite isolated in the 1970s after years of seeking to form alliances with African, Asian, and European countries.[3] But one would hardly know that the Zionists are ordinary political actors in a world of interests and ideologies when reading Butz or Thrasher.

The racial views of the Jews explicit in these Conspiracy Theories are also a baseless demonization. The problem is that Jews are not white in the ways either Thrasher and Butz depict. While neither explicitly defines whiteness, both imply it means being culturally and socially European as well as having pale skin. Neither of these categories apply to the Jews as a people, including Jews in Europe, unless one willfully ignores the history of the world prior to the last two hundred years. The exile in Europe looked very different across the continent: it lasted nearly two thousand years in places like Italy (where Jews had lived since Roman times), or more like 230 years in places like Russia (where they had been variously barred, restricted to the Pale of Settlement with few rights, and scarcely had a presence until the Russians acquired parts of Poland).[4] Further, until the early modern period (1500s), Jews in Europe constituted less than half of all Jews in the world.[5] Indeed, the absurdity of calling Jews white and European is all the more glaring since Jews not only have a continuous history in the land of Israel but also in nearby exile in the Middle East. Jews have an established history in the land of Israel from antiquity and from the Babylonian exile (about 586 BCE) onward in the Middle East, and then later in North Africa, places that can hardly be deemed culturally European or racially white. Indeed, redwood-sized family trees of Jews exiled to Babylon in 586 BCE rarely encountered Europeans in their multi-millennial presence in the region.

Furthermore, the local population in Europe and the Middle East treated the Jews not only as a separate religion but as a separate people both legally and in popular culture, and Jews for the most part voluntarily identified as such. In Europe, Jews had an inferior legal status that excluded them from working in many professions and determined where they lived. Indeed, Jews necessarily acted as a people apart, maintaining their own connections across political, ethnic, and cultural borders of the European states where they lived, preserving their customs and, in many cases, separate languages and dialects.[6] In fact, it was their transnational connections and their exclusion from being able to own land or join guilds that drove them to become successful merchants and bankers and also caused them to be further distrusted.[7] Jews in the premodern period continued to pray for a return to Zion, and nowhere did they view their places of residence as their historic or permanent homeland. And even when they renounced their Judaism as in Spain, their Jewish blood was still a snare that subjugated their social and political status.[8] It was also sometimes an excuse for the Inquisition to torture or burn them alive (auto-da-fé). It was only in the modern period that full assimilation became an option in theory though rarely in practice.

Jews were granted citizenship and national civil rights in Europe beginning in the nineteenth century up until World War I. This was a phenomenon embraced and advanced by the bulk of the Jews, who wanted to fully participate in civic life. For example, it was only in 1858 that Jews obtained the right to sit in the UK Parliament after many years of trying. Yet the particularity of Jews in Europe persisted after emancipation.[9] While Jews received full national citizenship and many assimilated culturally, they often continued to primarily socialize with other Jews. Further, Jews still maintained separate religious and cultural institutions even when these were modeled according to European culture (much like Black churches in the United States remained separate even though they were derived from European Christianity).[10]

Perhaps because of this otherness, large movements in Europe arose after emancipation that insisted on the distinct, even evil nature of the Jews. The Dreyfus Affair was an unwelcome reminder of this in supposedly enlightened France.[11] Indeed, the Nazi movement arose at the height of Jewish assimilation to European culture.[12] Many enlightened Jews who hoped and believed they could pass as Germans, Hungarians, or Poles learned that Europeans still considered them just Jews. As my father remembered his neighbors standing aside as the Jews were rounded up, he knew that they didn't think he was a Lithuanian. If being European means being white, that certainly meant Jews were neither white nor European.

Just as Jews in Europe were viewed as a separate people, so too were they treated distinctively in North Africa and the Middle East. Jews often had their own dialects and customs and were governed by different laws (whether in the Babylonian and Persian Empires, later in the Arab caliphates, and finally under the Ottoman Turks).[13] After the Muslim conquest of the region, they had to convert to Islam in order to become anything other than Jewish.

In the modern period, as Arab nationalist leaders and European colonial powers carved out states to replace the Ottoman Empire, the Jewish communities of North Africa and the Middle East were progressively oppressed and finally expelled.[14] Today, thirty thousand Jews remain in the Middle East outside of Israel from a community that once numbered some eight hundred to nine hundred thousand. It is those Middle Eastern Jews who fled to Israel, and their descendants, who make up more than half of the Israeli population. A popular Saudi historical television show, *Um Haroun*, depicts Jewish life both before and after the establishment of Israel. As one actor noted, "The show hasn't changed anything in history...Jews used to be in the Gulf. They have their cemeteries, their homes."[15]

Nor did things change after World War II. My father's family lived in Lithuania for many generations. In the mid-1990s, my father decided to apply for a Lithuanian passport thinking that Lithuania would one day join the European Union and that it might be nice to have an all-access pass to Europe post-retirement. He made an appointment with the Lithuanian consulate thinking that it would be a pro forma process for him to affirm his Lithuanian citizenship. They informed him that he needed all sorts of papers, including his birth certificate, proof of family residence via deeds, leases, or cancelled checks on a home, and so on. Despite the conversation taking place entirely in properly accented Lithuanian with my father's detailed description of his hometown and his knowing the name of the Lithuanian president in 1940 (trick question), the consulate official made it clear that unless he had kept all those papers through his four years in concentration camps and slave camps, there was nothing the consulate could do to help him with his application. While my father did see some Kafkaesque humor in the absurdity of the Lithuanian position, he was bitter that to these officials he was still just a Jew, to be dismissed as expeditiously as possible, and not a dispossessed Lithuanian citizen.

Even in the United States, where Jews have been most welcomed by the dominant white society and suffered far less than other minority groups, they have never been white. Though Jews could sometimes pass culturally, socially, and in appearance (especially after World War II), they have been viewed by other Americans and themselves as a separate group. For many decades, they produced Jewish culture in Yiddish, lived in Jewish neighborhoods, and founded a plethora of communal Jewish organizations.[16] Even Jews who lived as shopkeepers in smaller towns participated in Jewish life apart from the non-Jewish community. This contributed to the fact that, prior to World War II, European American society did not accept Jews.[17] It is well known that they were kept out of country clubs, universities (many in addition to Northwestern had quotas for Jews), and various neighborhoods. In many companies, there was a glass ceiling that Jews could not penetrate.

Since World War II, Jews have been allowed to reach the highest echelons of American society while also participating in distinct Jewish life. Jews have done very well in America, and in this respect, there is certainly no doubt that they suffer far less prejudice than African Americans and Native Americans and certainly have less fear of the police. And most Jews understand that their situation in the US has been much more comfortable than that of both African Americans and Native Americans.

I had an experience with my father that made clear this distinction and his view that, although we were not white as an identity, our white skin did have a positive impact on our lives in the United States. My father worked as a carpenter contractor. After work, he sometimes liked to go out for a beer or two with someone from the job, often at a particular watering hole about a half mile from our apartment. One particular evening when I was ten or eleven, my father was apparently having a third beer, and my mother was annoyed that he was not home and the food she was preparing was going to be overcooked. So, she sent me to the bar to tell him to come home (cellphones had not yet been invented) and, if he wanted, to bring whoever was with him, but to come home now. I gave my father the message—he frowned, put some bills on the bar, and invited his drinking companion, James, to come to our home for dinner. James accepted.

We got in my father's car to make the short drive home. A block later, a police car appeared with a siren and a signal to pull over. The two policemen looked in the car from both sides and saw my father at the wheel, James in the front passenger seat, and me in the back. Rather than ask about my father's driving, they asked about James and why he was in the car. My father politely responded that he was a coworker and they were picking something up. James said nothing. The two policemen then conferred out of earshot and gave my father a moving violation ticket for changing lanes without signaling. (Luckily, they didn't give him a Breathalyzer test.) My father took the ticket and said that he would be more careful.

Afterward, my father explained to me that the ticket was really for driving a Black person. For James, this was a benign outcome. Would my father have gotten a ticket with a Chinese or Japanese immigrant or a Syrian Jew in the car? Probably not. They are not white either, but they all have in some ways had it much easier than Blacks in the United States. My father also knew that, even though he had limited means, it was possible for me to reasonably aspire to be a doctor or lawyer in America, while for James's children the road would be much tougher due to school environments and outright discrimination. My father knew what systemic bias meant from Sveksna; he remembered too the difference that a smudge of black tar could make.

But Jews are not alone in suffering less prejudice than African Americans and Native Americans and not being white. Asian Americans (including Indians, Chinese, Koreans, and Japanese) also suffer far less prejudice than African Americans and Native Americans, and they are also not viewed as white.[18] The success and the relative benevolence bestowed on these groups compared to African Americans and Native Americans does not make them European or white. American society simply has a more positive appraisal of Jewish people than European societies did, while it has retained European racism against African Americans and Native Americans.

Nor does cooperating with the United States make someone white. Does Thrasher consider all people who cooperate with American security forces to be white? US security cooperation with India, with Mexico, or with Egypt does not make their citizens white.[19] Alternatively, are the Turks white because they oppress the Armenians, and are the latter in turn people of color? Nor does Jewish assimilation to European American culture mean they are white. Certainly, many Jews marry European/white Americans (the Jewish intermarriage rate among the non-Orthodox is about 70 percent over the last decade), and today more and more African Americans and Native Americans as well as Asian Americans marry whites. This does not mean that these African Americans and Native Americans are white. Indeed, Jews in the US, like other groups, are in a process of being absorbed by the dominant European American culture, but despite this assimilation (a process shared by Asian Americans, for example), they still maintain a separate identity and social and cultural ties, and view themselves and are viewed by others as a distinct group. As I explained in my first book, *Getting Our Groove Back*,[20] after two generations of intermarriage, Jewish identity is most often lost (except in cases in which the spouse converts to Judaism or is substantially involved in the Jewish community), but this is true for other identities as well.

Any visit to Israel will confront the visitor with the lack of visible whiteness and Europeanism of many Israelis (including some Ashkenazim). In the most gross and reductionist terms, if you travel across Germany and then Israel, you are unlikely to think you are meeting the same people, whereas a visit to New Zealand followed by a visit to the UK makes the origins of white New Zealanders clear. Given this history and this present, the insistence by the far left that Jews are hyper white is not true. Jewish demographics, history, and politics simply contradict Thrasher's claim that Jews are white.

Butz's view that Jews are fake whites who are infiltrating America is also hard to square with the reality that, for most of Jewish history, "white" Europeans did not consider Jews—even culturally assimilated ones—to be like them, that is to say white. Further, most Jews did not fake anything, but rather kept their names and sustained their identity as Jews in plain view, thereby distinguishing themselves from white Europeans. That being said, Jews were able to assimilate into European and white American culture far more easily than other groups, and a minority of Jews chose to do so by erasing their Jewish identity altogether.[21] It is for this reason that Jews appeared to be white for many African Americans.[22] But this minority of Jews who sought radical assimilation are not the ones Butz discusses in his book. And even my father, who shortened his name from Shajewitz to Shay when he became a proud US citizen, made no attempt to obscure his identity as a Jew.

Jewish support for Zionism in America is also consistent with a long history of American immigrant groups trying to, though not always succeeding in, influencing American policy in light of the interest of their home country. The immigration history of America has long meant that many Americans were interested in political realities elsewhere, such as Ireland but also Italy and Germany, to name but a few examples.[23] Such legacies have been a mainstay of American politics. Not only did such immigrant groups disagree among themselves, but they might disagree on American interests. The Cuban diaspora in South Florida is a case in point.[24] In many instances, they viewed American interests and their own cultural interests as aligned.

Butz's view requires an a priori acceptance that American and Jewish American interests are diametrically at odds and asserts that the latter are illegitimate. The inconsistency of this position is all the more glaring as he clearly does not think that German Americans ought to suppress their interests. A large number of American leaders during and after World War II were of German heritage, including Dwight Eisenhower, and most were appalled by the Nazis.[25] But others, including some of the most ardent isolationists and those most favoring a lenient treatment of Germany, were also German American.[26] Butz himself is part German American—does he suggest that this is in any way relevant? I presume he would consider it an affront to say that he is part of a plot to establish German world supremacy. Butz's views of whiteness are thus also based on misrepresentations of American history. Modern America is no doubt based on British culture (its language, laws, and political history), but it has also been influenced and shaped by other European immigrant groups with often diverse views. Even white America is made up of different subgroups with different ethnic solidarities, religions, and politics. The bottom line is that both Butz and Thrasher view the very skin of Jews as deceptive and dangerous.

Thrasher and Butz's Conspiracy Theories about Zionists are dependent on demonizing Zionist political actions—namely alleging that Zionism equates to racist and imperial colonialism. We previously noted Butz's words: "When in November 1975, an overwhelming majority of the United Nations, in a burst of intellectual clarity rare for the organization, endorsed a resolution declaring Zionism to be a form of racism, a truth as inescapable as 2+2 = 4, the US representative Daniel Patrick Moynihan, an otherwise impressive intellect, was reduced in astonishingly short order to hysterical yapping about the six million."[27] Thrasher, like Butz, dismisses any notion that Jews have a tie to the land, referring to Zionists as colonizers in numerous tweets. The problem is that this view flies in the face of basic logic.

Arabs are certainly one of the great peoples of world history, but there is no doubt that they and not the Zionists have an imperial past.[28] The great imperial peoples in history have typically had a major impact imposing their language and religion on others when colonizing indigenous lands, though rarely completely wiping out other cultures.[29] The Arabs are not an exception, having brought Islam and therefore monotheism to almost two billion people, something I discuss in my book on monotheism, *In Good Faith*.[30]

This influence, established through imperial conquest, has been impressive. In fact, along with the Chinese, the British, the Spanish, and the Russians, Arabs are one of the most impactful extant imperial peoples in world history. Among the Muslim imperial powers, which include the Turks and the Iranians,[31] they had a profound effect around the globe. Indeed, during the time of the caliphates, Arab armies colonized the areas they conquered, even creating new Arab towns such as Baghdad, where peninsular Arabs settled. It was also during this time that they Arabized the lands they conquered, establishing Arabic as the lingua franca in North Africa and the Middle East—though without displacing all indigenous languages. Tamazight (Berber), Aramaic, and written Hebrew survived—Coptic died as a spoken language sometime in the seventeenth century, though it survives as a liturgical one. If one is ever confused about who is a colonizer and who is colonized, there is a simple test: one of the best indicators of empire is the spread of language. Arabic, which started as a language spoken by a subgroup of tribes of one peninsula, became through these medieval conquests the lingua franca for twenty-five countries and 420 million people. Likewise, China's imperial past has been so enduring and successful that people often mistake it for a very large ethnic state when in fact China is replete with different peoples and languages.[32]

Religion is another. During this time, Islam became the dominant religion—the Amazigh converted to Islam, but some other communities such as the Copts, the Maronites, and the Assyrians resisted. Arab rule during this time did not lead to the genocide of indigenous peoples but certainly to their oppression. Non-Muslims were second-class *dhimmis* subject to additional taxes and punitive sanctions, and non-Arab Muslims were accorded a lower status than Arabs (even initially paying a tax similar to non-Muslims).[33] Arab imperialism had a clear ethnic and religious hierarchy.[34] And Jews, just like Kurds, Assyrians, Copts, Amazigh, and many other indigenous peoples in the Middle East and North Africa, fell under their imperial yoke during the caliphates (632–1258 CE), which practiced settler colonialism in conquered lands and encouraged Islamification and Arabization until the Ottoman Empire.[35] Although Arabs lost power to the Ottoman Turks, they remained provincial and local leaders and higher up on the Ottoman imperial hierarchy than indigenous or diaspora peoples in the area.[36]

Arab imperialism is a modern phenomenon as well. Arabs across North Africa and the Middle East revived the concept of Arab unity in the late nineteenth century. During World War I, Arab militants rebelled against the Ottomans with British promises via the McMahon-Hussein correspondence to grant them significant political power. After World War II, Arab nationalists took power and imposed Arabization policies in North Africa and the Middle East. The unity of this endeavor is evident in the creation of the Arab League in 1945.[37] Across Arab League countries, indigenous languages were prohibited from being taught and sometimes parents were prohibited from giving their children indigenous language names (Amazigh, Aramaic, Kurdish).[38] Non-Arabs were excluded from society; Copts, for example, were intentionally underrepresented politically and de facto excluded from high government positions,[39] Maronites who had fled Lebanon before 1945 could not return,[40] Assyrians were likewise persecuted.[41] In the case of the Kurds, cultural genocide turned into physical genocide under Saddam Hussein.[42]

These efforts at imposing Arab Muslim hegemony worked everywhere except in Israel and Lebanon. In both countries, the non-Arab population was too politically organized and powerful to be displaced. In the case of Lebanon, that balance deteriorated to the breaking point and is indeed the most practical advertisement against a one-state solution.

Although European imperialists partially colonized the Middle East in the nineteenth and twentieth centuries, it was of modest impact except for the self-serving considerations with which they drew national borders. Indeed since 1945, there have been no significant populations of European descendants in this region. Nor have European cultural norms remained. The only major influences have been on the legal system, and there only partially (the Napoleonic code or British common law is mixed with other legal systems like Shariah and Ottoman law in this area), and the political systems in the region have been influenced by modern states.

The borders are another issue. As an example, the Sykes-Picot Agreement of 1916 between France and Britain sought to split the Ottoman Empire into the world they imagined post World War I. In this they largely succeeded, creating the borders of modern Syria, Iraq, and Jordan and attempting to create borders between a Jewish and Palestinian state. But even this influence, though not unimportant, has not changed the overarching pan-Arab dynamic of the region in the postwar period.

Arab imperialism behind Palestinian nationalism is also evident to anyone who examines it. Most Palestinians are proud of their Arab heritage, and many clans can even tell you what part of the Arabian Peninsula they originally came from. The elites in particular identify with tribes from the Arabian Peninsula and can be identified by clan names such as Nusaybah, Tamini, Barghouti, Shawish, and Al-Zayadina, among others.[43] All the Arab League countries participated in the 1948 war to conquer all of Palestine and put it under Arab power. In the words of then Secretary-General Abdul Rahman Azzam of the Arab League, the conquest of Palestine would be "a war of extermination and a momentous massacre spoken of like the Mongolian massacre and the Crusades" if Jews would not preemptively surrender.[44] In the case of the Greek, Armenian, and Jewish diasporas, the respective Arab League governments' policies were oppression and expulsion.[45] The Jewish expulsion was tied to the Arab League's project of seeking full Arab control over Palestine, as they had in other countries. They could not tolerate the United Nations partition vote, which gave part of the land to Jews for whom it had been an ancestral home. They began to arrest Jews and stage pogroms. And thus, the bulk of Jews from North Africa and the (non-Israel) Middle East left by 1952.[46] So, while Arabs never created a unified empire that some had hoped for, Arab leadership and even supremacy has been central to the politics of all the countries of the Arab League (until the signing of the Abraham Accords in 2020) and to the aspirations of PLO chairman Yasser Arafat. Arafat was clear that Palestinians are an Arab people as he described in his 1974 speech.[47]

Finally, it must be reiterated that Jews remained in the land of Israel despite successive imperial conquests and expulsions.[48] The history of the Jewish Diaspora, according to the Bible, begins just 650 years or so after Joshua with the imperial conquest (by Nebuchadnezzar) that led Jews to their first exile. As the Jews faced this massive military defeat, Jeremiah the prophet gave instruction to those who had already left or were about to flee:

> Build houses and settle down; plant gardens and eat what they produce. Marry and have sons and daughters...so that they too may have sons and daughters... Also, seek the peace and prosperity of the city to which I have carried you into exile. Pray to the Lord for it, because if it prospers, you too will prosper.
>
> —Jeremiah 29:5–7

Imperial conquest led to the first of many subsequent waves of exile. The Jews took Jeremiah's pronouncement to heart as they stayed in Babylon—in what is today Syria, Iraq, and Iran (Persia)—and from there, Yemen and Saudi Arabia and other parts of the region.[49] Successive Diaspora Jewish communities also arose as subsequent imperial conquests shunted Jews elsewhere. When Jews again lost their sovereignty with the Syrian-Greek conquests (which led up to Chanukah), merchants established small communities across the Mediterranean.[50] With the Roman conquests, further trading outposts and communities were established throughout the Roman Empire as many Jews emigrated due to worsening conditions in Israel under Roman rule, which the Romans renamed Palestine. Then the Roman wars against the Jews caused deportations to what we now call Italy and across the empire. Nevertheless, Jews likely remained a majority in Roman Palestine until the fourth century, perhaps even later, while Samaritans, pagan Greco-Syriacs, and a large community of Syriac Christians also lived in the land.

Under the Byzantines, who adopted the land of Israel/Palestine and Jerusalem as a Christian spiritual center, Jewish communities outside of Israel/Palestine coped better than in their indigenous land, though some remnants in Israel/Palestine held on despite extreme hardship, including all manner of religious restrictions. Some emigration continued, and the community of Babylon became numerically the most important center of Jewish life, though Jews maintained a spiritual center in Israel/Palestine and possibly even a demographical majority if counted with Samaritans.[51] The Arabs ultimately defeated what was Babylon and conquered much of North Africa and the Levant, including Byzantine Palestine. After an initial period of grace under the caliph Umar, when Jews were allowed to settle in Jerusalem and elsewhere, subsequent caliphs became more repressive, and warring among Islamic rulers led to substantial non-Muslim emigration. Thus, by the time of the Crusades, Arabs had become a majority in the land of Israel/Palestine, although some scholars claim that Christians were more numerous than Muslims until after the Crusades.[52] The rise of a Muslim empire sent the Jews again on the move, primarily to neighboring Egypt and from there setting up far-flung merchant outposts and subsequently full-blown communities.[53]

By the Middle Ages, Jews had crossed North Africa to Spain and in the east into Afghanistan and Bukhara (in present-day Uzbekistan), which would become the main communities of the Jews from Muslim lands, including under the later Ottomans (during which time Spanish Jews relocated to Turkey and North Africa).[54] Also by the Middle Ages, Jews from Italy who had lived there since Roman times had fanned out into Germany, France, and England, creating the beginning of Ashkenazi Jewry,[55] only to reach Eastern Poland in the 1500s and Russia at the end of the 1700s after having been expelled from most countries in Western Europe.[56] Expelled Spanish and Portuguese Jews drifted out in small numbers into the world (including significant numbers to Holland and England),[57] but Jews only returned to the Western world from Russia in a great exodus when, as pogroms and oppression intensified, two million fled from the Pale of Settlement (the name of Russian lands where Jews were confined) and ended up primarily in the United States, Argentina, France, Germany, and England.[58] Then came the Holocaust, the expulsion of Jews from North Africa and the Middle East, and the mass exodus of Jews from the former Soviet Union.[59] While Jews have responded differently to these exiles, ranging from steadfast commitment to religion and identity to acculturation and complete assimilation into surrounding cultures, and many variations in between, the history of the Jews as a people who have both exercised sovereignty in their homeland and lived in the Diaspora is not a particular mystery.

The Jewish return to the land of Israel in the modern period, like the return of the Armenians to their homeland, occurred under a complicated set of circumstances. As discussed above, the Jews had never fully left their homeland, and over the millennia communities and groups of various sizes went back to Israel. Notably under Persian imperial auspices, particularly under the rule of Cyrus the Great, they returned from Babylon and rebuilt the temple in Jerusalem. But other such groups of various sizes returned later, thanks to more benevolent policies of individual imperial rulers during the Greek, Roman, Byzantine, and Arab periods, as well as during the Middle Ages and the Ottoman periods. Nevertheless, with each imperial conquest, Jews lived in larger and larger numbers in the Diaspora relative to the land of Israel until the Diaspora population dwarfed those remaining in Israel. Further, after the Roman conquest, these returning Jews did not create a large-scale political movement to regain political sovereignty. This changed in the nineteenth century, with growing nationalist movements in Europe and elsewhere successfully challenging the Ottomans and other empires. Jews also began to think seriously about a return to political sovereignty and hence developed the modern Zionist movement as a political movement of greater breadth than previous efforts. Their primary tactic was to buy land from local landlords and move there. Indeed, until 1948, this is the story of all Jewish settlements.[60]

Jews also sought the support of the international community for their project, in particular the Western powers that were dominant as colonial powers in the region. This alliance has been the source of much of the misrepresentation of Jews as an imperialist movement. However, the Jews acted no differently than people of other small nations like the Greeks and Armenians, who also sought political independence. Indeed, the Armenians were able to reestablish themselves in Armenia after living primarily in exile in Iran and Turkey thanks to the Russian Empire.[61] The Greeks also counted on European, especially British, imperial support.[62] That small nations allied with empires to achieve their goals does not make their goal imperialist; in fact, it usually made them vulnerable to changes in the policies of the empires they allied with, as occurred with Armenians who found themselves under Soviet control, or the Jews, who saw the British renege on their commitments. That the descendants of Arabs who initially sold land to Jews did not wish to share or give up any part of their political power is understandable, but it does not make them victims of settler colonialism. In fact, unlike the case of Armenia where Kurds and Azeris who had occupied Armenian lands were forced out,[63] the Arabs in Palestine not only remained but convinced their neighbors to go to war against the Jews to maintain control over all of Palestine.

There is an additional fundamental reason that the charge of Zionism as a settler colonialist enterprise from its inception is so slanderous—namely, that the Jews were offered the chance to be genuine settler colonists and vociferously rejected that route. Scholars well know that when the Sixth Zionist Congress opened in 1903, Theodor Herzl read a letter from Sir Clement Hill in which Britain would grant "the establishment of a Jewish colony or settlement" on 15,500 square miles of what is now Kenya (but was part of the Ugandan Protectorate at the time). The land in question had been staked out by the British Empire during the so-called scramble for Africa in the 1880s and decades later ruled and colonized by the same empire. Herzl reluctantly brought the offer up because of the escalating attacks and pogroms on the Jews in Europe. The situation was bleak, and the Kenya solution would offer a safe haven. Indeed, had this offer been accepted, millions fewer Jews would have been murdered in the Holocaust as the Jews would have had somewhere to go. But the founding members of the Zionist movement determinedly and loudly said no. This was at a time in which there was no certainty and on an objective basis, not a high likelihood that Jews would be able to return to their ancient homeland, given that the Ottoman Empire prohibited all Jews in particular, whether Ottoman subjects or not, from buying land in their ancient homeland and prohibited all foreign Jews from settling there. The British extended this ban to anyone seeking to purchase property. The Zionist movement wanted to return Jews to the place of their indigenous homeland and did not want the land of other peoples. In contrast, immigrants to the Americas, Australia, New Zealand, and South Africa, together with the Diaspora Jews who moved there, live on land that prior European settler colonists conquered, stole, and/or occupied from native populations. Finally, it is also worth mentioning that despite the above-mentioned restrictions, the Zionist movement bought (rather than conquered and seized) all the land they settled on before 1948, the vast majority of which was on very sparsely populated and largely uncultivated areas in the Jezreel Valley and Jordan Valley.

The far left's view of Jews as imperial colonizers thus requires ignoring reality. Jews have been repeatedly expelled and exiled from lands. They made do to survive as best as they could, sometimes prospering, many times struggling. It requires willful blindness to deny the Jewish presence in the land of Israel or to call them colonizers at any point in history. Indeed, while many Jews developed attachments to their countries of residence, over the last two millennia only a minority saw them as homelands and the majority saw them as places of exile. Certainly, one of the great political questions of our time is what to do in regions where indigenous people wish to reclaim land now that was seized by imperial conquerors. We have this very issue in the United States with Native American claims, but it is also present all over North Africa and in China (just ask those in Tibet) and parts of the former Soviet Union, now the Russian Federation.[64] Jews are one of very few peoples who have regained sovereignty after both imperial conquest and exile, the other being the Armenians. The Fiji Islanders were subject to imperial conquest but did not suffer a diaspora.[65] Yet, though neither Thrasher nor Butz's writings indicate any of this, it is all basic accepted history.

In this context, the two authors' support for Iran is all the more telling. Butz gushes with his admiration for Ahmadinejad's Holocaust denial and anti-Zionism. But what about Thrasher? Indeed, despite his dismissive words about Iran and ISIS as a journalist, Thrasher should have known that by August 2015 (when he tweeted about them), ISIS had already conquered various areas in Iraq and Syria, terrorizing and slaughtering Christian Assyrians and Kurds and Yazidis, and international ISIS affiliates had also gang raped women and beheaded Christians in Egypt and Libya.[66] Iran's track record of murdering critical journalists, political opponents (especially on the left), and members of its many national minorities is well known.[67] It is perhaps a point of pride of the leadership that the Iranian regime has murdered tens of thousands of its political opponents. Hundreds of gay men are officially recorded as being executed by the regime for the "crime" of being gay, although the more likely actual number is between four thousand and six thousand.[68] Throughout the 2010s, when Thrasher was already active as a journalist, Iran continued its assault on Kurds in the Iran-occupied eastern part of Kurdistan.[69] This can be added to the tens of thousands of Kurds murdered since the Iranian Revolution, and the thousands displaced.[70] The treatment of journalists in Iran or in ISIS-controlled territory does not merit a mention in Thrasher's tweets. Hundreds of journalists have been executed by Iran—the latest as of this writing is Ruhollah Zam, who was lured into Iraq and then kidnapped to Iran, convicted on a vague charge, and hung four days later. Suffice it to say that the lifespan of a journalist posting negative stories about the regimes in these territories is painful and short. Thrasher's tweet about white supremacy and police violence certainly stands on its own without the need to have the reader also agree with him about ISIS and Iran.

WHATSOEVER THINGS ARE
OF GOOD REPORT 1

WHY THEIR CLAIMS TO OBJECTIVITY ARE RHETORICAL TALL TALES (OR *BOLBE*, AS MY FATHER WOULD SAY)

Butz and Thrasher share with other Conspiracy Theorists a rhetoric of objectivity and morality. Conspiracy Theorists deny that their views are Manichean or their evaluation of the evidence faulty. They certainly consider themselves on the side of justice and morality, though how they articulate these perspectives depends on the theory in question. Butz and Thrasher share some commonalities and differences in this respect.

Both Butz and Thrasher appeal to intellectual and moral authority to underpin their arguments. Butz's *The Hoax of the Twentieth Century* is meant to show the supposed objectivity and scientific nature of his exposé. The book is over five hundred pages long and contains hundreds of footnotes. His objective is to convince the reader of his position through his meticulous argumentation and presentation. He relies on falsified *logos*. Thrasher, in contrast, feels no need to prove his point. Rather, it is his moral rhetoric (*pathos*) and appeal to other like-minded scholars (*ethos*) that gives his viewpoint legitimacy and authority. Thus, he references Angela Davis in particular, whose stature, already impressive, has grown further since the events of Ferguson, but others as well.

Included in their respective appeals are mentions of Jews who agree with them. The implicit assumption communicated by both Butz and Thrasher is that no Jew would be guilty of prejudice toward fellow Jews and so would necessarily evaluate the situation objectively. At first blush this seems reasonable, which is the problem of making arguments from *ethos*. This *ethos* is a fallacy based on an unwarranted elision of concepts. It is true that groups who experience racism, prejudice, and discrimination are well situated to describe their own experiences and that historians must examine this evidence. Much Holocaust research is based on survivor testimonies, for example. But as historian Deborah Lipstadt shows, professional historians triangulate survivor testimonies with other facts, accounts of other survivors, documents, and other forms of evidence.[1] That is to say, historians take the testimony of victimized groups seriously but also subject them to confirmation and scrutiny.

Butz and Thrasher assume that the views of members of a victimized group who deny this victimization or claim it is a manipulation should be taken unquestioningly. They offer these revelations of insider knowledge as complete confirmation. Scholars should not assume any testimony is automatically correct. (Of course, the evidence of the Holocaust is abundant and would have been clear even if, tragically, there were no survivors to give testimony.) This is why citing Jewish opponents of Zionism to bolster one's credentials as a nonprejudiced critic is a fallacy. It is a basic foundation of academic inquiry that all viewpoints must be subjected to scrutiny whatever the likelihood of someone lying or not. When the Jews who Thrasher and Butz cite are scrutinized (as will be discussed below), it becomes clear that they demonstrate the same intellectual shortcomings as non-Jewish opponents of Zionism. These defects include made-up facts, exaggeration, and distortion, all of which add to a cumulative slander of Zionists.

Butz's favorite go-to Jew, J. G. Burg, has given English language interviews describing Zionist conspiracies based on lies and distortions. The tenor of Burg's position is clear from a far-right interviewer's introduction of him:[2]

> Josef Ginsburg, who wrote under the pen name of "J. G. Burg," came to Toronto to assist Ernst Zundel's defense effort in the Great Holocaust Trial in 1988, at which time I was able to speak to this remarkable anti-Zionist Jew and to make extensive notes after each conversation. "Mr. Burg," as he preferred to be addressed, was the author of several booklets on such favorite Zionist subjects as the so-called Holocaust, the founding of the bandit-state of Israel, the so-called "diary" of Anne Frank, German "guilt," etc.[3]

Further in the interview, Eric Thomson states, "He [Burg] had toured the concentration camps of Auschwitz, Birkenau, Majdanek, Treblinka, Sobibor, and all the others in Poland as a member of the official Soviet inspection team, and he found no evidence whatsoever of any attempt on the part of the Germans to exterminate anyone and certainly not by means of lethal gas chambers!"[4] This is an astounding claim, contradicted by virtually all other eyewitnesses. Certainly, the Soviets who liberated Auschwitz found many physical indications of mass murder, including seven tons of human hair and hundreds of thousands of articles of men's and women's clothing and other physical evidence. On January 27, 2020, I had the privilege of meeting a few of the surviving Soviet soldiers who liberated Auschwitz at a seventy-fifth anniversary commemoration event. They spoke of the horror they witnessed, which stuck with them in such a fresh way even after all these years. Again, this too cannot be taken as truth in isolation but corroborates other physical and written evidence. Then we have the evidence of the perpetrators themselves, as Deborah Lipstadt has shown.[5] I also have my father's testimony of Auschwitz and why he felt so "lucky" to be sent with a work slave contingent to Warsaw. Had that not happened, he would almost certainly have been dead within a short while.

The Burg interview also includes the recitation of a Conspiracy Theory wherein Zionists manipulate the Nazis to establish Israel. Here he claims that the Nazis and Zionists collaborated in drafting the Nuremberg laws:

> "Yes," he said, "one of the Zionist collaborators was Rabbi Leo Baeck, who now lives in London, England."
>
> "What did Baeck do?" I asked.
>
> "He helped the Nazis define who was a Jew and who was a German and he suggested the adoption of the yellow, six-pointed star as the symbol of the Jewish nation."

There is no factual basis for this claim whatsoever. He also agreed that the Zionists declared war on Germany: "The Zionists never do anything for only one reason," he said. "Their declaration of war was given with at least a twofold purpose. One reason was their hatred of Hitler's economic program and his intention of nationalizing the Bank of Germany, which was owned by the Rothschilds, as are all so-called national banks today." Burg further insisted that Zionists declared war on Germany to conceal their collaboration. Given that in the inter-war period Zionists in Germany were openly seeking the support of Germans, this claim is yet another lie, not to mention an absurdity. The Zionists were without a state and army and in no position to declare war on an industrial superpower.

I will not attempt to dispose of the multiple entangled Conspiracy Theories in the Burg interview. But to mention just three, the statements that "all so-called national banks" are owned by the Rothschilds or that the diary of Anne Frank is a forgery or that Baeck created the yellow star, are absurdities. No national banks are owned by the Rothschilds, even though this canard is found in articles on the first page of a Google search that lists many national banks including those of Iran, Qatar, Saudi Arabia, Yemen, and Iraq. In 1980, as a result of so many slanders made against the veracity of the diary of Anne Frank, the actual diary was sent to the Netherlands Forensics Institute, where forensic scientists examined everything from Frank's handwriting (by examining letters sent to her friends before the war and comparing her penmanship to the diary) to the ink (when certain inks were available and where) to the paper, fibers, and glue. They issued a 250-page report that confirmed what was already known.[66] As Deborah Lipstadt put it, "While some may argue that the...Institute...used an elephant to swat a fly, once again it becomes clear the deniers' claims have no relationship to the most basic rules of truth and evidence."[7] Further contrary to Burg's claims, Rabbi Leo Baeck had nothing to do with the Nazi symbol of the yellow six-pointed star to depict Jews. A yellow badge had been used since the thirteenth century by various groups to identify Jews. The first time Jews were forced to wear a marking was in Poland, not Germany.[8]

Burg is not the only Jew to make stuff up. There are a number of Jewish Holocaust revisionists, all of whom view Zionists as the source of the Holocaust hoax. Revisionist sites in the Americas and Europe cite or mention Jews to corroborate their views. They have also been invited to Holocaust denial conferences in Iran. These Jews come from across the religious spectrum. They include Moshe Aryeh Friedman (who claims without corroboration to be a rabbi); David Cole, a secular Jewish filmmaker who has made films questioning the Holocaust; Professor of Medicine Roger Dommergue; Nathanael Kapner, a self-proclaimed Russian Orthodox monk raised as a Jew; the world chess champion Bobby Fischer; and Paul Eisen (the so called "rehumanizer of Hitler").[9] As the deniers do, these Jews claim that Zionists sought out the Nazis in order to collaborate with them, or that Israel has exploited the Holocaust for money and political gains. Like Butz, these figures publish in alternative revisionist presses and have little to no mainstream credibility in Western universities. Yet one cannot deny that they exist. The idea that no Jew would ever deny or revise the Holocaust is simply not true. While miniscule in number, there are Jews who think that Zionism and Zionists deliberately sought to harm millions of Germans and Arabs by lying about the Holocaust.

By contrast, on the left there are more Jews, particularly in academia, who tout Zionist conspiracies against Palestinians and other people of color. In her tweets as a public intellectual and her writings as an activist for Jewish Voice for Peace, Prescod-Weinstein has advanced a number of conspiratorial claims. In a December 2018 tweet she wrote, "Genocide ben Netanyahu referring to an article in Haaretz claiming that Netanyahu's son says he'd 'prefer' if 'all the Muslims leave the land of Israel.'" In an essay "Black and Palestinian Lives Matter: Black and Jewish America in the Twenty-First Century,"[10] she speaks of the "successes of the Zionist mission (including the creation of Israel in tandem with the expulsion of Palestinians)."[11]

I am not going to defend the indefensible tweets of Yair Netanyahu, but both sentences from Prescod-Weinstein insinuate conspiracies that are not there. In the first instance, the accusation of genocide is just a moniker, but the insinuation is clear. Netanyahu's misguided son is just one person, but as the son of a prime minister, he is mentioned so as to suggest an inherited view among Zionists ("ben" means "son" in Hebrew). Yet this insinuation is utterly false. Zionism never required the genocide of Palestinians, only their recognition of Jewish connections to and sovereignty in at least part of the land of Israel. In fact, the Zionist movement upheld Palestinian cultural autonomy and citizenship within Israel and for most parts of the Zionist movement, sovereignty in another part of the land. One has only to look at neighboring countries like Iraq, where not only forced assimilation to Arab culture but actual genocide occurred against the Kurds, to understand how far Israel's policies are from genocide.

Her description of the "expulsion of Palestinians" as a success of Zionism is written as a factual claim, in this case pointing to genocide since she de facto includes the whole people in the sentence. Yet it is totally false. No unbiased historian claims that the Palestinian people were expelled wholesale in 1948 with the objective of a total ethnic cleanse—the scholarly consensus is that they were encouraged to leave by the Arab states that declared war on Israel and in other cases fled because they feared for their own safety. There are only isolated instances that have been grossly exaggerated in which Jews encouraged or forced Palestinians to leave their homes, and even in those isolated instances many stayed in other parts of Israel. After the war, about 160,000 Palestinians remained, and they and their descendants comprise about 1.6 million citizens of Israel presently. (There are another 300,000 Arab Israeli citizens who live in East Jerusalem, which was annexed by Israel in 1967.) There was and is no genocide of Palestinians by Israel, yet certain scholars like Jasbir Puar strangely complain that too few Palestinians are killed given the situation, because, she alleges, Israel prefers maiming.

Given the frequency with which the allegation of genocide is used against Israel, a quick review of the numbers is in order. In 1949, the UN considered about 700,000 Arabs as displaced; sixty years later, in 2019, the UN counted 5.6 million official Palestinian refugees. This is in addition to the fact that Palestinians in Israel run their own schools, speak their own language, and have their own political parties. They are also a majority of the citizens in the neighboring state of Jordan. Thus, the notion of genocide used by academics when it comes to Palestinians is a complicated theoretical construct that is hard to decipher given the reality of high population growth, cultural continuity, political representation, and citizenship elsewhere in the region. In contrast, Hamas's goal to expel every Jew from "the river to the sea" to make sure that there are no live Jews in Israel comes close to genocide, but most precise are the calls to kill all Jews in a holy war by extremist Islamist clerics and some Palestinian faction leaders, which are explained away by these same academics as being mere hyperbole or populism. We are reminded of Butz explaining away Hitler's promises to rid Germany of Jews as being some sort of metaphor by a politician and not something he was serious about.

False claims about Israel committing genocide, which have the objective of asserting that Israel is a criminal state and therefore should be dismantled, won't bring peace. Rather, it is more likely to embolden extremists—those who truly wish to expel or kill the Jews—under the false banner of a defensive act of national liberation from an imperialist colonizer. Further, using genocide in this context devalues the word and the too many cases in the world where there is real genocide occurring. Instead, the political aspirations and objectives of all parties involved should be a part of a negotiated solution.

Prescod-Weinstein makes other conspiratorial claims as well. She argues that Zionists conspire to uphold white supremacy globally and thereby harm people of color. She writes, "American police have been trained by Israeli organizations in methods of control that are often deployed against Black communities, for example in Ferguson."[12] This is also a conspiratorial accusation. Israel's cooperation with the US is in counterterrorism, a strategy that has become necessary especially since 2001 and has saved many lives.[13] To call it "methods of control" to be used against citizens willy-nilly is a grave distortion of the truth. As previously noted, most of the very infrequent interactions between American and Israeli police relate to nontactical issues.

In terms of her view that Zionists require "compulsory allegiance to Israel," Prescod-Weinstein doesn't feel obliged to do so, nor does any Jew or non-Jew I know. In most campus humanities departments, the opposite is true. It is very uncomfortable to be pro-Israel in most university departments and safe to reveal this only after receipt of tenure.

Likewise, she insinuates a Jewish conspiracy to silence opponents in a tweet from January 7, 2019: "I really hope that this isn't because a bunch of Jews pressured a Black civil rights organization not to give an award to a Black woman because of her solidarity with Palestine because...it makes Jews look like an all-powerful cabal." Jewish groups, like all other ethnic and cultural groups, protest actions they disagree with. When other groups actually do protest awards, she does not say it makes them "look like an all-powerful cabal." This criticism is particularly ironic given the current trend toward "cancel culture" by some on the far left.

Finally, Prescod-Weinstein also argues that American Jews have had their values distorted by the Zionists. She writes that while Jews in the past supported African Americans, "much of the community rests on the laurels of activist Jews long dead...This assimilation of white Jews is inextricably tied to the rise of the Zionist State of Israel. [...] There is a clear connection between Jewish American support for Israel's current form and the production of harmful and sometimes violent anti-Jewishness in the United States."[14] This alleged connection is without factual basis. In her view, Zionists are an evil cabal causing harm to people of color, to the United States, and to Jews.

Prescod-Weinstein is not alone; rather, her views are the orthodoxy of Jewish Voice for Peace (JVP) and organizations that, like the Institute for Historical Review, reject Jewish national self-determination as racist and murderous. Jewish Voice for Peace has the support of a number of very prominent Jewish academics, including Judith Butler, head of the Modern Language Association (MLA), Daniel Boyarin, Shaul Magid, Sarah Schulman, Avi Shlaim, and Noam Chomsky, among others, as well as prominent public intellectuals and artists like Naomi Klein and Udi Aloni. In its literature, it expresses the main anti-Zionist Conspiracy Theories that are circulating in the academy today, as well as efforts to advance Boycott, Divestment, and Sanctions (BDS) campaigns. JVP is the main point of reference to Jewish testimony for scholars like Thrasher. Yet with all of JVP's organizing and support, Jewish anti-Zionists most likely comprise about 5 percent of Jews and certainly no more than 10 percent,[15] and even these numbers are much higher than those of Holocaust-denying Jews. The main reason for this discrepancy, which we will discuss in further detail later, is that the racial nature of far-right ideology has meant that even if Jews agreed with Nazis, they would still be dangerous to those Jews, whereas far-left ideology will accept Jews who conform ideologically. But in either case, Jews are required to view their own normal claims like national self-determination as sinister projects to harm others.

By way of a short digression, the reader might note that I have rarely used the term "anti-Semitism" other than to cite or analyze statements by others such as the JVP. That is because the distinction between anti-Semitism and anti-Zionism confuses rather than explains. The term "anti-Semitism" was invented in 1879 to obscure the plain intent of the word in use at that time, *Judenhass*: "Jew Hate." Because putting it in such blunt terms was not polite enough and dissuaded some potential supporters, Wilhelm Marr, a German politician, employed a popular theory of his day, scientific racism, that made his loathing of Jews easier to express in a mannerly way.[16] So, with his coining the term "anti-Semitism" and his subsequent formation of the Antisemitic League, he could make his true goals sound higher minded and less objectionable through what I will call a word bomb—that is, a loaded term encapsulating a theory, usually a false one. The word bomb's *ethos* or *pathos* overpowers any rational discussion. The bottom line was that Marr hated Jews. He did not distinguish between Jews who were religious or secular or who wanted self-determination and any other Jews.

The whole debate in academia about the difference between anti-Semitism and anti- Zionism is a diversion. The reason is simple: the majority of anti-Zionists are in favor of the national self-determination of scores of other peoples; however, they categorically reject the national self-determination of the Jews in any form, including all articulations of the two-state solution. This perspective is clearly unprincipled. Be for or against Zionism, that is to say the national self-determination of the Jews (who long remained stateless), but if you are against it, be against national self-determination on principle including for the Tibetans, the Kurds, the Armenians, or any other ethnic/national group who has been conquered by an empire. Zionism is simply the idea of Jewish national self-determination. The notion of discrimination, recrimination, and demonization against Jews—and not other groups—who happen to hold that idea as legitimate contradicts every other idea that academia holds dear. Yet somehow in the case of Jews this distinction is made—if a Jew has the wrong opinion about Jewish self-determination, they have whatever is coming to them no matter where they live or what else they think. Wilhelm Marr, a proto-Nazi, and the extreme left both figured out how to do that through the use of fancy terminology. Sadly, many JVP Jews embrace these terms that attempt a distinction that does not exist. Were any of these anti-Zionist JVP Jews mentioned above to change their opinion on Israel, JVP would judge them fair game for demonization.

This is not a rhetorical point. Norman Finkelstein was a "rock star of the Pro-Palestinian movement." He was paid to do more than forty speaking engagements a year (most university departments have discretionary budgets for visiting speakers), until he said he couldn't tolerate the "disingenuousness [of BDS] --- they don't want Israel [to exist]... It's a cult." BDS supporters reacted with ferocious fury, calling him a "comrade at heart with Alan Dershowitz" and removing him from the paid speaking tour. Even Israel supporters were perplexed by the BDS fury; as one put it, "he consorts with Hamas, he's hostile to Israel in every possible way, and yet he comes up short on this one."[17] Entering JVP is a bit like The Hotel California—you can check in but you can never check out, at least not without being vilified.

Confirmation from members of the very group one is criticizing is just a rhetorical device. The claims against Zionism by the Jews mentioned above and others like them, like the claims of Butz and Thrasher, must be judged on their own merits. Very smart people like Butz and Thrasher can show very low standards in evaluating Jewish history, Zionism, and the Holocaust. So too can very smart Jews. As another example shows.

I first learned about corroborating Jews at Northwestern during my Introduction to Existentialism course taught by Professor David Michael Kleinberg-Levin in the fall quarter of 1976, or just before the January when Arthur Butz made his splash. We were in the midst of reading *What Is Called Thinking?*,[18] Martin Heidegger's very difficult book that aimed to explain all of reality and our place in it. Clearly it was a good read for this class, and Professor Kleinberg-Levin was such a stunningly good teacher that I believed I could understand what I was reading. What I did not know when I was assigned the book was that Heidegger was a Nazi. It was not in his biography on the back of the book, and the internet had not yet been invented. Someone in a discussion group brought it up. But not to worry, we were assured by the graduate teaching assistant; Heidegger just faked being a Nazi. None other than Hannah Arendt, whose Jewish credentials as a member of the liberal intelligentsia were unimpeachable, had so attested.

Indeed after 1950, when she and Heidegger first met again in Germany, Arendt became his main ambassador in the United States, arranging translations of his work, helping him to sell his manuscript for *Being and Time*,[19] and finally definitively seeking to restore his reputation in the public sphere in an important essay in the *New York Review of Books* (1971), where she not only disputed his Nazism but claimed he had practiced "spiritual resistance" to the regime.[20] Arendt was not just a Jew; she was a heroic Holocaust survivor.[21] She was arrested in 1933 by the Gestapo for "Zionist" activities and fled to France, where she stuck with Zionist organizing and saved hundreds of Jewish children by helping them flee Europe to British Mandatory Palestine through a program called Youth Aliyah. After the Nazi invasion of France, she was again imprisoned, this time for the charge of being Jewish, but managed to escape and made her way to the United States in 1942, where she settled for the rest of her life. Hannah Arendt displayed tremendous personal courage and was a hero who deserves to be remembered as such. By the time she reunited with Heidegger in Germany in 1950, she had become a public intellectual. She wrote about Jewish as well as European and American politics and culture for both Jewish and nonsectarian American journals. If Arendt thought Heidegger's involvement with the Nazi Party was just a mistake that he quickly rectified after understanding the nature of the regime, then, QED, he must not have been a Nazi. Except she was wrong.

The problem is not simply that Arendt was wrong because of freshly discovered facts but that she was in no place to evaluate Heidegger's Nazism. Arendt left Germany in 1933, under conditions which made communication quite difficult. She had no direct knowledge of any of Heidegger's Nazi activities, and most of the details she only learned after the war, a full decade after Heidegger led a university as a member of the Nazi Party. To complicate matters, what she did learn about Heidegger before meeting him in 1950 led her to criticize him.

Someone who did have direct knowledge of Heidegger and with whom Arendt corresponded at length was Karl Jaspers. Arendt's dissertation advisor, Jaspers was a philosopher who had refused to accept Nazi authority and was forced into retirement in 1937. He remained in Germany during the war in fear of deportation on account of his Jewish wife. Jaspers knew Heidegger personally and knew of all his activities during the 1930s. It was Jaspers's letter to the Freiburg Denazification Committee in December 1945 that tipped the balance against Heidegger, forcing him into retirement rather than allowing him to return to teaching.[22] In it he writes, "He [Heidegger] and Alfred Bauemler and Carl Shmitt are the—among themselves very different—professors who attempted to reach a position of intellectual leadership under National Socialism. In vain. They made use of real intellectual capacities and thereby ruined the reputation of German philosophy. An aspect of the tragic nature of evil arises therefrom."[23] Jaspers maintained this negative view of Heidegger even after Heidegger was allowed to teach again in 1951. It turns out Jaspers was right all along.

While debates have raged over Heidegger's Nazism over the last seventy years, Heidegger's personal notes, his so-called Black Notebooks first published in 2014, have closed the matter.[24] They contain too many harsh references to Jews and positive references to Nazis to leave any room for doubt. Further, they demonstrate beyond any doubt that Heidegger's appraisal of Jews and their history did not meet basic standards of analysis. For example, rather than consider their political status as a Diaspora people, Heidegger judged the Jews as "worldless"[25] in an ontological sense with no place of authentic being. Further, he called the concentration camps places of "self-destruction," another portrayal hard to square with the reality. He also wrote that the Germans were the real victims of the Jews because the latter were guilty of "repressing our will for the world."[26] Such a strong and conspiratorial accusation of some half million people's impact on about seventy million Germans surely begs some elaboration. Heidegger does not give any. By the way, I think most would agree that it is good that Nazi Germany did not conquer the world.

The case of Arendt's defense of Heidegger leaves us with a final point. Arendt's defense of Heidegger resembles similar defenses by non-Jewish Germans, relying on minimizing and reinterpreting his actions in favorable ways that are hard to square with the facts. The same is true of the views of Jewish Holocaust deniers and of Jewish anti-Zionist Conspiracy Theorists who make the same arguments as their non-Jewish peers. What we must add is that Arendt had countervailing information and she chose to ignore it. For even though Arendt did not have access to the Black Notebooks, she knew of Jaspers's opinion (even sharing it for a few years) and that of other critics. She simply dismissed them as she had her own theory of Heidegger. Yet, the graduate teaching fellow who led the discussion said to take Arendt's word for it because she was a Jew and a Holocaust survivor. I did. Like many students, I took what were presented as facts in class as truth.

Communists also expediently employed useful Jews. As will be discussed in more detail later, during his reign, Vladimir Lenin set up a committee of stalwart Jewish communists by the name of Yevsektsiya. Yevsektsiya was to be in the business of terrorizing other Jews and denigrating anything Jewish, all in the service of the party and undermining any remaining authentic Jewish leadership.[27] Lenin wanted to offer the Jews of Russia an alternative model that would allow them to be one with the greater communist proletariat, with the understanding that they would have to relinquish Judaism, Zionism, and their distinctiveness (bourgeois character) as Jews. Stalin employed the same playbook and in 1941 organized the Jewish Anti-Fascist Committee, whose job was to oppose Zionism and to appeal to American Jewry.[28] Over time, most of the leaders of the committee were murdered on Stalin's orders via various contrived operations, including the Night of the Murdered Poets and the Doctors' Plot. Luckily, Stalin was summoned to a surprise interview with his Maker, which staved off escalating brutal anti-Jewish oppression.

Useful Jews are not just a twentieth-century phenomenon. The Hebrew prophet Jeremiah tells the story (chapter 40) of Gedalia, a Jew, who King Nebuchadnezzar appointed governor of Jerusalem and the Judean area. King Nebuchadnezzar had at that point just destroyed the Jewish Temple in 586 BCE and taken most of the inhabitants back to Babylon for a life in exile. Nevertheless, he allowed a remnant to remain, and once Jews in the surrounding lands of Moab, Ammon, and Edom heard this, they started coming back to Judah. The Ammonites, who often fought Jews, did not like the idea that Judah might be rebuilt to even a modest degree. They preferred the devastation that Babylon had wrought and hoped for anarchy. So, the king of Ammon found a useful Jew by the name of Ishmael ben Nethaniah who was willing to get close to Gedalia and assassinate him. Ishmael was not sufficiently discreet, so word leaked out and Gedalia was warned. He could not believe that a fellow Jew would seek to assassinate him, so he allowed Ishmael unfettered personal access. Ishmael seized the first opportunity to murder Gedalia, and with that any remains of Jewish sovereignty ended in Judah until Cyrus allowed the Jews to return in 538 BCE. The date of Gedalia's assassination remains a fast day among observant Jews even today.

WHATSOEVER THINGS ARE
OF GOOD REPORT 2

HOW ENCOUNTERS WITH REALITY CAN INOCULATE AGAINST CONSPIRACY THEORIES

We cannot all be experts in everything, so we generally take the word of "experts" and even more so our cherished teachers. But sometimes by chance, circumstance, or our own choices, we are faced with a discrepancy between reality and what we are taught.

In my case, being the child of a Holocaust survivor, knowing my father's family was murdered and that my father lived through work camps, concentration camps, and slave labor, I simply have too much personal knowledge of the Holocaust to take Butz's claims about a "hoax" seriously. When my father led the ritual feast of the Passover seder, he did it in a way that was clear that he understood what slavery really is and, in a way, I am thankful I do not begin to comprehend.

I would, however, have perhaps been more susceptible to Thrasher's arguments had I not spent my junior year abroad in Israel in 1977–1978. Like most liberal Americans, then and now, I opposed racism and colonialism. I also knew very few Jews outside of the world of either Holocaust survivors or third- or fourth-generation Jews. So even though theoretically I understood there were Jews from such far-flung places (to me) as Iran and Bukhara, they were not really on my radar. Nor did my sense of Jewish history and Jewish texts provide me with much initial direction. I was a refugee from the horrors of the 1970s Hebrew schools. I would have rather eaten cardboard than read the Bible until I got some background when I transferred to Ida Crown Jewish Academy. Basically, had I not known more about Israel and had some Jewish education, I might have been vulnerable to pondering a Thrasher predecessor's views that Israel is a racist—mainly white—colonialist country.

Instead, my year in Israel gave me a backdrop that most American students, and a majority of American Jews, do not have. Only 45 percent of American Jews have ever visited Israel, while an overwhelming majority of those who are not Haredi—those orthodox Jews who reject many aspects of modernity—go to college. So, most Jews get their information from the college environment and American news sources, both of which convey in varying degrees a lack of context along with bold-faced false information about Jewish history and Zionism. Given the power of the university discourse about Israel and the relative lack of alternative views, it is not surprising that a small but rising minority of American Jews have been persuaded. But having spent a year in Israel, where I traveled the country extensively and learned Hebrew to an advanced level, I could recognize that much of what the far left contends about Israel does not represent reality. None of what I learned is all that controversial; it just isn't taught at university or reported by the media.

I arrived in Israel for my junior year abroad with the standard preconceptions. Most importantly, I thought all Jews looked like the ones I grew up with from East Rogers Park (my neighborhood in Chicago) and fellow students at Northwestern. The American Jewish community is overwhelmingly made up of Jews who lived in European lands over the past two centuries (especially Russia and neighboring countries), and though often dark haired like my family, they generally—though not always—have pale skin. It took about ten minutes at the airport for me to learn that my father, who had told me that Jews were not white, was right (as he was often, despite my initial reflexive skepticism). I knew in some abstract way that Israel was the "ingathering of the exiles" from around the world, but it only became concrete then that this meant from places other than Europe.

Another thing that changed for me was the timeline and geographical framework of Jewish history. Though I knew Jews had lived in the land of Israel in antiquity and also in Babylon at some point, my understanding of Jewish history was very centered on the immediate past in Eastern Europe. If someone had asked me to give a summary of Jewish history around the world, my response would have been patchy, like summing up British history with a bit about the ancient Britons, the Magna Carta, Henry VIII, the Civil War, the British Empire, Queen Victoria, and a lot about the twentieth-century UK. But this too changed during my year in Israel. As I began to take advanced Hebrew lessons, lived with a Mizrahi (Middle Easterner of Jewish descent) roommate for three months, and learned the history of Jewish communities from antiquity to 500 CE, I started to learn an accurate story of Jewish peoplehood.

Many Jews are used to thinking that the Jewish people are only Ashkenazi or Sephardi. Ashkenazi specifically means German and Sephardi refers to Jews from the Iberian Peninsula. In practice, Ashkenazi Jews dwelled primarily in Northern and Eastern European and had some of their own religious practices, while Sephardic Jews lived in Southern Europe and Northern Africa. Mizrahi Jews had many similar religious practices to Sephardi Jews, but not all are Sephardi—some Mizrahi Jews have lived in the same lands of exile from 586 BCE. The Jews living in predominantly Muslim and Christian lands had both prayed to return to the land of Israel and maintained their Judaism while also being valuable parts of the local communities (with leading roles in the arts, commerce, literature, and in some cases politics)— when they weren't being persecuted. During that time, conversion, some intermarriage, and cultural integration also occurred in North Africa and the Middle East, as it had in Europe. So, these Jews took on visible, economic, and linguistic characteristics of everyone else who lived in the area. Just as Yiddish became a Jewish dialect of medieval German, Judeo-Persian, Judeo-Arabic, Judeo-Berber, Aramaic, Amharic, and Ladino were the spoken languages of these communities concurrent with the majority language they came from. I had grown up with Jews having Eastern European accents. When I first met Iraqi Jews at Hebrew University, I noticed that their Hebrew had a distinctly Arabic tinge and their mannerisms and sensibilities were Middle Eastern. One time, I went to the *shuk* in the Old City of Jerusalem with a Mizrahi Jew who was a fellow student, and all the negotiation was done by him in Arabic. The Arabic accent of an older Yemenite Jew I met was so strong, I could barely understand his Hebrew. At first, I thought he was speaking to me in Arabic.

While I knew all too well the recent history of the Jews of Europe, the recent history of other Jewish communities became more real to me as well during that year at Hebrew University. It was not simply that I saw many Jews with darker skin than me—*Israel was half Mizrahi.* I learned that Mizrahi Jews had participated in the modern Zionist movement, founding neighborhoods in Tel Aviv and Jerusalem before 1948, as well as villages and agricultural settlements. I also learned that the great return to Israel, as with the Ashkenazi communities, came after World War II. About eight hundred thousand Jews fled the Middle Eastern Diaspora communities that had been their homes in most cases many centuries longer than the Jews of Europe had spent in their countries. The majority came to Israel by emergency evacuations. A smaller number went to France, England, Italy, and North America. They left because Arab nationalists not only enlisted to fight and control Palestine; they Arabized their home countries, alternately terrorizing and extorting Jews and other non-Muslim and non-Arab populations. Most Jews left with only a suitcase and felt lucky to have their lives.

Certainly, leaving was not easy, and not only because of the poverty that followed. It was an incredible upheaval—even while praying for a return to Zion, many Jews had become very acculturated and attached to their Diaspora communities. In Europe, some Jews had become German and French nationalists, rejecting their Jewish identity altogether, while others completely denied nationalism and became communists. The vast majority of Jews from North Africa, the Middle East, and Asia identified as Jews and welcomed the creation of a Jewish homeland. They harbored intense disappointment at the betrayal of their fellow citizens who had rioted and forced them out. Had they not been hounded out, most would not have moved to Israel. In this respect, Jews are not different from many other diaspora communities—moving is hard, especially to a new state at war with its neighbors, with few economic resources. Most Armenians have also remained in the diaspora rather than move to post-Soviet Armenia, though like Jews, many are great patriots who support their homeland and their brethren.

My first dorm room from July through October was a direct link to that history. It was a set of hovels called Shechuni HaEleph. This dorm complex, in which two students were crammed into a room without heat, was previously used to host entire families who arrived in that exodus from North Africa and the Middle East (Iraq, Yemen, and so forth). Many Holocaust survivors had lived in similar transit camps in Israel when they arrived. Other survivors, like my father, went to North America, South America, and Australia. We shivered in Shechuni HaEleph under the blankets on cool October nights and realized that entire families had lived there for many winters without heat.

While in Israel, I had the unexpected delight of attending prayer services conducted by Yemenite, Moroccan, and Iraqi Jewish communities, all different strands of Mizrahi Jews. What was amazing to me was that although I recognized the services very well, there were substantial differences between them due to a more than seven-hundred-year separation of Ashkenazi Jews from Mizrahi Jews. The replies during the service were very different, and the *kaddish* and many readings had significant wording differences. Nonetheless, there was a strong sense of a shared history and peoplehood despite these differences.

My encounters with Palestinians in Israel also informed my understanding of how life in the Diaspora can change communities without destroying their peoplehood. I was lucky enough to have been in Israel at a time when Israelis and Palestinians could both move relatively freely in the area. So, I traveled into the Sinai, the Gaza Strip, and across the West Bank on public buses. From those travels, I have vivid memories of Bethlehem, Shiloh, Jericho, Sharm el-Sheikh, Mount Sinai, and Saint Catherine's Monastery. Bethlehem was predominantly Christian at the time and was very welcoming to tourists. Israel was in a constant economic crisis, and the Israeli currency, then the lira, suffered frequent devaluations. The devaluations were so bad that the government subsequently scrapped the lira and started a new currency, the shekel. The upside to me was that my meager funds denominated in US dollars now allowed me to afford travel all over the country.

I discovered that Hebrew University had a Hillel, a Jewish campus organization. Like its American counterparts, it too had free food at events. I was intrigued by one of their programs for foreign students, which was to match us with Israeli Arabs who lived in the Galilee. I was paired with a high school senior who lived in a village in that area. When I arrived, I realized the village was not large, but it did have one modest-sized high school that my new friend attended. I stayed at his home for a few days as we communicated primarily in Hebrew, which was the best common language we had. I got to know his family, who were wonderfully gracious and warm, and we spoke a lot about life and occasionally, cautiously, about politics. We also maintained a frequent correspondence when I was back at Hebrew University. He visited me there as well.

Aside from politics, my Palestinian/Arab/Muslim friend was in many ways culturally indistinguishable from my Mizrahi Jewish friends. If you visited the HaTikva Market in Tel Aviv, which catered to Mizrahi Jews, in conjunction with an Israeli Arab market in the Galilee, the sounds, smells, tastes, and language would be hard to distinguish. Yet there was also a world of difference. He and his family participated not only in the broader Arab culture but adhered to their politics and their religion. He viewed himself as part of a different people from me, whereas I shared a sense of peoplehood with the Jews in Israel, including those who sounded more like him than my father.

Too many American Jews and Americans in general rely on their own limited experience or false discourses that all Jews are Ashkenazi/European Jews. And neither university experience nor American media corrects this false view. In fact, though many American Jews of my generation list themselves as white in the US census and view themselves and consequently most Jews as European, it is because they unfortunately do not grasp Jewish life outside of its American context. In the United States, the majority of the ancestors of American Jews did live in Russia and Eastern Europe but, as explained above, were never assimilated or considered as European before arriving in the US. Additionally, American Jewish history is a tiny slice of Jewish history in the Diaspora. For credentialed scholars, this ignorance is shocking and paradoxically is a very white, Eurocentric view of the world that should rightly be decried. The history of the Jewish people is far from the categories, frameworks, and theories the far left peddles. It is akin to history denial.

It was during that year in Israel that I got a better understanding of the history of Jews in the land of Israel. I was fortunate to have another wonderful teacher, Professor Isaiah Gafni. Dr. Gafni helped me bridge the gap in my conception of the history of the Jewish people and the land of Israel. I recommend any of his books, but particularly his three books on Babylonian Jewry. I took his class both semesters on the history of the Second Temple and then the Talmudic Period, which ended with the Muslim Arab conquest of the land of Israel. The first class began after biblical narrative, which ends in the time of Ezra and Nehemiah and the story of the rebuilding of the Temple. Unlike during much of the First Temple biblical period, throughout the Second Temple period, the Jewish people were only very briefly sovereign.

Rather, they lived under successive imperial powers: first Persian, then Greek, Roman, Byzantine, and finally various Muslim empires.

Under each ruler, the Jewish people/Israelites had to contend with different limitations and forms of oppression. In its most benign form, submission meant paying tribute as occurred under the Persians, who allowed the Jews to rebuild the Temple but not reinstate the monarchy. Under the Greeks and Romans, the situation became more difficult. Greek rule was truly a settler colonial empire model that subjugated populations through cultural assimilation. The Ptolemy/Syrian-Greek rulers established many military colonies throughout the land, which locals had to feed. Further, the military men were encouraged to marry local women, a form of forced assimilation. Thus, the Greeks attempted and to some measure succeeded in Hellenizing a hard-to-estimate percentage of Jews. This Hellenization would not only harm the Jews but divide them between those who resisted and those who accommodated and later promoted Greek rule. This tension would lead to the revolt against the Ptolemaic King Antiochus, in which the anti-Hellenistic Jews led by the Maccabees prevailed. That victory is celebrated by the holiday of Chanukah. Greek rule and internal tensions caused warfare and economic hardship, which led many Jews to leave the land of Israel. The Jews were not the only people to lose their sovereignty during this period; the Greek and Roman Empires covered much of the Mediterranean basin and reigned over such previously powerful states as Egypt, Babylon, and Persia, themselves former empires, as well as smaller states such as the city states of Phoenicia, which were also Hellenized to lesser and greater degrees.

The Romans then conquered many of the lands previously ruled by the Greeks. Roman oppression and further internal divisions quickly caused two Roman-Jewish wars. The Jewish War (66–70 CE) was memorialized by Flavius Josephus. We learn of the later Bar Kokhba Revolt (132–136 ACE) against Rome from various Roman and Jewish sources. The Jews fought so tenaciously that Rome particularly celebrated their final victories. One can visit today the Arch of Titus in

Rome, which was built after the conquering generals returned home. Sadly, these wars led to massive civilian losses, the destruction of the Temple, and the exile and enslavement of large parts of the surviving population. The Romans renamed the Jewish land of Israel to Palestine and Jerusalem to Aelia Capitolina. The rump Jewish community did not totally disappear; rather, it remained via scattered villages, especially in the northern part of the country. These communities would remain as the Roman Empire divided into eastern (Byzantine) and western empires. Jews who remained in the area that was Israel were largely under Byzantine imperial rule. Economic and religious oppression was the main feature of the Romans' Christian heirs—synagogues could not be built, and Jews were at times expelled from areas, forcibly converted, or subjected to random violence.

One of the highlights of Dr. Gafni's classes were the field trips. There we could see the ruins of the different actors of the period. We visited vestiges from Hasmonean kings, who for a short time under the Greeks reestablished a ruling dynasty and ruled semi-autonomously. We also saw evidence of the continuity of Jewish existence and ritual in the region despite imperial pressures. The presence of *mikvehs* (ritual baths) in Jewish cities and villages was a clear distinguishing mark. We noted the presence of settler colonists from the Greek period, whose villages, unlike Jewish villages, had pig bone remains. (The Jewish rejection of pork came at a high economic cost since pork was among the cheapest available sources of protein.) We visited synagogues built during Greek and Roman rule and non-Jewish structures as well. Shockingly to my twenty-year-old self, since the Arab conquest was to be many hundreds of years in the future, none of the non-Jewish remains were from groups of Arabic origin. Though highly impoverished, a diminished Jewish community in the land of Israel continued to produce great scholars and composed the Jerusalem Talmud during the Byzantine period through the early fifth century, despite the Byzantines formally prohibiting rabbinic ordination. The Jews remained in Israel, small in number but present in the subsequent Islamic empires, and in the interim Crusader period (where they barely hung on).

Dr. Gafni would take out his (well-worn) Hebrew Scriptures or part of the Talmud, show us a site, and read aloud a text as we would gasp at how the ancient descriptions were perfectly consistent with what was before our eyes. One biblical passage has always stuck with me, and that is when Jeremiah is asked by God to do something so unusual, he questions God: "Here are the siege mounds raised against the city to storm it…Yet You God said to me 'buy the land for money and call in witnesses.'" (Jeremiah 32:24–26) Jeremiah is in prison for foretelling that Jerusalem and the Temple will be destroyed. While in prison, his cousin, who is about to flee the destruction as the Babylonian troops are massing, comes to him and asks Jeremiah to purchase his land (as close relatives were expected to do in biblical times). Jeremiah follows God's command by making a public ceremony in the prison, counting out the money, and exchanging the deed. "Thus, says the Lord…'take these documents, this deed of purchase, the sealed text and…put them into an earthen jar, so that they may last a long time…houses, fields, vineyards shall again be purchased in this land.'" (Jeremiah 32:13–15)

Talk about optimism! The land of Israel is about to be decimated, with many people killed, and here is Jeremiah buying land! Even a real estate newbie knows that this is a bad deal. But this is the story of an indigenous people tied to their land. Others may possess the land, but the indigenous people still believe they own it because their deed is in "an earthen jar" that will last millennia. I learned later that the Jerusalem Talmud contained a discussion about when foreign invaders seize and settle land, and concludes that this property is legally considered to be stolen. The center of Jewish life moved from the land of Israel to the Diaspora outside the land of Israel (in the Diaspora itself, many centers would come and go) after the Roman wars, but Jewish life never ended in Israel.

This is what I learned from the field trips I took with Dr. Gafni and others: the archaeology of Israel evidenced by professionally executed, peer-reviewed excavations demonstrates with certainty that there is a deep and continuous connection between the Jewish people and the land of Israel.

Absolutely, there is another story to tell of the Muslim conquerors and some of their descendants who make up the core of Palestinian communities as well. Their presence as inhabitants, unlike those of the Greek and Roman Empires, remains to this day, as do many of the mosques, fortifications, and in some cases castles they built. And like the British who colonized the United States and now feel deeply American while also part of a greater Western culture with its roots in Britain, the Palestinian people's history and connection to the land is centuries old and with clear roots in the Arabian Peninsula, and thereby remains part of a greater nexus of Arab and Muslim history. It is even more entwined because Islam is informed by Jewish texts and ideas as well as local traditions. Peace will have to be negotiated between both sides, but it will never come by fabricating a false history.

PART III

WHATSOEVER THINGS ARE HONEST 1

AN INTELLECTUAL TRADITION OF FAR-LEFT AND FAR-RIGHT ANTI-ZIONIST CONSPIRACY THEORIES

Although we have focused on two particular scholars at one university, Butz and Thrasher are not solitary figures. Intellectuals and university professors are supposed to adhere to standards of truth and morality; however, we find that in practice, there have been both voices of truth and goodness as well as falsehood and evil. The story of the blood libel well illustrates the power of intellectuals to do harm as well as good. Historians thought for a long time these ideas were popularized by common folk, but research has shown otherwise. It was intellectual elites who were able to get this meme established in the mainstream.

The earliest account of blood libel comes from England in 1144. The libel was in turn linked to a Conspiracy Theory that Jews from all over the world met and conspired yearly to choose a country where they would murder a Christian child for ritual purposes. In her book *Blood Libel: On the Trail of an Antisemitic Myth*,[1] Magda Teter tells the story of how the prince-bishop of Trent, Johannes Hinderbach, took the murder of a boy, Simon of Trent, and turned it into a blood libel. He made a particular effort to get the story out in such a way that ensured that neither secular nor religious authorities were allowed to investigate or intervene. Only he could relate and prosecute the alleged crime, which led to the execution of several Jews. By cleverly suppressing any other version of the libel, Hinderbach made his narrative "the acknowledged truth." Teter notes that subsequent scholars accepted the Simon of Trent story because it was taught to them as truth from the supposedly authoritative source of Hinderbach. Hugo Grotius, one of the wisest sixteenth-century thinkers to whom humanity is still deeply indebted, was confounded by the blood libels because they made no sense to him from his experience with Jews, yet that was what was written in authoritative books that he studied. So he too accepted blood libels as truth.

In addition to the lineage among intellectuals we discussed in the previous chapter, both Butz's and Thrasher's specific Conspiracy Theories are basically standard reiterations of far-right and far-left postwar anti-Zionist Conspiracy Theories respectively. For this reason, we need to consider a brief history of this genre.

The story of modern far-right anti-Zionist Conspiracy Theories starts with the Nazis and neo-Nazis. As mentioned earlier, Hitler wrote in *Mein Kampf* (published in 1925) that he opposed Zionism because it would be "a Jewish state in Palestine," which would only serve as an "organization center for their international world-swindling...a place of refuge for convicted scoundrels and a university for up-and-coming swindlers." His words were not merely rhetoric. It is well established that Hitler not only sought to murder the Jews of Europe but of British Mandatory Palestine as well. He met with the Mufti Amin al-Husseini, with whom he shared his goal of the destruction of British Mandatory Palestine, but confided that his plan could not yet be made public.[2]

Indeed, recent archival data has demonstrated that he would have succeeded were it not for the famed Desert Rats of Britain's Eighth Army at El Alamein under the leadership of Field Marshal Bernard Montgomery,[3] which prevented the Germans from advancing eastward into Egypt. After Germany's defeat in the war, the Nazis went underground and their views were largely ignored and discredited. Yet by the 1960s, they were once again publicizing anti-Jewish conspiracies under the banner of Holocaust denial.[4] Now, we are used to reading about Holocaust revisionism as anti-Semitic conspiracy, but it cannot be stressed enough that Holocaust revisionists unanimously blame Israel/Zionists for what they call the Hoax and vilify the Jewish state. As Deborah Lipstadt writes in her landmark book *Denying the Holocaust*,[5] Holocaust denial became inexorably tied with delegitimizing Israel.[6] In 1962, the French journalist Paul Rassinier created a splash with *The True Eichmann Trial or The Incorrigible Victors*, which claimed that the continuing war crimes trials were part of a Zionist and communist strategy to divide and demoralize Europeans. In America, the history professor Harry Elmer Barnes published the 1964 article—whose title could not identify the "enemy" more clearly—"Zionist Fraud,"[7] which laid "the chief blame for misrepresentation on those whom we must call the swindlers of the crematoria, the Israeli politicians who derive billions of marks from nonexistent, mythical and imaginary cadavers."

By the 1970s, these sorts of publications proliferated in the US and in Europe, with cross-pollination between the two and in some cases funding from Saudi Arabia.[8] In 1973, the American English professor Austin App published *The Six Million Swindle*,[9] followed by the British National Front politician Richard Verrall's *Did Six Million Really Die?*[10] in 1974, both accusing Zionists of fabricating the Holocaust and conspiring to manipulate the Allies into doing their bidding. Inspired by these books, and hoping to break through to the mainstream, David McCalden and Willis Carto founded the Institute for Historical Review (IHR) in California and its publishing arm the Noontide Press and the *Journal of Historical Review* in 1978. Butz joined the editorial board of their journal. The institute not only united the hitherto less-publicized voices across the US and Europe devoted to manufacturing global anti-Zionist conspiracy but also strove to give them academic legitimacy. Butz was a pivotal player in this early effort to legitimize Holocaust "revisionism" in the academy.

From the 1970s onward, far-right Conspiracy Theorists in the United States not only continued to come from the academy, they also tried to achieve scholarly credibility. Indeed, most major far-right figures have come from or remained in the academy since the 1970s. William Luther Pierce, who was a physics professor before he left for a job at Pratt & Whitney to finance his far-right activism, headed the National Alliance, a far-right educational organization.[11] Kevin MacDonald, a professor of evolutionary biology at California State University, Long Beach, is another example, as is John Hartung, a professor of anesthesiology at the State University of New York, a key witness in the David Irving trial in Austria. Irving, a British historian known for his Holocaust denial, likewise explained it as a Zionist hoax, though he did not teach at a university.

As Lipstadt shows, the IHR also made several attempts to gain legitimacy within the academy. The editors tried to hold a conference in a University of California building,[12] and their publication of a journal reproduced the veneer of a scholarly periodical. Other attempts were made by the IHR to engage student newspapers and academic organizations. Lipstadt also demonstrates how Bradley Smith and Mark Weber, both far-right activists, formed the Committee for Open Debate on the Holocaust and placed advertisements in university newspapers questioning the Holocaust's historicity under the organization's aegis. While no student editor approved of the content, many falsely believed that they had to print it as a matter of protecting the First Amendment, including the *Daily Northwestern*. In fact, the First Amendment is about limiting government censorship and does not apply to newspapers approving advertisements. As Lipstadt shows, college newspapers had no problem refusing advertisements on all kinds of other topics.

Another strategy of the IHR was to buy the mailing list of the Organization of American Historians (OAH) and send members complimentary copies of the *Journal of Historical Review*.[13] Other instances included publishing revisionist work in the OAH newsletter, soliciting various history professors in support of Holocaust revisionism, and picketing at American Historical Association conferences.[14] None of these efforts have yet succeeded in getting far-right anti-Zionist Conspiracy

Theories about the Holocaust into the academic mainstream. Yet far-right academically trained Holocaust revisionist intellectuals are consistently tied to anti-Zionist Conspiracy Theories, and far-right professors and intellectuals use terms like the "Zionist Occupied Government" to describe the US, or the "bastard state," and accuse Israel of committing genocide enabled by the Holocaust hoax.[15] The active organizing and strategizing of these far-right intellectuals indicates that they have no intention of tapping out. They sincerely want everyone to read their books. On the far left, the story is vastly different.

Like Butz, Thrasher's views are standard anti-Zionist conspiracies, albeit on the far left. While unlike Butz, he is not a central player, some of his intellectual role models, especially Angela Davis, are. Further, unlike far-right anti-Zionist conspiracies, those on the far left have a profound impact on the academy. Far-left intellectuals and activists have been central in promoting distortions about Zionism since the 1960s in the universities and have largely succeeded. As with their far-right counterparts, far-left anti-Zionist Conspiracy Theorists have their roots in pre-WWII party propaganda, in their case Soviet and various Arab League parties. The Soviet state opposed Zionism from the outset.[16] Though the Bolsheviks opposed racial anti-Semitism, they publicly sought to eliminate Judaism as a religion (as they did with non-Jewish religions).

It is less well known how central opposition to Zionism was to this project. In 1918, the Jewish section of the Communist Party, the Yevsektsiya, was approved by Lenin to help bring about a communist revolution among the Jewish masses. The stated objective of the Yevsektsiya was "destruction of traditional Jewish life, the Zionist movement, and Hebrew culture."[17] Indeed, the Yevsektsiya was particularly fierce in its opposition to Zionism, in addition to Jewish culture and religion, calling for its "total liquidation" at the Third All-Russian Central Executive Committee in 1921.[18] For communists, Zionism was a form of bourgeois nationalism, a false ideology meant to distract workers from international working-class solidarity.

Taking a less destructive tack, in 1924 the Soviets also established the Jewish Autonomous Oblast, a territory dedicated to Jews, which they hoped would offer an alternative to Zionism while seeking to allow Jews some form of national recognition. But this soon changed in the 1930s, when Stalin shifted to a policy of more open Russification.[19] During this time, not only did he continue to outlaw Zionism but many members of the Yevsektsiya were purged. Stalin also severely reduced the number of Jews in the top echelons of the party following the Molotov-Ribbentrop Pact. Stalin's vote in favor of the creation of Israel in 1948 was not ideological; rather, he presumably ordered a positive vote on strategic grounds, thinking the new state would join the socialist bloc (to which it was more ideologically aligned) and figuring whether or not the new state would survive, it's mere creation would hasten the British decline in the area. Nevertheless, Stalin swiftly returned to anti-Zionist form, purging his own wartime creation of the Jewish Anti-Fascist Committee, many of whose members supported Zionism, because of his renewed opposition to Jewish culture and because of his concern that Zionist Jews could be an American fifth column.[20] Thus, by the 1950s, Soviet anti-Zionist propaganda was re-entrenched, with intellectuals playing an important role in its dissemination.

After World War II, unlike the Nazis and other far-right parties, communist and Marxist parties did not go underground; rather, they remained in power or came to power. Communist intellectuals were the only players in the Eastern Bloc and remained important in the West even during the Cold War.[21] For despite the exodus of many intellectuals from the Communist Party in response to Stalin's crimes against humanity, and persecution of suspected communists during the McCarthy era, a small number of university faculty remained committed communists or fellow travelers (people sympathetic to communism who did not however officially join the party) and a larger number remained intellectual Marxists of various stripes throughout much of the postwar period in the US, but especially since the 1970s.[22] Openly Marxist journals continue to be a mainstay of English language academia in both the social sciences and humanities, while more generally radical (a term that includes various Marxist, anti-capitalist, anti-imperialist viewpoints) ones developed and remain widespread as well. Marxist analyses of Zionism have consistently viewed it as an illegitimate form of reactionary bourgeois nationalism.

While the American players in disseminating Marxist anti-Zionism and anti-Zionist Conspiracy Theories are too numerous to list, a few stand out. Unlike the far-right *Journal of Historical Review*, which struggles for academic consideration, one of the premier journals among anglophone radical intellectuals, the British-based but transatlantic *New Left Review*, has since its inception in 1960 consistently represented Zionism as a European settler colonial enterprise.[23] Not all of the articles presenting this erroneous position can be viewed as Conspiracy Theories. Yet this esteemed journal certainly set the stage for the increasing acceptance not only of the anti-Zionist perspective but even of its more conspiratorial iterations in the academy.

Other players have been prominent public intellectuals, and in the American context no one has been more important in the last few decades than Angela Davis. Davis provides the direct line between communist anti-Zionist Conspiracy Theories and younger American scholars like Thrasher. Thrasher proudly traces his intellectual genealogy to Davis, whose own consistent communist views are unwavering. Davis's current views on Zionism draw from classic Soviet propaganda and Conspiracy Theories, which as previously mentioned described Zionism as a racist, imperialist, fascist movement aimed at destroying global national liberation movements and the Soviet Union.[24] Davis's perspective is not surprising for someone who had ties to a Marxist-Leninist organization in high school, studied with Marxist intellectuals in university, and then officially declared herself to be communist and joined the party in 1968[25] (though she formally left CPUSA in 1991, she still considers herself a communist ideologically). Indeed, she joined Arafat as the keynote speaker of the 10th annual 1973 World Festival of Youth and Students and described her support for his views.

[Arafat] always acknowledged the kinship of the Palestinian struggle and the Black freedom struggle in the United States, and who, like Che, Fidel, Patrice Lumumba, and Amilcar Cabral, was a revered figure within the movement for Black liberation. This was a time when communist internationalism—in Africa, the Middle East, Europe, Asia, Australia, South America, and the Caribbean—was a powerful force. [26]

In a 2017 interview, she describes her own connection with Palestinian viewpoints in a manner identical to the Soviet Zionologist discourse that defined Zionism as racist Western settler colonialism and imperialism. Her insistence on the parallel between Israel and the United States underscores this point.

Palestine has always occupied a pivotal place, precisely because of the similarities between Israel and the United States—their foundational settler colonialism and their ethnic cleansing processes with respect to indigenous people, their systems of segregation, their use of legal systems to enact systematic repression, and so forth. I often point out that my consciousness of the predicament of Palestine dates back to my undergraduate years at Brandeis University, which was founded in the same year as the State of Israel. Moreover, during my own incarceration, I received support from Palestinian political prisoners as well as from Israeli attorneys defending Palestinians.[27]

Davis's current perspective on Zionism is thus based on a totally orthodox Soviet and Pan-Arabist one, which she—along with other communist and far-left intellectuals—has continued to perpetuate now thirty years after the Soviet Union's demise.

Davis's current contribution to classic Soviet anti-Zionist Conspiracy Theories has been to perpetuate them in the post-communist world and to add the claim of an exact parallel between Palestinian and African American oppression and liberation in the context of the expanding incarceration rate of African Americans. Davis claims to make this connection within an international framework of understanding oppression, which lends the comparison an aura of objectivity; however, this designation is exaggerated to say the least, since her only consistent focus outside of the US is Palestine, which as she describes to Frank Barat, she mentions all the time.[28] As she writes: "Well, I think we constantly have to make connections. So that when we are engaged in the struggle of racist violence, in relation to Ferguson, Michael Brown, and New York, Eric Garner, we can't forget the connections with Palestine."[29] Indeed, the whole purpose of the book *Freedom is a Constant Struggle*, published in 2016 in the wake of Ferguson, is to promulgate a bogus connection between Palestinians and racism in America. Unsurprisingly, her updated claims about the evils of Zionism, like those of Butz or the Soviet Zionologists who shaped her views, are also conspiratorial. She takes small facts to make not only exaggerated, but false arguments. For example, she cites the attendance of US police officers in training courses in Israel (of which very little was tactical) to allege that Israel is the center of a global conspiracy to incarcerate people of color, or what Frank Barat calls in his interview with her "the reproduction of the occupation."[30] Or she insinuates that Israel is at the heart of global imperialism and fascism. See her statement for the 2020 BDS Apartheid Week events:

> In Palestine, the US, Arab countries, Latin America and Asia, the people who are seeking to maintain systems of oppression and racial domination are sharing ideologies, strategies and weapons. For example, police strategies have been transnationalized, with US and Israeli police departments exchanging tactics. And the

global prison industrial complex is being tested in its most extreme forms in Palestine.[31]

She also charges that the Israel lobby is extremely powerful, repeating the common claim of its conspiracy to manipulate others:

There are a lot of similarities, precisely because BDS has chosen to follow the root of the antiapartheid struggle toward a hopefully more global sense of solidarity by using the method of mass boycott. I guess what is different is the existence of a powerful Zionist lobby. Certainly there was a powerful apartheid lobby, but it did not have nearly the influence as the Zionist lobby, which can be seen in terms of Black religion; its tentacles reach into the Black church, there have been direct efforts to, on the part of the state of Israel, to recruit significant Black figures. And I don't know whether we experienced that level of sophistication during the antiapartheid era. Certainly the Israeli state has learned from that movement.[32]

Unlike Butz, however, Davis is rarely questioned about the conspiratorial nature of her arguments. No one questions her how racism in America, which progressives argue began in 1619, could now be significantly aggravated by Israel, which was founded in 1948, or Zionism, which held its first convening in 1897. No one questions her how Israelis are somehow the only group in the world that can brainwash visiting otherwise intelligent upstanding citizens of other countries to return as violent racists. Remarkably, neither in academia nor in the media does anyone pose challenging questions as to her fixation on Zionists as a uniquely all-powerful malevolent force. This is due to her stature as a civil rights activist, which even those who disagree with her communism do not usually question. It is also due to her own approach to activism. In particular, she does not grant interviews other than to sympathetic media outlets. She appears mostly on *Democracy Now!*, which is almost as hostile to Zionism as she is. She also does not participate in debates.

Thus, with no actual evidence, Davis's updated Soviet-era Conspiracy Theories have now become accepted truths in much of the humanities, repeated through a younger generation of scholars like Thrasher and Jasbir Puar, without ever being called out for what they are. Further, since she adopts the official communist line of rejecting anti-Semitism (understood very narrowly as rejecting racial anti-Semitism while opposing sovereign Jewish culture, religion, language, and politics), she has been given access to all the major universities to do this. Davis has given major addresses at Northwestern alone four times, in 1989, 2001, 2009, and 2014. In her most recent talk, on May 19, 2014, she filled an auditorium and received a standing ovation. Davis often mentions Palestine whatever the topic, which she herself admits is a conscious strategy in *Freedom Is a Constant Struggle*. On this occasion, she spent time talking about the Palestinians and compared Israel to South Africa. She said, "When we look at Palestine, we are compelled to acknowledge the modes of racism, apartheid for example, which we assume were abolished with the end of South African apartheid, have not been deposited into the dustbin of history."[33] Davis does not even bother to establish why "we are compelled" to see things this way with data or evidence. While guest speakers should and often do generate debate in the university community, all of the *Daily Northwestern* articles reported that Davis and her pronouncements were treated as revealed truth. Davis's views are now dogma, not arguments. It is no wonder that Thrasher's conspiratorial tweets and public pronouncements have gathered mostly loud applause and certainly made no difference to his prestigious appointment, despite constant claims that academics are being silenced by a Zionist cabal.

Finally, Davis was on the Russell Tribunal on Palestine and is one of the most ardent advocates of the Boycott, Divestment, and Sanctions (BDS) movement against Israel. The Russell Tribunal was ostensibly a people's tribunal established, in her own words, to promote peace in the Middle East. In practice, it was staffed by a jury of known opponents of Jewish self-determination, who consider Israel to be a European settler colony.[34] One of its primary organizers, Frank Barat, actively supports the BDS movement against Israel and is also featured in the introduction in Davis's *Freedom Is a Constant Struggle*.[35]

It is important to be clear about the goals of BDS, which rejects Zionism as a national liberation movement, deeming it to be a white settler colonial construct, and therefore wants an end to all of Israel. The importance of this point cannot be overlooked. BDS was established in 2005 along the lines of the international boycott against South Africa in opposition to apartheid. As Cary Nelson writes in his book about the BDS movement and the American academy, *Israel Denial*, the BDS movement is clear in its desire to eliminate the Jewish state. He quotes BDS founder Omar Barghouti who says "accepting Israel as a 'Jewish state' on our land is impossible."[36] Indeed, their goal is an Arab Palestine in the entire territory. Moreover, BDS as an organization advances all of the falsehoods and conspiracies Thrasher and his many colleagues advocate about Israel as a European settler colonial state, Israel's intention to harm people of color, and its nefarious influence in the United States. To advance these views, BDS holds an Israel Apartheid Week across university campuses globally every year, where they invite speakers to give talks on Israel's imagined monstrosities.[37] In 2020, Davis, an avid supporter of Israel Apartheid Week, claimed as mentioned earlier that "the global prison industrial complex is being tested in its most extreme forms in Palestine."[38] The last part of this sentence is especially jarring not only for its false claims but for its utterance by a public intellectual who has said nothing about China or North Korea's penal system, not to mention the USSR's gulags and prisons, despite her close alliance to global communism. Davis is perhaps the most important opponent of the Jewish state and proponent of anti-Zionist Conspiracy Theories in America today.

While I have focused on Thrasher as a case study, I could well have chosen other Northwestern professors. Indeed, a sizable number of Northwestern professors in the humanities and social sciences are openly involved in promoting anti-Zionism and even anti-Zionist Conspiracy Theories, like Thrasher, with no opposition to their career advancement and with little counter-influence. They do this, as Cary Nelson explains, in a number of ways, which actually cover the gamut of professorial influence.[39] They promote and/or support BDS, produce anti-Zionist scholarship, and/or uncritically teach anti-Zionist sources in their courses or introduce anti-Zionist material in unrelated courses; they demonize Israel on social media, or they support or welcome speakers who promote anti-Zionist Conspiracy Theories. Northwestern faculty in the social sciences and humanities are relatively representative of American faculty in general in major universities in their proud support for all of these measures. In discussing all of these anti-Zionist initiatives, whether conspiratorial or not, it is important to recall that we are talking here about activities that promote the rejection of Jewish national self-determination as racist and illegitimate. With regard to BDS, Northwestern faculty have been involved in its different arms: they have signed calls for either general or discipline-wide or university-wide cultural boycotts,[40] academic boycotts,[41] as well as economic boycotts.[42] Jessica Winegar, who we will discuss in greater detail shortly, was a leader of the call for the American Anthropological Association's boycott. It is also reasonable to assume that a sizable number of Northwestern professors voted in favor of various disciplinary associations' BDS resolutions even if they did not sign the petitions initially calling for them, since those referendums which lost did so by relatively small margins. Other BDS-related petitions at Northwestern that have been supported by Northwestern faculty included the petitions for a moratorium on speaking at University of Illinois at Urbana-Champaign until Steven Salaita's reinstatement,[43] or signed petitions in support of anti-Zionist scholars like Angela Davis[44] and Stephane Hessel,[45] or campaigns to boycott specific conferences at

Israeli universities.[46] Northwestern scholars have also been active, like Thrasher, in demonizing Israel on social media and in articles for the general public.[47] Finally, a large number of Northwestern faculty have been supportive of or silent with regard to anti-Zionist speakers,[48] and Northwestern has consistently had an Israel Apartheid Week. In short, some students in the social sciences and humanities will encounter anti-Zionism, even conspiratorial anti-Zionism, without any rebuttal from faculty during their time at Northwestern. Indeed, there is almost no faculty Zionist activism and no Zionist equivalent of anti-Zionist/ pro-Palestinian scholarship at Northwestern.[49]

Of these many Northwestern scholars, two will be highlighted as examples of the nature of far-left anti-Zionist Conspiracy Theories on American campuses like Northwestern. The first is Jessica Winegar, a professor in the Department of Anthropology, a part of the core faculty of the Middle East and North African Studies program, and director of the Alice Kaplan Institute for the Humanities. A leader in the American Anthropological Association and an academic journal editor, Professor Winegar was awarded a prestigious book prize for her first book. Her second book, coauthored with Professor Lara Deeb of Scripps College, *Anthropology's Politics: Disciplining the Middle East*,[50] claims that anthropologists face a Zionist conspiracy to censor the discipline.

The book starts from the premise of responding to "sexism, racism, Islamophobia, and obstruction of any criticism of the Israeli state—that all of us face in our work in colleges and universities, no matter our discipline, foci, and backgrounds."[51] To prove their point, the authors cite a few controversial teachers who they said were "targeted...for taking anti-Zionist political positions...being Palestinian, [or] simply asking scholarly questions that call Zionist assumptions into question."[52] Yet, as they admit, despite exhaustive research, there are "only two cases in which anthropologists have come under such...assault."[53] The authors further report that despite the fact that "the vast majority of our interlocutors have not personally experienced such menacing opposition to their tenure or retention, they still expressed apprehension...and fears that they could easily be targeted by right-wing and/or Zionist organizations."[54] The authors consider this fear to be well founded when they state, "Indeed, anthropology is not immune to compulsory Zionism in the academy, and many fear that if they criticize Israel, they will be called an anti-Semite and/or a self-hating Jew and then suffer career consequences."[55] They also reported that faculty members, even after achieving tenure, "took great care to avoid being targeted by student spies...A few reported actively watching for moles in their classes."[56] Winegar in a separate article wrote that professors "are afraid" to teach about the Israeli-Palestinian conflict.[57]

Winegar thus promotes the anti-Zionist Conspiracy Theory that Zionists are out to silence opponents to the Jewish state despite the book's self-contradictory claims and its own conclusive presentation that most of the evidence is to the contrary. Certainly, Zionists oppose anti-Zionists, and vice versa, yet Winegar's claim in her book that there is a "compulsory Zionism" in the university is baseless for several reasons. First, a large number of anthropologists, including Winegar, are actively and conspiratorially anti-Zionist and have experienced no impediments or detriments to their careers.[58] Winegar relates in an interview that after 9/11, "we wanted our main disciplinary institution, the American Anthropological Association [AAA], to take a public stand against racist attacks on Arab and Muslims in the US, the invasion in Iraq, and the apartheid wall that Israel was building—issues that we saw as interrelated and linked to the new War on Terror." She was a lead activist in encouraging the AAA to take such a stand. In November 2015, members of the AAA voted 1,040 to 136 to place a referendum on a boycott of Israel on the following spring's all-member agenda. The Boycott, Divestment, and Sanctions resolution was defeated with 2,423 against and 2,384 in favor, a very tight margin.[59] In the wake of the close defeat, the AAA decided to make it clear that, just shy of a boycott, it would issue a censure of the government of Israel, write official letters to various ministries in Israel, and take other pro-Palestinian actions both alone and in partnership with sister academic associations.[60]

Another example also makes this point clear: an alternative resolution on Israel, though critical of the country in that it "called for the end to the occupation while also rejecting the boycott," garnered just 14 percent of votes (196 in favor, 1,173 opposed) at the November meeting.[61] It is likely that a pro-Zionist resolution would have received no votes at all.

It can't be stressed enough that all of the anti-Zionism proponents in the AAA were hired and, in many cases, promoted and received tenure without apparent discrimination based on their opinions, which is consistent with "the vast majority" of their colleagues facing no backlash and only two cases within the profession cited as examples. Many more than two anthropologists during this time frame did not receive tenure for a host of reasons. The scholarly contributions of the two anthropologists they cite versus other anthropologists contemporaneously receiving or being denied tenure were neither analyzed nor compared in Winegar's book. Yet despite the lack of any quantifiable evidence, and Winegar's own admission to knowing it, she and her colleagues still insisted they are being oppressed by Zionist forces and some worry about "moles" and "spies" in their classes. In other words, Winegar *feels* she is being oppressed despite the facts pointing to the contrary, and this is apparently proof enough. At no point does she consider whether it is appropriate for a whole profession to feel afraid of and oppressed by a force that seems to have had no negative impact on them.

Winegar's book *Anthropology's Politics: Disciplining the Middle East* assumes that Zionism is extraordinarily evil. Indeed, the book is incomprehensible if that premise is not accepted. An attempt at a description of Zionism only takes place within one paragraph on page 18[62] and that description is garbled, but before the paragraph ends, the reader already knows that "compulsory Zionism" is executed and enforced within academia. The book is written from the sole perspective that Zionists are all bad and are behind any bad things that happen to the good folks who don't comply with compulsory Zionism. Anyone critical of BDS or of anti-Zionism is portrayed in a sinister

light and specific terms are meant to be taken by the reader as ominous, such as "Hillel rabbi," "pro-Israel faculty and students," and
"local Zionist community."[63] Their "outcry" is presumed to be illegitimate, subversive to truth, and disingenuous, as opposed to anyone
who corroborates Winegar's narrative.[64] The only actors in the book
referred to anywhere near as negatively are "Americanists." Proponents
of BDS are lauded without exception for their courage and truth telling. With a few exceptions, the references to Zionists are all via academics who are opposed to, upset by, or infuriated by Zionism. The
only positive references to Jews are to those Jews who oppose Zionism.
Christian Zionists are criticized and, according to the authors, feared
as well. There are vague references to the forces that the Zionists use
to thwart those who do not comply. The lack of criticism for those
who follow the narrative of anti-Zionism and the reliance on hearsay
and prejudiced feelings with respect to people like "Hillel rabbis" and
"pro-Israel faculty and students" is a complete departure from normal
academic norms, but the book was published by Stanford University
Press. Northwestern University funded "some of the research" for the
book. "Many undergraduate and graduate students helped."[65] The
book is an argument from *pathos* and *ethos* dismissing traditional
scholarly *logos*.

Winegar's book *Anthropology's Politics* essentially accepts the
Conspiracy Theory that Zionists are causing great harm to anthropologists. Indeed, she has written that there is a "massive collusion between
education, the media, and US and Israeli state policy on this issue."[66]
However, she notes hopefully the trends and states that the days of
this collusion "are, in fact, numbered."[67] (One is reminded of Butz's
hope in his 2003 preface to *The Hoax* that Holocaust revisionism is
"successful" in making Zionism a "dying monster.") Her views and
those of her interlocutors are accepted as true and are neither examined
nor deemed falsifiable by Winegar. One can oppose the existence of
Israel without also believing that Zionists are expending vast resources
mendaciously undermining academic anthropologists. However, for

Conspiracy Theorists, the collusion and power of the opposition is vast and palpably everywhere to be found.

A second example of a Northwestern faculty member actively promoting BDS, anti-Zionist narratives untethered from facts, and anti-Zionist Conspiracy Theories is another anthropologist, Associate Professor Sami Hermez, who is the director of the Liberal Arts Program at the school's Qatar campus. He has authored scores of articles and essays arguing essentially for boycotts of anything having to do with Israel or Israelis, whether in Israel or the rest of the world. He noted in an article that "whether it is legal or not to collaborate with Israel should not be of concern, rather, the question is whether this collaboration should exist on moral grounds."[68] This is a somewhat forgone conclusion for Hermez, as he seems to only reference or cite authors who are at the extreme of anti-Zionism. In a course he taught called Anthropology of Palestine, all the authors were advocates of boycotting or ending Israel. Indeed, Hermez does not differentiate between within or outside the 1948 borders in his advocacy for BDS. In addition to promoting BDS, Hermez also teaches blood libels as fact. One text he assigned for class was an article by Diana Allan and Curtis Brown[69] in which the al-Dura incident is recited as fact. The al-Dura incident consists of the allegation that Mohammad al-Dura was killed on September 30, 2000, by the Israel Defense Forces (IDF) while he was being cradled by his father as depicted by France 2 television and subsequently picked up by every major media outlet in the world. However, it turns out this version of events was a lie. Whatever did happen that day, it is next to impossible, based on his position and on the physical evidence, that the IDF killed him as portrayed by France 2. The book *Contre expertise d'une mise en scène* (roughly, *Re-evaluation of a Re-enactment*)[70] by Gérard Huber goes even further, making the case that the entire event was staged. *The Atlantic*, in an exhaustive examination reported in the article "Who Shot Mohammed al-Dura?"[71] concludes that what was portrayed could not have happened. In other words, the al-Dura incident was a hoax in the form of a media-savvy blood libel. While I do not know if other countervailing articles were offered in Hermez's class, it is still disturbing that a hoax, or at very minimum highly disputed allegations, are being taught as a matter of fact at Northwestern.

Finally, Hermez openly lauds political leaders who promote anti-Zionist Conspiracy Theories. For example, he has argued that Hassan Nasrallah of Hezbollah should be considered in the same league as Mahatma Gandhi, Nelson Mandela, and other similar leaders. He contends that "history has not yet judged Sayed Hassan Nasrallah, but he will likely be judged, as he is now, for using arms to free a nation...Violence cannot be viewed in a one-dimensional realm that is always destructive...we must view violence in its intersection with parallel nonviolent movements...In the end, we must recognize that it is only by managing both violence and non-violence in our lives, rather than surrendering to any one means, that we can achieve total control over our futures."[72] Hermez is unperturbed that Nasrallah has said, "If they [Jews] all gather in Israel, it will save us the trouble of going after them worldwide."[73] Or that he is on record claiming, "If we searched the entire world for a person more cowardly, despicable, weak and feeble in psyche, mind, ideology and religion, we would not find anyone like the Jew. Notice, I do not say the Israeli."[74] Or that in his view Jews are the "grandsons of apes and pigs" and "Allah's most cowardly and greedy creatures."[75] Nasrallah routinely touts the Conspiracy Theory that the Zionists are to blame for destabilizing Lebanon. *Ethos* should not be acceptable when the references to reliability are bad role models. Nasrallah is not a name I would put in the same category as Gandhi or Mandela. Prior to Northwestern, Hermez held posts at Harvard, the University of Pittsburgh, and Oxford in the years after he wrote "Judging Hassan Nasrallah" and has continued his activism for BDS throughout his career, all without having any apparent "career consequences."

It is ironic that Butz contends that the Nazis were far too nice to cause anything as evil as the murder of the 6 million Jews while

Hermez venerates the leader of an organization that seeks to be in a position to murder every last Jew on the planet.

My father would have listened to the way Winegar and Hermez present the anti-Zionist side—without any criticism and criticizing the Zionists as all evil while saying at the same time Zionists squelch any criticism—and said, "No matter how thin you slice a salami it still has two sides." (This saying's origin is attributed to Baruch Spinoza, without the salami.)

While there are no openly espousing Holocaust denying faculty at Northwestern beside Butz, there may be some who keep their views to themselves. A case in point is Dr. Bart Van Alphen, who was a Northwestern neuroscience researcher by day but also operated a Twitter account styled as "Bart VanCaveman" in which he posted highly offensive racist, anti-Black, anti-Jewish, and neo-Nazi tweets. Van Alphen committed suicide in 2021 after his identity was unmasked.[76]

As Cary Nelson describes in his book *Israel Denial*,[77] not only are the faculty of entire disciplines opposed to Zionism, but Conspiracy Theories increasingly pass muster and are even applauded. Nelson's book about hatred of Israel on the left, like Lipstadt's about hatred of Israel on the right, deserves to be read on its own. I would like to draw on one of the examples of Nelson's careful research that shows the way anti-Zionist Conspiracy Theories now pass as scholarship: Jasbir Puar. A professor in the Women and Gender Studies Program at Rutgers, Puar has built her whole career around fantasizing about how any good thing done by a Zionist is really a conspiracy to hoodwink the rest of the world. The similarities between her reasoning and that of Butz are striking.

Puar's book *The Right to Maim*[78] makes many conspiratorial allegations. One is that Zionists practice organ harvesting. Israel provides emergency health care in places afflicted by natural disasters, to victims of conflict who cross the Syrian border to get treatment, and to Palestinians. It also trains Palestinian medical professionals in the territories. Puar argues that organ harvesting must be the real motive for such Israeli medical aid. This shocking allegation is made without a shred of proof. At Vassar, Puar stated the following: "These pivotal elements...are also about the machinery of biopolitical control itself, the experiment of expanding and entrenching power to such an extent that at certain moments it can barely be recognized as this incorporative mechanism. Israeli computational sovereignty is invested in entities and populations far below and beyond the human form and territories far more complex than the proper ownership of land that is invested in the control of controlled self. Algorithmic computations are rationalized in the service of a liberal yet brutal humanism and humanitarianism."[79] Puar later claims, "Technologies of measure, algorithmic computing and architecture and infrastructure—prehensive gendering operates at the sub, para and intimate levels as body parts and the kinds of changes that come with epigenetic deterioration take hold. In the context, then, of Palestine, hacking is not a computational metaphor, rather a distinct practice of reshaping the forms of human bodies and parts informed by computational platforms."[80] She also alleges that Israel deliberately seeks to stunt the growth of Palestinian children. These conjured allegations would not be considered as scholarship were it not that the target is Israel.

Puar also promotes a fictional claim about why Israel has been so progressive in protecting the rights of LGBTQ individuals, including offering asylum to some gay Palestinians. She asserts that Israel does this to burnish its image through duplicitous "pinkwashing." Even saving LGBTQ Palestinians is somehow a condescending gesture to her. She fails to note that Israel as a matter of policy stopped prosecuting homosexuality in 1953, long before academia paid any attention to this human rights issue. Strangely, she morphs this argument into a complaint about the global obsession with the Holocaust. She writes, "It is my contention, or at least deep suspicion, that as long as the Holocaust remains the dominant trauma of the modern era, [Jews and Christians are allied] against Islam as a fundamentalist force and does so within the spaces of liberal secular feminist practices and queer scholarship."[81]

Finally, Puar claims that Israel deliberately maims Palestinians who confront the Israel Defense Forces as part of a vile conspiracy to minimize the number of fatalities. In contrast to what one might infer from disproportionate press coverage of the Israeli-Palestinian conflict, the fact is that the percentage of civilian casualties compared to other conflicts around the world is quantitatively quite low.[82] In Puar's view, since Israel is evil, there must be an ulterior motive behind this, so she invents an Israeli policy that she says is to maim Palestinians rather than kill them in conflict. While she can find no real evidence of any of this, she asserts that the absence of evidence makes her case all that much stronger, which the reader is supposed to recognize is because Zionists are so good at being evil that they cover all tracks.

It is sometimes hard to make sense of Puar's writing, but it is clear that if Zionists take any act, it is to oppress and deceive the rest of the world. In fact, Puar admits that it really doesn't matter if her allegations are true. In a speech at Vassar, she said she "stretches the speculative into the now."[83] She does so because it is important to get as many people involved in BDS as possible. This is not so much because she thinks BDS itself would succeed but because "we need BDS as part of the organized resistance and armed resistance in Palestine as well. There is no other way the situation is going to change."[84] From this and other of her writings, it is correct to infer that BDS is intended to provide the intellectual cover for the ultimate destruction of Israel. Despite the fact that she admits to presenting her speculating/fantasizing as fact, not only is Puar unchallenged but she has received bountiful accolades from academia. In 2018, she was awarded a National Women's Studies Association prize for her book *The Right to Maim: Debility, Capacity, Disability*. And as of 2021, she is being welcomed as a visiting professor at the University of Chicago's Pozen Family Center for Human Rights.

The situation in the social sciences and humanities across the United States is so undeviating that in the 2010s, BDS resolutions passed in the American Studies Association, the Association for Asian Studies, the

African Literature Association, the National Association of Chicana and Chicano Studies, the American Anthropological Association, the Native American and Indigenous Studies Association, and the National Women's Studies Association.[85] Radical Black intellectuals, of which Thrasher is a part, are no exception. The Black Radical Congress's endorsers are composed of prominent Black radical intellectuals, poets, and artists, as well as socialist and communist activists who personally endorse BDS.[86] In this respect, Thrasher is a conformist. In fact, he would have had a difficult time and most likely not been accepted as a graduate student in American studies at New York University (NYU) if he were a Zionist. The American Studies Department at NYU proudly advocates for boycotting the school's campus in Tel Aviv but nowhere else.

BDS contentions in its public pronouncements of nonviolence are often opaque.[87] And while some BDS resolutions have failed since Ferguson, the prominence of BDS among progressive social movements has risen. BDS backs the Hamas government in Gaza where Israel has no control (although along with Egypt, it controls Gaza's borders). Hamas's charter pledges to militarily eliminate Israel.[88] Hamas leaders unabashedly stated throughout the May 2021 conflict that their goal is to eliminate all Jews from "the river to the sea." As leaders of BDS have publicly admitted, the goal of BDS is not just related to the West Bank and Gaza but to the elimination of the state of Israel. Indeed, its major demands, which not only include ending the occupation of the West Bank and Gaza, but the right of return of all Palestinian refugees, as expansively defined (meaning ending the Jewish character of the state of Israel), effectively eliminate Israel and lead to the creation of a Palestinian Arab state with, at most, a Jewish minority.[89]

Far-right and far-left anti-Zionist Conspiracy Theorists in the academy and periphery have influenced contemporary political movements as well. Many intellectuals freely move between the academy and activism. On the right, the Institute for Historical Review has become the "scholarly" arm of a growing nexus of white supremacist anti-Zionist groups across America and Europe that has included or currently includes organizations such as Aryan Nations, National Alliance, the National Socialist Movement, and the National Socialist Vanguard, as well as the British and French National Front, among many others, some of which also operate militias.[90] In many cases, the links between the IHR and these organizations are direct. Willis Carto, one of the founders of the IHR, also founded the National Youth Alliance, one of the largest white supremacist organizations in the US. Carto was also behind the creation of the populist white supremacist party headed by David Duke. As noted above, however, the IHR has not reached more mainstream conservative movements despite its goals to influence the right more generally.

In contrast, far-left intellectuals, who often have strong political ties, activist involvement, and/or party affiliations, have managed to promote BDS within larger, more mainstream progressive organizations. The example of the Women's March stands out. In 2019 three of the Women's March co-chairs—Linda Sarsour, Tamika Mallory, and Bob Bland—resigned over accusations of anti-Semitism including support for anti-Zionist Conspiracy Theories and Theorists.[91] Angela Davis, who supports BDS and advances anti-Zionist Conspiracy Theories, appeared at events for progressive movements unconnected to the Middle East and yet manages to connect them to Palestine. Others, such as Sami Hermez, have held positions in mainstream organizations like the UN and the World Bank.

One anecdote on the power of far-left anti-Zionist conspiracies advanced by intellectuals helps to make its influence clear. At the University of California, BDS circulated a petition—influenced by Davis's Conspiracy Theories about Israeli ties to racism against African Americans and signed by hundreds of organizations and individuals—that tied US police brutality and the murder of George Floyd by a former Minneapolis police officer to Israel. The proof: in 2012, some members of the Minneapolis Police Department attended an FBI seminar in conjunction with the Israeli Consulate of Chicago that included a few Israeli law enforcement members.[92] The allegation that choke-holds or kneeling on the neck of a target was taught at that event is false. Those techniques are not used or permitted by Israeli police. By contrast, the use of these techniques was permitted by the Minneapolis police according to its own regulations from either 2002 or 2012 and was in de facto use since at least the 1990s. There is no evidence that Derek Chauvin attended the conference, and the other three officers involved were hired well after the conference.[93] Nonetheless, in the view of the UC BDS organizers, this transient unconnected meeting dangerously polluted the minds of several members of an otherwise mundane US police force and transformed them into racists, who in turn influenced others in the department to become brutal racists.[94] This is parallel to Butz's view that Zionists somehow poisoned the minds of Americans who came in contact with them at the Nuremberg trials. A former FBI official involved with these trainings stated there was "no hands-on training and no tactical training" at the seminar in question. He further said that "recent programs have included sub-jects such as improving relations between law enforcement agencies and minority communities, and recruiting in minority communities."[95] It should also be noted that the Minneapolis Police Department also conducted seminars with the UK, German, and other foreign police forces.[96] Despite this information, the Minneapolis police/Israel con-spiracy was embraced by far-left activists who tried to enshrine it as a new standard for campus government resolutions. Were this sort of Conspiracy Theory purported for any other country or ethnic group, it would be immediately dismissed by academics as nonsensical and illus-trating prejudice. As of the time of this writing, Dr. Winegar had as her profile photo on Twitter a collage of George Floyd, the Palestinian flag, and the wall at Israel's border.[97] Again, conflating these unconnected issues with potent *pathos*.

Also, unlike anti-Zionist Conspiracy Theorists on the far right, those on the far left have influenced the general media. A generation of reporters for the *New York Times* have gone to universities where prejudice against Jewish self-determination is unquestioned and unquestionable, thereby making anti-Jewish prejudice "undetectable" to graduates. The *New York Times*, which is *the* bastion of the mainstream media, has permitted blatant anti-Jewish hate books to be approvingly cited. In the *New York Times Book Review* of December 13, 2018, an interview of Alice Walker appeared in the "By the Book" column.[98] She is quoted as recommending *And the Truth Shall Set You Free* by David Icke. Mr. Icke's book, among other things, claims the Jews are behind anti-Semitic attacks, that Hitler was Jewish and an agent of Zionism, that the Holocaust didn't happen but at the same time the Jews funded the Holocaust, that *The Protocols of the Elders of Zion* is an accurate account of history, and so forth. Jews also are deemed as both fake white and hyper white at various points in his depiction of them as cunningly manipulating whites who live to oppress people of color. In a detour that reminds one of Butz's ancient Roman excursions, Icke also takes time to attack the Talmud and its evil impact on society. In his view, it is the evilest book ever written. In a December 21, 2018, interview, Walker defended and expanded on her recommendation of Icke's book.[99] Alice Walker is an important author whose work *The Color Purple* is rightly a classic. But it is unimaginable that anyone could recommend any book like *And the Truth Shall Set You Free* with similar accusations toward any other group on the planet without the *New York Times* editing out the reference or making clear note of the hateful nature of the contents of the book.

Similarly, on April 25, 2019, the *New York Times* international edition published a cartoon that could have been published by *Der Stürmer*, the Soviet-era *Pravda*, or the Iranian regime–controlled *Donya-e-Eqtesad*. After initially downplaying the incident, public outrage forced the *Times* to apologize, offer sensitivity training to certain journalists, and make a ritual sacrifice of firing two staff cartoonists who had nothing to do with the offensive cartoon. Bret Stephens in his *New York Times* column asked, "How have even the most blatant expressions of anti-Semitism become almost undetectable to editors who think it's part of their job to stand up to bigotry?...its publication was an astonishing act of ignorance of anti-Semitism at a publication that is otherwise hyper-alert to nearly every conceivable expression of prejudice, from mansplaining to racial micro-aggressions to transphobia."[100]

For those who think bad ideas have no teeth, the links between anti-Zionism, anti-Zionist Conspiracy Theories, political parties, and even states with military capacities should be an eye-opener.

WHATSOEVER THINGS ARE JUST

A POLITICAL TRADITION OF FAR-LEFT AND FAR-RIGHT ANTI-ZIONIST CONSPIRACY THEORIES

While our focus is on Conspiracy Theories within academia, the rubber meets the road when ideologies are implemented in the political system. Opposition to Zionism and the promulgation of Conspiracy Theories about Zionism have been central to far-left and far-right political organizations, parties, and governments. Many people associate the far right with racial anti-Semitism and the far left with principled opposition to Israeli policies. But the far left has made the false claim of an alliance between white supremacists and Zionists. In fact, all postwar parties or movements on either extreme have opposed Zionism. Further, the obsession over Zionism is equally central, conspiratorial, and irrational on both extremes. Below is a brief survey of each in turn.

Contrary to claims on the far left, all far-right political movements since World War II have rejected Zionism, not merely Jews. Soviet propaganda tried to equate Zionism with Nazism[1] through various lies, whether by distorting the nature of the Haavara Agreement of 1933 (in which Nazi Germany financially benefited from sixty thousand Jews desperate to flee the country to British Mandatory Palestine) or falsely claiming Zionism is a racist ideology (even though converts to Judaism can become Israeli citizens). Any look at what the Nazis and neo-Nazis said and did shows this comparison to be bogus.

As mentioned, Nazi anti-Zionism is as old as Nazism itself. Hitler not only rejected Zionism in *Mein Kampf*, he also had concrete plans to murder all the Jews in British Mandatory Palestine. Nevertheless, it is important to emphasize that anti-Zionist Conspiracy Theories became even more prominent on the far-right view during and after World War II.[2] We not only find a growing number of books decrying the Holocaust as a Zionist conspiracy, but claims about Zionist conspiracies become core worldviews to postwar Nazis and far-right parties and advocates.[3] Whether in Europe or the US, far-right (otherwise referred to as white supremacist) and neo-Nazi groups and parties were united in their Nazi view of Zionism as a conspiracy to injure the United States, Germany, Europe generally, and all real white people. Their use of Zionism was more than a synonym for Jews. They explicitly rejected Jewish national self-determination, as Hitler and the Nazis did, because it is an expression of Jewish power. The increasing use of the term "Zionism" rather than "world Jewry" or "international capital" or "the Jews" in the writings of the far right after World War II is simply a continuation of Nazi ideology. The formation of Israel was a disturbing development for the neo-Nazis and white supremacists, and their opposition to Jewish power was increasingly an opposition to Zionism.

Postwar German Nazis, the far right, and now the alt-right in America have overwhelmingly and actively opposed Zionism in their writings and actions. Nazis in postwar Germany fervently opposed Zionism. From Holocaust functionaries, to propagandists, intelligence officers, and SS generals, Nazis went to work against Zionism in countries at war with Israel, such as Egypt, Syria, and Iraq.[4] Nazis staffed Egyptian president Gamal Nasser's anti-Zionism Institute for the Study of Zionism in Cairo.[5] Nazis also worked for the Syrian army.

Post-World War II American far-right groups also actively combated Zionism. A brief survey of top American far- and alt-right leaders makes this clear. Take Francis Parker Yockey, for example, a law-yer and far-right philosopher who deeply influenced leaders such as Willis Carto, who headed a series of far-right groups, including the Liberty Lobby (1958–2001), the National Youth Alliance (1968–1974), the Institute for Historical Review (1978–present), and the Populist Party (1984–1989). Yockey was connected to all of the Nazi and fascist groups in the 1940s in America and Europe. In 1948 he wrote *Imperium: The Philosophy of History and Politics.*[6] He believed Zionist Jews controlled the US. After World War II, like many German Nazis, he sought out anti-Zionists in the Arab world. He met Nasser and wrote propaganda for the Egyptians, as he viewed Egypt as the best opponent to Zionist power.

Another anti-Zionist example is William Luther Pierce, who was the head of the National Alliance (1970–2013), the organizational heir to the American Nazi Party and the center of white supremacy in the United States. As mentioned earlier, Pierce worked first as a professor and then as an advanced researcher at the aerospace manufacturer Pratt & Whitney. During the Yom Kippur War, he tried to force the defense contractor McDonnell Douglas into canceling military contracts that sent armaments to Israel by buying shares in its stock and putting for-ward a shareholder motion at the annual meeting. He failed, but had he succeeded, he well knew that the lack of American arms would have been catastrophic. His was the first attempt to harness US public com-pany shareholder power to boycott or harm Israel. This strategy has been adopted by the far left as part of BDS.

Other far-right/white supremacist/neo-Nazi leaders have been simi-larly consistent in their opposition to Zionism. Kevin MacDonald, men-tioned above, is a long-time white supremacist, a leader of the white supremacist American Freedom Party (2009–present), and an ardent opponent of Zionism. His book *Understanding Jewish Influence: A Study in Ethnic Activism*[7] devotes a great deal of energy to the evils of Zionist power. The same is true of David Duke, perhaps the most visibly active American white supremacist, who has sought power both in white supremacist organizations like the Ku Klux Klan and in mainstream politics. His book *Jewish Supremacism: My Awakening on the Jewish Question*[8] describes the evils of Zionism and the crimes of Israel. On social media and elsewhere he has repeatedly called for freeing Palestine.

In the late 2010s, a new generation of far-right activists such as Richard Spencer tried to unite the far right by rebranding it as the alt-right. Spencer is widely viewed as coining the term because he launched altright.com and AltRight Corporation.[9] Others include Patrick Casey of the organization Identity Evropa, Bradley Griffin of the journal *Occidental Dissent*, Mike Peinovich of the blog *Right Stuff* (who has a radio show gruesomely called *The Daily Shoah*), and Andrew Anglin of the message board website Daily Stormer. Yet as with old wine in new bottles, their views are the same as those of previous generations. A survey of their writings and podcasts shows that they not only advocate white supremacy (usually in the form of an ethno-empire or state) and an end to immigration, they also oppose Zionism as hostile to white interests.[10] The fact that Jared Taylor, the leader of the New Century Foundation and editor of its journal *American Renaissance*, has been attacked for not sufficiently criticizing Zionism (which he is indifferent to, not supportive of) by others on the alt-right is telling.[11]

The way populist right-wing parties, in contrast to far-right parties, have sought a rapprochement to Israel actually underscores the ubiquity of opposition to Zionism on the far right. Many left opponents of Zionism emphasize the rapprochement between right populists (whom they deliberately do not distinguish from neo-Nazis, unlike many researchers and scholars[12]) in Europe and Israel in the last decade as evidence that Zionism is white supremacist.[13] Special mention is given to a younger generation of Western European leaders like Geert Wilders of Party for Freedom (The Netherlands) and the Alternative for Germany, Tom Van Grieken of Flemish Interest (Belgium), and Matteo Salvini of the Northern League (Italy), all parties established since the 2000s. Other supporters include authoritarian Eastern European leaders like

Viktor Orbán of Fidesz (Hungary) and even Vladimir Putin, who have been around since the 1990s.[14]

But it turns out that the analysis must be much more nuanced. These new right-wing populist parties openly support Israel as a means to signal (whether accurately or not) that they are *not* far-right parties and that they reject the white supremacy of the further right. Wilders and his Party for Freedom, for example, initially refused to work with the old National Front and Freedom Party in the 2000s, calling them fascists, agreeing to work with them only after they rebranded (both changed leadership and directions in the 2010s).[15] On the other hand, Alternative for Germany uses its pro-Israel rhetoric as a cover for minimization and dismissal of Germany's perpetration of the Holocaust.[16] While there is reason to be skeptical about the populist right's self-definition—I think right-wing populism is dangerous for many reasons, including its stance on immigration and its authoritarian bent—it is clear that the leaders of populist parties believe their support for Zionism draws a bright line between them and the far right. In fact, they believe that support for Zionism insulates them from being accused of racism, which the far right happily embraces. It is incumbent to differentiate between cases in which support of Israel and the disavowal of anti-Jewish hate is real and those cases in which it is just a façade.

A few examples about the far right and alt-right will suffice. David Duke had urged white supremacists to vote for Donald Trump because of his immigration policies, but he publicly refused to endorse him because, as he said in a *Daily Beast* interview, "Trump has made it very clear that he's 1,000 percent dedicated to Israel, so how much is left over for America?"[17] At the same time, he publicly praised Ilhan Omar for her rejection of Zionism, tweeting, "By defiance to Z.O.G. [Zionist Occupied Government] Ilhan Omar is NOW the most important Member of the US Congress!"[18] He even endorsed 2020 Democratic primary candidate for president Congresswoman Tulsi Gabbard due to her support for isolationism and criticism of Zionism.[19] To her credit, she softened both stands immediately upon hearing of Duke's endorsement. In an explicit endorsement of a far-left initiative, Duke tweeted on December 2, 2018, "May our hearts fill up with Boycott. Divest. Sanctions." The hashtag Kikebart has been used by white supremacists to reject Breitbart for its support for Zionism.[20] The alt-right has named anyone who supports Zionism and rejects white supremacy as "alt light," effectively dissociating them from the movement.[21] Richard Spencer, the head of the alt-right, is an avid opponent of Zionism and declared in 2018 that the Trump moment was over, and other white nationalists agreed, citing among other things a "kike infestation."[22] Arthur Butz's rejection of Zionism and specifically his adoption of anti-Zionist Conspiracy Theories makes his views utterly conformist with the far right and neo-Nazis.

While the terms "far left" and "far right" are not often used to characterize dictatorships in the Middle East, Islamist movements also promote state-sponsored anti-Zionist Conspiracy Theories—most notably the Islamic Republic of Iran, where Ayatollah Khomeini's writings on the evils of Zionism are well known.[23] Iran has in fact been a center of the merging far-left and far-right anti-Zionist Conspiracy Theorists at their Holocaust conferences, which have been attended by the likes of David Duke in 2006—who also made an appearance on Syrian television a year earlier.[24] Until recently, Saudi Arabia, another arguably far-right dictatorship, now in a period of purported reform, was a state sponsor of anti-Zionist Conspiracy Theories.[25] Indeed, the ubiquity of these Conspiracy Theories can be seen by the measures that the Saudis have recently taken, such as the removal of anti-Zionist material from schoolbooks under the new reform measures. Changes include, for example, the removal of a history book chapter titled "The Zionist Danger."[26] But even with these improvements, the situation is still ambivalent to put it generously, as Israel is not depicted on maps in Saudi Arabia, Zionism is still described as racist, and the name "Zionist enemy" is usually given for Israel.[27]

Though our focus has been on the present far right, it is nonetheless worth noting that the authoritarian right in Europe and the

Americas has also consistently rejected ties with Israel since World War II. The three European right-wing authoritarian regimes of the post-war period—Franco's Spain, Salazar's Portugal, and Greece's postwar government and military junta—did not recognize Israel and had no diplomatic relations with it.[28] They did, however, have full diplomatic relations with Israel's enemies, such as Syria, Lebanon, and Iraq. Greece and Cuba, two authoritarian right-wing countries in 1948, had both voted against the partition of Palestine and the creation of a Jewish state (neither Portugal nor Spain were members of the UN at the time).

The picture is similar with authoritarian-right regimes in South America. Voting on the UN's 1975 "Zionism Is Racism" resolution (UNR 3379) fit the pattern as authoritarian-right-led countries such as Brazil and Portugal voted in favor, while other authoritarian-right military dictatorships such as Bolivia, Paraguay, Argentina, Chile, and Guatemala abstained.[29] The latter group (with the exception of Guatemala, which was not a Nazi refuge) also refused to extradite Nazi war criminals. Other authoritarian-right regimes such as prerevo-lutionary Iran and Turkey also voted in favor of UNR 3379, reflecting their Islamic perspective. The bottom line is that no ideologically right authoritarian government supported Israel in the UN in connection with the "Zionism Is Racism" resolution of 1975. Other postwar pop-ulist right-wing parties like Jean-Marie Le Pen's National Front and Jörg Haider's Freedom Party of Austria opposed Zionism well into the 2000s.[30]

Far-left parties globally have all opposed Zionism in the postwar period. While the Soviets promoted racial equality and national libera-tion movements across Asia and Africa, they had opposed Zionism as a form of bourgeois nationalism since the first Russian Revolution and the establishment of the Communist International (later Cominform).[31] Stalin's stunning momentary decision to vote in favor of the creation of Israel was either divinely ordained or tactical as suggested above. Swiftly, the USSR became the primary arms dealer and benefactor of Egypt, Syria, and Iraq, Israel's most powerful enemies, in the 1950s

and '60s.[32] All countries within the Soviet orbit and all communist parties supported by the USSR, including the American Communist Party,
openly and vigorously opposed Zionism and espoused anti-Zionist
Conspiracy Theories.

Far-left parties and political movements have also continued to
oppose Zionism since the fall of the Soviet Union.[33] Since 1990, the
American Communist Party may have reformed and rejected one-party
rule of the proletariat and violent revolution in favor of basic democratic rights, making it no longer officially nondemocratic. But it still
very much opposes Zionism.[34] In addition, the democratic socialist bloc
in American and Western European politics is increasingly opposed to
Zionism itself, not just to Israel's policies in the West Bank, based on
their support for BDS. This is true of Democratic Socialists of America,
which has endorsed BDS.[35] It is also true of the Green Party in the
United Kingdom and Canada and the African National Congress in
the Republic of South Africa. In fact, the Socialist International organization, which includes 140 global political parties and 35 parties in
government at the time of the vote in 2018, endorsed BDS.[36] It also
called for a military embargo on Israel.

It is important to note that while the postwar anticolonial movements on the left rejected Israel, Israel had initially reached out to them.
Had Israel been an actual opponent of these postcolonial countries,
then the communist rejection of Zionism would have at least been
rational. In fact, the opposite is true. An outlook favoring the national
liberation of all peoples was foundational to Zionism's own self-understanding as a movement for national liberation. Theodor Herzl viewed
national self-determination for African people as one of the goals of
Zionism, as he wrote in *The Jewish State*:

> There is still one other question arising out of the disas-
> ter of nations which remains unsolved to this day, and
> whose profound tragedy, only a Jew can comprehend.
> This is the African question. Just call to mind all those

terrible episodes of the slave trade, of human beings who, merely because they were black, were stolen like cattle, taken prisoner, captured and sold. Their children grew up in strange lands, the objects of contempt and hostility because their complexions were different. I am not ashamed to say, though I may expose myself to ridicule for saying so, that once I have witnessed the redemption of the Jews, my people, I wish also to assist in the redemption of the Africans.[37]

In the 1950s, Golda Meir made a rapprochement with African states the center of her foreign policy. As she described:

Independence had come to us, as it was coming to Africa, not served up on a silver platter, but after years of struggle. Like them, we had shaken off foreign rule; like them, we had to learn for ourselves how to reclaim the land, how to increase the yields of our crops, how to irrigate, how to raise poultry, how to live together and how to defend ourselves...We couldn't offer Africa money or arms, but on the other hand, we were free of the taint of the colonial exploiters because all that we wanted from Africa was friendship. Let me at once anticipate the cynics. Did we go into Africa because we wanted votes at the United Nations? Yes, of course... But it was far from being the most important motive.[38]

Israel's first prime minister, David Ben-Gurion, also favored reaching out to Asian and African nations. Ben-Gurion even remarked in 1959 that China and India would one day replace the Americans and Soviets as the greatest powers in the world.[39]

While many leaders initially responded warmly to Ben-Gurion's and Meir's no-strings outreach policy, as happened with Kwame Nkrumah, the prime minister of Ghana, diplomatic ties and technological cooperation did not lead to the long-standing alliances the Israelis had hoped for with Asian and African countries.[40] Most African countries formerly broke diplomatic relations with Israel in 1973, hoping in part that support for the Arab League would lead to donated oil and investments, a promise that was not fulfilled. Prior to 1973, Israel attempted to prioritize African liberation above its relationship with South Africa, even offering to donate to the Organisation of African Unity's liberation fund. However, after 1973, when Israel's international isolation was most acute, it strengthened its ties with its few allies, including, unfortunately, South Africa, while continuing to denounce apartheid. This cemented the break with other African countries. African relations with Israel remained strained until recent years, when they have become much less cold and, in some cases, warm. One signal of the shift occurred in 1997, when South African president Nelson Mandela accepted an honorary doctorate degree from Ben-Gurion University of Israel. The same timeline holds more or less with Asia, which followed the Arab League due to trade and strategic considerations. There is simply no history of Israeli opposition to people of color.

Likewise, Zionists in the United States openly supported the civil rights movement. Many American Jews, like my parents who tended to be very liberal, donated, worked, volunteered, and sometimes demonstrated for various aspects of the civil rights movement. Most of these liberals were Zionists, as were top religious figures like Abraham Heschel. In other words, there is no history of Zionist Jews opposing civil rights in the US. In fact, no Jewish organization opposed the civil rights movement. The rejection of Zionism among many African American intellectuals cannot therefore be ascribed to a rational opposition to a hostile political movement. Rather, its roots are in the far left.

The communist and Arab origins of anti-Zionist conspiracies among many African American and African intellectuals to which Thrasher is heir can be clearly traced. The Communist Party, which included many Jews, was also a major source of African American intellectual and political leadership in the civil rights era.[41] The party attracted and recruited many African American youth and students, who would go on to become preeminent political leaders and intellectuals, like Angela Davis (who was recruited to Advance, a Marxist-Leninist youth group associated with the Communist Party, while in high school in New York City). In addition, many prominent Black intellectuals and writers who associated with or joined the party included Langston Hughes, Richard Wright, Ralph Ellison, and Chester Himes, and activists such as Benjamin Davis Jr., a New York city councilman. In the 1960s, many of these Black communist intellectuals were joined by the New Left and Black Nationalists, both of which opposed Zionism, due to their closeness to third world national liberation movements and the mostly Soviet sponsorship.[42] Thus, by the 1960s the radical or far-left stream of the civil rights movement firmly opposed Zionism and in some cases, as with the Black Panthers, even expounded the anti-Zionist Conspiracy Theories of the Soviets and the PLO; as the Black Panther Party Minister of Defense exclaimed, "The Jewish people have a right to exist so long as they solely exist to down the reactionary expansionist Israeli government."[43] In contrast, the Black churches, Black political figures in both major political parties at the city, state, and federal levels, and the Black Congressional Caucus continue to be largely supportive of Israel, if at times critical of its policies.[44] In the words of Martin Luther King Jr., "When people criticize Zionists, they mean Jews. You're talking anti-Semitism."[45]

The consistent focus of the far left and far right on anti-Zionist Conspiracy Theories underscores their irrationality politically. Indeed, one of the distinguishing features between a genuine conspiracy and a Conspiracy Theory is the likelihood of a given actor to have the sinister intentions and the wherewithal to put them into practice. In the case of anti-Zionist Conspiracy Theories, there is a large disconnect between the actual power and influence of the Israeli government or Zionist Jews and the claims made against them. Even today, Israel may have a very strong and well-trained army, but it is certainly not a superpower like China or the US and could hardly, as a nation of barely more inhabitants than New York City, take on the hundreds of millions of Europeans or billions of people of color as Thrasher would have it. But what is even more striking is that the anti-Zionist Conspiracy Theories on the left and right existed in the 1950s when the state of Israel could barely feed its citizens and almost went bankrupt, and when its fledgling army could not defend against sniper attacks from the Jordanian side of Jerusalem.

This point merits repeating since most people do not understand how quickly pre–World War II Jewish Conspiracy Theories became anti-Zionist Conspiracy Theories on the far right after 1945. Nor do they understand how the far-left anti-Zionists became obsessively opposed to Israel when Israel was fully socialist and welcomed collaboration with the Marxist nonaligned world. Butz and Thrasher's views are part of a longer tradition. In countries where the far left or far right governed, intellectuals were co-opted to take the party line on all manner of subjects, including Zionism. In democratic countries like the United States, as we have seen, far-right and far-left intellectuals and political movements have tried to influence the academy, students, and the broader public, though in different ways. As previously discussed, while the far left faced government persecution during the McCarthy era in the US, its intellectuals have by and large found refuge in the academy. In contrast, the far right has faced social, though not state, sanctions, and its intellectuals have remained outsiders in the academy. It is telling that Thrasher openly celebrates his left-wing political affiliations, while Butz masks his neo-Nazi links under more opaque language. In either case, the question remains what to do with the fact that respected and even outstanding intellectuals are also Conspiracy Theorists.

PART IV

IF THERE BE ANY PRAISE 1

WHY THE GOLDEN RULE IS FUNDAMENTAL TO SCHOLARSHIP AND SOCIETY

In my view, the best way to counter the popularity of anti-Zionist conspiracies in the university is to reemphasize the fundamental mission of universities by emphasizing mottos like Northwestern's and more precisely its echoing of the Golden Rule. In short, the ideas expressed in Northwestern's motto are able to provide a framework to dispute the Conspiracy Theorists' claims to truth and inoculate people from this errant type of thinking because of their intellectual and moral axioms and their universality.

Intellectually, the motto claims that there is one truth. Every individual can have valid feelings, but when it comes to factual events, only one thing actually happened, and that is what must be reported for it to be a "good report." This does not mean that we always have enough evidence to be confident about what is true but rather that we have a shared lived world that we can understand in common terms. We come from different cultures, but we must all agree that mercury is poisonous.

Morally, the motto communicates the principle that there is one humanity. The use of the term "brethren" is derived from the idea that all humans are brothers and sisters. It also expresses the view that justice is both necessary and must be applied to everyone equally. Something is just because it is a principle that applies to all humans in relation to the same action. Stealing is an action we can define irrespective of the status or ethnic background of one group or another. The motto thus echoes the Golden Rule by affirming that people ought to examine views, thoughts, and acts along the same principles as they would want their own views examined.

Academics might dismiss the motto as a Christian Scriptures, old-fashioned, Eurocentric view of reality. Rather, its content is appropriate to all the global religious and humanist ethical traditions that also accept the Golden Rule. These include the major Abrahamic faiths of Judaism, Christianity, and Islam; the Indian and Chinese religions and philosophies like Hinduism, Buddhism, Jainism, Confucianism, and Taoism; and many Native American and African spiritual traditions. It is also incorporated in the UN Declaration of Human Rights.[1] Expressed in its negative form, the Golden Rule reads as follows: "Do not do unto others as you would not have them do unto you." In its positive form, it is, "Do unto others as you would have done unto you." As mentioned in the introduction, like the Jewish sage Hillel, I prefer the negative form of the Golden Rule, as it is the most modest and most universal. I can't think of any flaw or case in which I would not accept this version. But whichever form you choose, the Golden Rule leads to a recognizable standard of universal justice, since what applies to any human applies so universally. It also mandates an accepted understanding of truth. It is a scholarly and ethical standard that the university and its students and faculty should embrace.

Keeping Northwestern's motto and the Golden Rule in mind gives us the conceptual tools to properly evaluate a situation or event. Let's take the case of the theory that X conspired to murder Y. If one follows the intellectual principles, then one requires facts and evidence to establish a conspiracy. To establish that X is a murderer, there needs to be physical evidence or reliable witnesses to the crime as well as a probable motive. Further, the facts and evidence must be evaluated by people who are capable of evaluating it. We rely on accredited forensic scientists to interpret evidence for us. If there is a question that the forensic scientists have been paid off, that they are prejudiced against the accused, or that evidence has been tampered with (all of which are possible), then this too would require evidence and a motive. Perhaps the police falsified the forensic reports, also possible, but that would need to be proven. Or alternatively, the murder might have happened in a country where such things do not need to be established (e.g., a dictatorship that can freely frame people or convict them without evidence), and here too we would need prior examples of this or evidence. If all of the evidence has been meticulously cleansed, then we could be left with the hypothesis that X murdered Y without being able to prove it.

Can someone or a group in a nontotalitarian country successfully frame another person and get away with it? Yes, it is possible, though rare because of all the planning it entails and likelihood that something could go wrong. We would still be left with X's claim to have been framed. Someone operating by the motto and the Golden Rule would have to evaluate the evidence of all these scenarios. Further, the Golden Rule requires us to examine X's actions fairly. Let's say X is particularly despicable, or even has a prior record of assault; we still cannot apply a lower standard of evidence to X. Alternatively, assume X is a pillar of the community or a celebrity; we still cannot dismiss the evidence or decide that there should be a higher standard of evidence required to convict. That would diminish the justice that Y and all the rest of us deserve. The Golden Rule and the motto require individuals or groups to be treated equally as human beings and also for the accusation to be investigated thoroughly.

The axioms of the motto and the Golden Rule provide the intellectual and moral criteria to distinguish between real conspiracies, possible conspiracies, and Conspiracy Theories. Conspiracy Theories are characterized by insufficient or ambiguous evidence at best and at worst fabricated evidence, distorted evidence, or even no evidence at all. So, for example, *The Protocols of the Elders of Zion* conspiracy is based on a forged document of a fictitious meeting—that of the fictional Elders of Zion.[2] A good chunk of the book is plagiarized from a novel by Maurice Joly parodying Napoleon III. If it weren't so sad that so many people accept *Protocols* as real, it would be funny that a novel can be repackaged so effectively. The Conspiracy Theory of QAnon offers no evidence that there is a cabal of pedophiles run by Barack Obama, Hillary Clinton, and George Soros planning a coup. Rather, like all Conspiracy Theories, it is based on the claim that the cabal has covered their tracks. Neither QAnon or *The Protocols of the Elders of Zion* can be substantiated by a person who follows the Golden Rule or the motto.

Likewise, the McCarthyistic Conspiracy Theory that communists infiltrated all parts of American society and that many people who had left-wing views were actually communist/Soviet agents would have shriveled under the standards of the motto.[3] While some Americans did belong to the Communist Party (which was indeed funded by the USSR) and wanted America to become communist, and McCarthy's allegations against Alger Hiss were possibly correct, that was insufficient evidence. But more to the point, McCarthy, as a powerful senator, made claims that went far beyond any evidence to imagine a conspiracy of greater breadth, coordination, and far more participants than was true or could have been true.

In contrast, genuine conspiracies can usually be proven through direct evidence. For example, we know that Théoneste Bagosora ordered the mass killing of Tutsis through eyewitness accounts of speeches and telephone calls.[4] He was also an advocate of Hutu Power ideology, for which there is plenty of evidence. Similarly, we know that the CIA covertly tested LSD on people in the 1950s and 1960s; though many documents relating to this operation were destroyed, others were kept and declassified in 1977 and later in 2001, proving the claims along with the evidence of survivors.[5] Or for example, we know that the tobacco industry had evidence that linked lung cancer and smoking as early as the 1950s but buried it.[6] The key distinction between the two is the attitude toward evidence. Those who follow the Golden Rule and the motto simply cannot jump to the conclusions that Conspiracy Theorists do.

The moral axioms of the motto and the Golden Rule also require people to judge others fairly. In practice this means treating people according to evidence and without prejudice based on ethnicity or gender, group identity, or any other identifier that treats an individual as a statistic rather than a human being. This means that when there is evidence, one can, without contradicting the Golden Rule, judge people or even whole groups or societies as acting immorally. And sadly, using the Golden Rule prism, we find many, if not most societies in human history have fallen woefully short. Examples abound. This is certainly the case of the proponents of the Hutu Power ideology as mentioned above. This ideology claimed that Tutsis are dishonest by nature and seek only their own power and glory. This claim therefore justified Hutu supremacy in the eyes of Hutu Power proponents. This ideology relied on a view of Tutsis as entirely bad, without providing evidence that Tutsis were consistently dishonest or that all their actions could be reduced to seeking their own power and glory. Rather, the ideology had a characteristic common to all racist frameworks in that it attributed precise characteristics and actions to a group merely by virtue of their belonging to that group, something that is contrary to the Golden Rule. In contrast, we can argue based on the Golden Rule that the advocates of Hutu Power did in fact act wrongly because they coordinated a genocide of the Tutsis. These acts were murderous and evil.

Another clear example is the Italian Mafia. Using the principles of the Golden Rule, we can establish that the Mafia is a criminal organization, for it engages in racketeering, intimidation, murder, and corruption. We can certainly trace specific crimes to the Mafia itself. To argue the Italian Mafia, or any other Mafia, is simply a cultural organization does not square with the evidence we have about its activities and ideology.

The motto and the Golden Rule can likewise offer a framework for distinguishing between just moral criticism and unjust moral criticism. The glum reality is that many people claim that their political opponents are immoral. One extreme historical example is how Hitler described the need to wipe out the Jewish people as defensive.[7] He said that the Jews were the predators victimizing Germans. Given that today all sides use moral justifications to justify their opinions, the path to clarity is the Golden Rule. One has to take a step back and look at the claims of both sides (without assuming anything about either group) and then examine the evidence for the claims. Is there any truth to the Nazi claim that they were the victims of a capitalist/communist Jewish plot to destroy Germany? That Jews were acting offensively? The answer is no, for a number of reasons.[8] One, there was no evidence of a coordinated Jewish plot of any kind—the Jewish community was politically and religiously diverse. Two, the Jews were unarmed and small in number compared to the Germans, who had other much more powerful enemies such as the French, who did put in place the Versailles Treaty measures to curb German power. This is just one example of how the Golden Rule and the Northwestern motto enable one to look into the claims of all groups. I encourage readers to try this with a political argument they oppose. Indeed, very few people come out and say that they or their own group is factually or morally wrong. Racists in the US South argued they were on high moral ground. But moral justifications that don't follow the Golden Rule are not moral.

Applying the Golden Rule is thus a framework for critical thinking that places facts and individual morality, not ideology, at its center. While critical thinking is a ubiquitous term in the university, few people think of it in terms of the Golden Rule. Rather, today the notion of critical thinking has been debased. Sadly, critiques of a situation, process, or event today typically depend entirely on one's preferred intellectual, political, and moral criteria. In many disciplines, we can find examples of Marxist critiques of capitalism or nationalism as well as many other topics. The same is true of liberal and conservative approaches to the same topics. The problem of such critiques is that they are often based on theories that are themselves open to criticism. In some cases, these theories are even the first stepping-stones to more nefarious and even deadly Conspiracy Theories. As Quassim Cassam indicated, most Conspiracy Theories are tied to a broader political agenda and therefore ideological worldview.[9] These worldviews can and should be subject to critical appraisals by honest intellectuals.

WHATSOEVER THINGS ARE
OF GOOD REPORT 3

HOW A REASONABLE THEORY CAN BE ABUSED AND HOW A BAD THEORY CAN BE EXALTED

The motto and the Golden Rule are good rules of thumb for recognizing when theories go off the deep end. According to the *Merriam-Webster's Collegiate Dictionary*, a theory, whether in the sciences or the social sciences, is "a plausible or scientifically acceptable general principle or body of principles offered to explain phenomena." In all academic disciplines, theories are only as good as their explanatory power. If evidence contradicts them, then it is back to the drawing board, so to speak. Long-accepted Newtonian physics was put into question by Einstein's theory of relativity. No problem.

The social sciences and humanities are replete with theories. No theory should be sacrosanct. There are, for example, theories of language. Some view language as predating logic and others see logic as subsidiary to language. Historians and philosophers have theories about the main engines of history. Marxism (which today is better known as an ideology) is in fact a theory about history that claims that history can best be understood by evaluating conflicts between classes.[1] Historians have been using the Marxist theory of history to try to explain specific events such as the French Revolution to see if Marxism has some additional explanatory insights on them. Theory thus informs the questions historians ask, but good historians will not select or suppress evidence for the sake of a theory.

Both Butz and Thrasher are involved in theories and facts in their academic work. Butz teaches control systems theory in his class, and as mentioned, he invented an algorithm relating to Hilbert's space-filling curve. Butz's specialty is electrical engineering, and therefore his work deals with the reality of how electrical systems work. Thrasher is a journalist and therefore his work is focused on discussing the reality of events and processes, particularly in his areas of expertise, namely race in America, LGBTQ issues, and public health and the intersection of all three. Thrasher is transparent about the theories that influence his journalism, first and foremost decolonial theory. As he tweeted in 2019, "I find it hard to trust any professor or academic, in ANY field, who has never taken a graduate class in ethnic or women's or queer or Black or Native or Asian American studies. There's no excuse. Someone who's not used one course like this by force or elective isn't trustworthy." That same year he wrote, "There are two ways to try to avoid the fatigue of what I call 'native informant syndrome' @Jamiles 1. Therapy (w an anti-racist trained therapist) 2. Demanding my colleagues & the field adopt an anti-racist, decolonial approach. (Usually fails.)" A year before he tweeted, "We desperately need a society in which people Borderlands, Ethnic Studies, Decolonial Studies, Chicano Studies, African/American Studies, and great articles like this @BostonReview piece by @matthewblongo." For Thrasher, decolonial theory is the only legitimate way to understand the world. Given the centrality of decolonial theory in his work as a journalist and the place of anti-Zionist Conspiracy Theories not only in his view of current affairs but in those of so many in the humanities and social sciences, it is vital to understand decolonial theory's relationship to Northwestern's motto and the Golden Rule.

At first blush, decolonial theory seems to align with the motto and the Golden Rule. Decolonial theory is closely related to postcolonial theory, and both challenge the notion of Western/European/white supremacy and reject European imperialism.[2] They also repudiate the ways in which Western frameworks of understanding and examining the world are purported to be universal. Therefore, the defining aspects of decolonial theory do not at first glance contradict the Golden Rule or the motto. As stated numerous times, the Golden Rule rejects the innate supremacy or superiority of any given group. Groups can be judged on their moral actions, but these can change over time and should be evaluated as such. Other features of society such as technological advances and expertise are certainly worthy of examination, but they don't according to the Golden Rule justify any form of rule over other peoples. By any measure, imperialism and colonialism are contrary to the Golden Rule.

To put it in individual terms, if you are a child who "invents" a way to lock a door that does not have a lock (e.g., you tie it shut), you still don't have a right to lock your younger sibling inside. To use another individual analogy, if I own a house, by what right should I take over my neighbor's house as well? Or do I have the right to tax my neighbor for them to have the privilege of staying in their own home, or to kill them or enslave them or exile them as empires did, or to require them to speak my language and follow my customs and adopt my religion and pay tax to me as still others did, or to seize their house and leave them a decrepit shack in the neglected part of the backyard, as still other empires have done, all the while claiming the indigenous people deserved it, or that they were somehow inferior, or that I was actually helping them?

The other objective of decolonial theory, namely that our knowledge about the world should not mistake Western culture for universalism, is something else that aligns with the motto and the Golden Rule.[3] Certainly, the Golden Rule is an ethical system that is common to cultures around the world, and the notions of evidence or observations about the world are also features of many societies. Decolonial theory has rightly pointed to the fact that much of our knowledge of colonized societies (especially oral societies) is based on the accounts of European colonizers, whether missionaries or anthropologists. Thus, our data about these cultures and the reason for the studies in the first place must be comprehended in the context of the interests and worldviews of the colonizers, who did not in most cases apply the moral or intellectual axioms of the Golden Rule. Since scholars have questioned European supremacy, we have come to a clearer understanding not just of historical processes but even of the knowledge of colonized peoples—previously dismissed as primitive or irrational but actually cultures abounding with valuable insights and contributions about the world in which they lived, whether in medicine, engineering, philosophy, the realm of arts, or other facets of human experience.

Decolonial theory would therefore seem to be a positive framework within which to study Jewish and Israeli history on its own terms. Given its critique of Western hegemony, it seems natural that decolonial theory should be an important framework for understanding Jewish history. Indeed, Jews have lived in both Muslim and Christian lands, the latter in large part in Europe. A lot—though not all—of what we know about Jewish communities from the Roman period to the nineteenth century was written by Christian Europeans and not by the Jewish communities themselves. Who would argue that *The Merchant of Venice* was an accurate depiction of what Venetian Jewry thought of itself? A decolonial approach would take into consideration European attitudes toward Jews in evaluating the evidence.[4]

Jewish texts could certainly use some decolonizing too. A lot of academic writing about the Bible, particularly the Five Books of Moses, is written from the perspective of Christianity, which for many centuries viewed itself as the replacement for Judaism. As the late Rabbi Jonathan Sacks pointed out, even among atheists in academia there is a difference between "Christian atheists" and other atheists.[5] Therefore, a decolonial perspective of Jewish texts, like that of the texts of other cultures, requires understanding the prejudices or outlook of the writers or sources about Jews, whether Roman or modern European. Yet those who preach decolonial theory have been among the greatest critics of Israel. How did that happen?

Decolonial theory derailed when it departed from the motto and Golden Rule because of intentional selective application. In theory, decolonial theory should be universally applied to all imperial or supremacist groups. Thus, we should take a critical perspective of Chinese sources about Tibet or Arab sources about Kurds. Unfortunately, when we go beyond the proverbial first blush, we can see that decolonial studies as overwhelmingly applied today in the American academy has become problematic due to its myopic focus on modern European colonialism and its erroneous use of solely European colonial categories to understand the world. Though there are some exceptions to this rule, they have not fundamentally changed the general trend.[6]

This focus is not entirely surprising given the hegemony of European powers in the last several hundred years and their devastation of precolonial societies, especially in the Americas. But that adoption has meant forgetting the rest of the history of the world. It has meant either ignoring, downplaying, distorting, and even in many cases justifying or exulting other colonial and imperial legacies, whether they be Chinese, Turkish, Russian, Iranian, and Arab—all of which have premodern imperial/colonial histories as well as modern ones.[7] This is unjustifiable from a scholarly perspective. These large-scale exclusions of non-European empires make Jewish history incomprehensible since Iranians, Turks, Arabs, and other ancient empires all ruled over large portions of Jews. Even more incomprehensible is that these empires are not only spared the imperial critique of decolonial theory, but thousands of years of their imperial histories and abuses are distorted and waved away.[8]

The absurdity of these apologies is clear. I will give just two examples: the Iranian Safavid Empire sent the majority of Armenians into exile, resulting in the deaths of tens of thousands, and the Ottoman Empire began mass slaughter of Armenians, Georgians, and Assyrians even before the Armenian genocide.[9] In ignoring or soft-peddling these imperial legacies, scholars are vindicating the legacy propaganda of these imperial powers. Indeed, twentieth-century Turkish, Iranian, and Arab imperialists (not to mention Chinese) have used their defeat at the hands of Europeans and Americans to recast themselves as anti-imperial,[10] while in fact they have oppressed indigenous peoples in classic imperialist fashion within their borders, including the Uyghurs and Tibetans (China); Kurds, Bahá'í, Jews (Iran); Kurds, Maronites, Assyrians, Amazigh, Copts, and Jews (Arab League countries)[11]—the list goes on and on.

Further, with its insistence on racial categories used in European contexts such as white, Brown, and Black, which are deliberately weaponized or irrelevant in other imperial contexts, decolonial theory distorts history. Applying the category of Brown to Iranians from a European or American colonial framework (and the subordinate status this entails) is misleading given Iranians' own self-understanding as a superior civilization with its own past and present of self-justified oppression of non-Iranians. To mention the Chinese regime for a moment, it employs the largest mass incarceration program of any country in the world; is systemically suppressing, degrading, and delegitimizing several ancient cultures; and is liberally using population transfers to extinguish Muslim separatists, among which are the Uyghurs.[12] Its efforts to exploit natural resources from Africa rival those of Europe.[13] This doesn't even begin to catalog China's attempts to assimilate large parts of the world via economic and technological domination. Also very seriously, China has attempted to exploit many countries through its Belt and Road Initiative, its ownership of critical ports and other infrastructure in developing countries, and its technological dominance via 5G gear, chip production, and the like. Yet the critique of the United States or Europe from decolonial theorists and academia writ large drowned out most criticism of China for decades to a disproportionate degree because China does not fit the Eurocentric model of colonialism.

Decolonial theory has also departed from the motto and Golden Rule in its distortion of evidence, as we see in its approach to Zionism.

One reason decolonial theory has largely succeeded in presenting the Zionist movement as a European settler colonial movement is that proponents can correctly state that certain aspects of the Zionist movement were influenced by European nationalist movements. For example, the central European nationalist idea that all peoples (at least European ones) have an innate character finds echoes in Zionist teachings. Likewise, the simultaneously European nationalist and/or imperialist notion (depending on where applied) that some peoples have an innate charge to pioneer and redeem land is also present. Thus, elements of the secular Zionist movement's discourse and approach certainly have echoes of European nationalism and imperialism.

Yet in this respect Zionism is hardly alone. Most of the non-European national movements of the modern period have been influenced by European nationalism in some way as well.[14] But that is not clarifying either, as the idea of a people wishing to govern themselves (in whatever form) is neither a modern nor European idea. Focusing on particular commonalities to the exclusion of all the many other features of Zionism creates a totally distorted understanding of Jewish self-determination.

Indeed, a cold look at the facts shows that Israel has none of the features of a European empire.[15] The Jews had no home state or metropole from which to colonize (a feature of all European colonial projects); rather, they had been a stateless Diaspora across Europe, the Middle East, and indeed much of the world. They had an ancient history in the region, including a state, so they viewed themselves as a national liberation movement, reviving a national language rather than imposing an imperial language on native peoples. The list of differences is very long and the list of similarities very short. The fact that some Zionist Jews lived in Russia does not make Zionism a European project, and it was never part of an imperial colonial one. Certainly, the Russian czars did not see it that way. The British conquest of Palestine was a British imperial project and was coupled with British support for Arab leaders who battled a British rival, namely the Ottomans. Zionist attempts at gaining the favor of the British for a Jewish homeland can hardly be compared to the British Empire's own colonization of Canada or Australia. Nor can Zionism be reduced to European nationalism, since the desire to return to sovereignty in Israel has been part of the prayer service for Jews since late antiquity.

Despite these obvious facts, decolonial studies obsesses over the unfounded narrative that Israel is a European settler colonial movement.[16] This characterization is not an accident. It was one of the great PR victories of Yasser Arafat in particular that he deliberately branded Zionism as European imperialism and settler colonialism bonded together in one evil coupling. Arafat's own reshaping of Palestinian politics is complicated, but from the founding of Fatah by the Arab League at the height of pan-Arabism to his ascension as the leader of the PLO in 1969, at the height of Soviet anti-Zionist propaganda, he was central in shaping the narrative about Israel as a settler colonial enterprise against indigenous Arabs.[17] The activism of decolonial professors for BDS and a unitary Arab Palestine is no coincidence, as anti-Zionism is woven into the popularization of academic decolonial theory.

Another way that colonial theory departs from the motto and the Golden Rule is in its inconsistent application of values and definitions. Decolonial theory's ambivalent attitude to nationalism and cultural continuity demonstrates this problem. On the one hand, it reaffirms the cultural continuity and national identity of colonized peoples and therefore the value of their self-determination; on the other, it coexists with postmodern theories that promote the invented nationalities and ever-changing nature of European peoples. Thus, European cultures and nations have been viewed through the lenses of "invented traditions" and "imagined communities" based on two classic books by Eric Hobsbawm, *The Invention of Tradition*, and Benedict Anderson, *Imagine Communities*,[18] as well as books such as *The Invention of the West: Joseph Conrad and the Double-Mapping of Europe and Empire* by Christopher GoGwilt and *The American West: The Invention of a Myth* by David Hamilton Murdoch.[19] In fact, a random search on

WorldCat (a comprehensive library index) with the word "invention" and any number of European countries or cultures will bring up scores of articles and monographs. In contrast, one is hard pressed to find the invention of Iroquois culture, or Mayan civilization, or the Maori people. Rather, these cultures are rightly examined as living cultures with historical precedents.

In the case of Israel, since an increasing majority of scholars view Jewish and more specifically Israeli history as European, Jewish history has been deconstructed with particular vehemence. Not only has Zionism been written off as an entirely invented European contrivance but the Jewish people have as well. Like it or not, Zionism has been around for three thousand years and has not been recently invented. An entire school of history on Jewish antiquity called biblical minimalism is based on the idea that the Jews hardly existed as a people until the Greek period (although troublingly for its proponents, this period begins around 338 BCE, which still puts Jews in Israel about a thousand years before Arabs). Thereafter, Jewish history is primarily defined by its surrounding cultures. Prior to the Greek period, the history of the area is largely defined by other peoples. See such works as Niels Peter Lemche's *The Canaanites and Their Land: The Tradition of the Canaanites*, Keith Whitelam's *The Invention of Ancient Israel: The Silencing of Palestinian History*, and Thomas L. Thompson's *The Mythic Past: Biblical Archaeology and the Myth of Israel*, which have become academic bestsellers and have largely monopolized the discourse.[20]

Not that Jews are alone. In general, decolonial theory has focused exclusively on modern European colonialism in the Middle East, ignoring preexisting empires. Even other non-Arab groups in the Middle East have been recast as European inventions and treated as puppets, as though they did not have their own history and politics. Thus, in a recent book on Assyrian history by Adam Becker,[21] Assyrian nationalism is turned into an American invention, as though the Assyrians, who have been incredibly well documented since antiquity, had no national history. Becker is also an adamant supporter of BDS. An entire generation of students has been taught false theory rather than actual history. Just like such outstanding scholars as Hugo Grotius and regular students just like me, I assume that these students take the word of their teachers as truth. Johannes Hinderbach was profoundly astute in his mendacity.

Decolonial studies should fall under a far larger rubric of the study of empire and imperialism regardless of the race, creed, or religion of the imperialists. That would be consistent with the motto. The stringent focus of decolonial studies on Europe and its use of racial categories derived primarily from European colonization has transformed it into a false theory rather than what it was supposed to be, which is a field of critical inquiry. It is all the more problematic that decolonialism is not entirely false or without merit; rather its selective and distorted application has transformed it into an overarching academic principle. It is akin to trying to understand geometry by recognizing one corollary as a law, but without any knowledge of the seven postulates or an inkling that these postulates exist.

Unfortunately, most of these distortions are hidden behind word bombs. Word bombs are phrases or terms that are packed with faddish jargon. They create a screen that obscures the theory's departure from solid facts. These word bombs work because they signal to others that one is in the know. They become a kind of code among an elite to signify smartness even when they are camouflage for lies.

To add to the distortions created by decolonial theory for Jewish and Israeli history, one final point must be addressed: the deconstruction of Jewish texts. One of the theoretically positive features of decolonial thinking has been to overthrow the monopoly of European philosophy and religion as universal truth and to include in university classes other philosophical and ethical traditions, including those from oral societies. Diverse philosophical and religious traditions are given due respect, at least in theory, within the post/decolonial discourse in the humanities[22]—that is, *except* for Judaism. Decolonial studies have sought to deconstruct Jewish texts for their supposed canonical or Western origin. Courses on the Bible focus predominantly on Biblical criticism, which does not seek to interpret and consider the content of the biblical text—namely its philosophical and ethical framework—but rather is consumed with how specific parts of the texts were pieced together at different dates under a myriad of hypotheses, all for presumed political or ideological purposes.

The originator of biblical criticism, Julius Wellhausen, was also, as it turns out, a harsh critic of Judaism (and hated Jews).[23] His theory is all conjecture and thought experimentation. No one has ever identified any actual source material of J, E, P, D, or any of the other speculated foundation texts of the Hebrew Scriptures. That is not to say that the theory is impossible; it is just that there is not a shred of proof. If a problem is suggested with the theory, a new source text or hypothetical redactor is proposed, which makes biblical criticism unfalsifiable. Inexplicably, the Bible is decomposed to a degree not applied to any other European text. Today one still reads Plato's *Republic* or Hegel's *The Phenomenology of Spirit* for their ideas, not primarily as a reflection of contemporary Greek and German politics. Yet one can take many courses on the Bible in university without understanding the main teachings of Jewish texts and its worldview. (I took one advanced Jewish text course at Northwestern, and it was a circular intellectual exercise that I will discuss a bit more later.) The parallel would be taking a class in Western civilization where one is told that the Greeks and Romans are an invented people mainly influenced by the Persians and Egyptians, who had no new ideas and with no real legacy across time in the European civilization that followed, and whose texts should be understood mainly in terms of the political dynamics during the time of the later editors, never once considering the ideas of Plato, Aristotle, Cicero, and Plutarch.

In contrast, according to the motto and the Golden Rule, to understand any text, one must give it a "sympathetic reading," which does not mean that one has to pre-agree to its conclusions, but one has to take the time to consider the work seriously. I gave Butz's book a sympathetic reading because I had to comprehend where he was coming from and how his reasoning worked. The same goes for Thrasher's writings. One needs to first understand how the author's reasoning works and the underlying philosophy of his or her views. Once that is done, sensible analytical work can begin. This is part of the Northwestern motto of seeking out whatsoever is good. It may be that there is nothing good to find, but one must try.

Dr. Devora Steinmetz has made the point that a key to Talmud study is the practice of trying to figure out how statements by the other side could be correct. That doesn't mean concluding that what the other person said is right, but analyzing someone else's statements in a way we would want for our own statements means looking at others' statements to see if they could be plausible. In the Talmud, the editors go through incredibly complicated thought gymnastics to see how they can reconcile what seems to be unreconcilable. The editors assume that every rabbi who makes a statement has to be accorded the supposition of being right. No view is simply rejected *a priori*. This is what can make Talmud study so difficult, at times obscure, and at times so energizing. When one figures out how a strange assertion could unexpectedly be right in a certain circumstance, it is an aha moment—"Oh, that is what he meant! I did not think of that case; it is not relevant to my life, but it must have been important to that rabbi. I wonder why?" It forces you to change your perspective to that of the other. This is a virtue that is both intellectual and moral, which is what Northwestern was trying to accomplish with the motto.

Through decolonial and postmodern theories, the general picture of Jewish history has become totally distorted for an American student in the humanities. Indeed, Jewish studies departments, though ubiquitous on American campuses, woefully often have an intense focus on modern European Jewish history and secular Jewish culture to the detriment of all other aspects of Jewish history and civilization.[24] Thus, Franz Rosenzweig, Martin Buber, and gender studies are ever-present, yet one is hard-pressed to learn anything about Iranian or Yemenite Jewish history or Jewish law or biblical political theory (though there are exceptions). At Vassar, the Jewish Studies Department was one of the sponsors of Jasbir Puar's Conspiracy Theory lecture. In all likelihood, an American learning about Jews and Judaism in an American college will learn the history of Jews as a people with an astonishingly short past in the land of Israel, who have been influenced by other empires to the point of being a non-people, and who in the modern period mendaciously parachuted into a land where they never lived as newly conquering European colonizers. The reality is that Jews are not an invented people. The question should be: Why have academics invented a theoretical construct that they falsely equate with the Jewish people?

The distortion of Jewish history is part of a broader picture about how theory can go bad. The process is fairly straightforward. When theory is not applied universally or ignores facts, it morphs into a false theory and/or a dogma and ideology, which has a cascade effect of obliterating academics' perception of obvious facts. This is demonstrated by a famous social science experiment known as "the invisible gorilla," which is viewable on YouTube.[25] Christopher Chabris and Daniel Simons report on an experiment they conducted in which six people, three wearing black shirts and three wearing white shirts, pass two balls around while moving in circles around each other. A group of viewers is asked to watch a video and count the number of passes only between the players wearing white shirts. The exercise, which can last a minute or two, requires some concentration. During the passing, a woman wearing a gorilla suit marches into the middle of the scene, stops and pounds her chest a few times, and leaves. After the video ends, the viewers are asked about the number of passes and then they are asked about the gorilla. About half of participants are sure that no gorilla appeared. More than 75 percent of those who didn't see the gorilla are sure that there was no way they could have missed it even if they were focused on counting the passes. Some who are shown a replay of the same video insist they are being tricked, that it must be a different video from the one they first watched.[26]

By looking at the world only under decolonial theory as it is currently practiced, many academics miss or downplay all kinds of other relevant facts, such as wholesale human rights abuses. For example, the treatment of the Uyghurs in Saudi Arabia is woefully neglected even though their position is truly dreadful. Saudi Arabia leverages them to behave as the regime desires because of their fear of being deported to China, where they face incarceration in reeducation internment camps or worse.[27] Yet because neither the Saudis nor the Chinese neatly fit decolonial theory, they are rarely mentioned—though as an ally of the US, the Saudis are sometimes singled out as white by proxy.[28] At most, lip service is paid to these abuses. No movements arise to counter them like the large-scale and international BDS movement. The same can be said of the Iranian eradication of the Bahá'í or of Turkey's treatment of the Kurds. When Iranian border guards beat fifty-seven Afghans in early 2020 and threw them in the Harirud River, there was no outcry from decolonial adherents.[29] Or when the entire Sikh and Hindu communities of Afghanistan seek to immigrate to the US because of the continuing murder of their members by other Afghans, there is no far-left complaint.[30] Under decolonial theory, it is not justifiable to criticize any aspect of a group if they are deemed to be oppressed by white colonialists. This type of thinking distorts the facts to suit Manichean categories. People are either all good or all evil. There is no nuance, only ideological motivated groupings.

This vision problem can lead to sabotaging scholarship itself. One archaeologist who is active in the Middle East told me that when the biblical minimalists first started showing up at academic conferences, actual archaeologists openly laughed during their presentation sessions because they weren't even doing archaeology. Literally, they were writing polemics bashing the veracity of archaeological finds based on weird interpretations of soggy secondary literature. But the power of orthodox anti-Zionism in the university is such that archaeologists learned it is better to remain quiet and not jeopardize project funding.

In 1999, the Waqf, which oversees the Al-Aqsa Mosque that sits on the Temple Mount in Jerusalem, conducted an excavation that involved the destruction of an area that might have been a two-thousand-year-old passageway within the Second Temple.[31] The remnants of whatever was there was crushed, put into trucks by tractors, and dumped in a landfill. In 2007, another excavation and renovation led to the destruction of another possibly ancient architectural feature of the Second Temple. Normally the academic archaeology community would be up in arms if any ancient structure anywhere in the world was treated as an excavation project with the remnants dumped in the garbage. But here the archaeology community outside of Israel was mum. Why? Because the incident could only be viewed via the guiding theory that there were no Jewish people then, or that they were somehow really Europeans, or that the Al-Aqsa Mosque was built on vacant land so there can't really be a meaningful Second Temple remnant to be concerned about. So, there is zilch to protest. The gorilla, they insist, can't be in the video. In short, because many academics view the world through the filter of flawed decolonial theory, they suffer from academically induced intellectual macular degeneration. It is bad for academia but much worse for the victims or even artifacts that cannot be seen. As the Bible notes, "without vision the people will perish." (Proverbs 29:18)

If the motto and the Golden Rule can be used to assess various theories, they can also be used to detect a related phenomenon: the creation of false theories based on the dubious use of facts. This is the case with Butz. In contrast to Thrasher, Butz does not cite a scholarly theory in *The Hoax of the Twentieth Century*. Rather, his narrative implies a theory about the world without ever stating it. For Butz, the dominant theory of history is a type of German supremacy, though it is caught in a struggle with Zionism "as the dying monster."[32] Butz does not come straight out and call for German world domination or white supremacy. Nor does he name his own theory and method. Instead, he focuses on uncovering "the facts" of the great hoax. But in uncovering Zionist enemies, he presents Germany as a righteous victim. He defends Hitler as a politician who exaggerates as many politicians do and as a leader who simply wanted to end the Jews' bad influence in Germany[33] and so on. The inference throughout his text is that if only Hitler had been a bit harsher and more realistic, he might have overcome the evil British and Americans.

Butz's theory of German supremacy can also be detected in what is absent from his book. There is no criticism whatsoever of Nazi imperialism or any other form of imperialism. The silence is earsplitting. Imperialism has a long history in German lands. His views on ancient history are also instructive in this regard. He writes that the Jews of Talmudic times had also exaggerated Roman massacres in Roman Palestine.[34] Butz portrays himself as a wide-ranging scholar opining on the Talmud and ancient history and demonstrating a dislike and dismissal even of Jews who have been dead for two thousand years. According to him, the Jews had not only grossly exaggerated their victimhood in the modern era but elsewhere—in ancient Alexandria, for example, they had even massacred the Romans.[35] Nowhere is there a contemplation of Rome's imperial policies in Palestine. According to Butz, the Jews were living in their land and not trying to subjugate anyone else, so why shouldn't the Romans conquer them? In short, he views the great Roman imperialism as reasonable and justified.

Butz's implicit theory has other features of German supremacy and neo-Nazism. He generally has a poor opinion of Russians. Butz alleges that in certain cases, Jews were put into ghettos "for security reasons to protect against the oncoming Russian onslaught."[36] At the same time, he alleges that the Soviets took in Jews who had been deported,[37] which Butz does not seem to think was smart. We are told Jews learned laziness from Russians, as he notes that Jews at Auschwitz were "working with the lethargy taught to them by the Russians."[38] In addition to their brutality, Russians are depicted as unclean, as "Russians were one of the principal sources of typhus."[39] (In many instances, Butz claims typhus was the primary source of the modest number of Jewish deaths in the concentration camps.)[40] Putting aside the dubious nature of these claims, for which no credible evidence is offered, for Butz an essential point is that all of these features are inherent to the people themselves. In sum, Butz generally asserts that Russians are inferior whites. Blacks are mentioned only once in his whole book,[41] as their status seems clear to him. Americans and British whites are on a high level but not at the German level because many are duplicitous and others are dumb and susceptible to being hoodwinked by Jews.

Finally, Butz's obsession with the Jews is characteristic of neo-Nazism. He hates Jews and seems to think most white Americans are just too stupid or hoodwinked to understand his Jewish Conspiracy Theories.[42] In contrast to the German people, not only are the Zionists conniving hoaxers who cheat others out of money, they are dangerous to even associate with. For example, Butz asserts that Jews mysteriously used gaslighting and deception to cause non-Jewish professional investigators who they came into contact with to extract false confessions, thereby condemning innocent Nazis. In some ways, Butz is unselfconsciously admiring of his imagined Zionists. They managed to secretly place hundreds of forged documents for investigators to happen upon, baffling German witnesses to confess to being perpetrators, participants, and enforcers of the murder of millions of Jews. While all these Germans confessed, remarkably they all had different motives for their testimonies, so befuddled were they by the Zionist agents and their unwitting allies. And even more amazingly, the Zionists infiltrated and induced the judges and the prosecutors to overlook blatant perjury and shoddy evidence.[43] Thousands of Jews conspired in broad daylight and were so good at it that it went unnoticed and without a single leak. Butz ticks all the boxes of a Conspiracy Theory.

There are few defenders of Nazism or even of German, European, or American imperialism in today's universities. At the same time, however, white supremacy/European imperialism/neo-Nazism has grown on the dark web and unites millions of people globally in a false theory. Decolonial theory, in contrast, is now canonically sacred among a large number of academics, especially in the humanities and social sciences and increasingly in all politically progressive movements. Many young students coming out of the university are as sincerely convinced of these "truths" as their teachers are or the Aramean army was. The roots of these problems are compounded by the lack of knowledge of most American Jews to even respond. In my Jewish communal work with American Jews of my generation—the vast majority of whom are university educated—I spoke with many who are convinced of some of the most extreme and controversial stances of biblical criticism and have limited knowledge of global Jewish history, and the knowledge they do have is very concentrated on the Jews in America or Europe or on the Holocaust. Further, many American students are often unaware of the underlying ideological biases in the way they were taught to view and process events.

There is a wide gulf between a totally false theory and a useful but distorted one. False theories must be abandoned, but the distorted ones might be repairable. Good theories are useful and should be embraced, along with a nonprejudiced reading of history. The motto and the Golden Rule can guide academics and the rest of us on this triage. Both can also help with ideologies more generally.

WHATSOEVER THINGS ARE
OF GOOD REPORT 4

HOW TO EVALUATE IDEOLOGIES CRITICALLY

While ideologies have parallels to theories in that they propose principles to understand the world, they are much more all-encompassing in
their focus on politics, economics, and society. Scholars sometimes go
so far as to propose a correspondence between religions and ideologies,
though many ideologies do not have teachings about the supernatural
or deities. The Golden Rule and the motto of Northwestern can provide a critique of ideologies in a corresponding manner to what we
have described in the previous chapter.

There are lots of ideologies present in America today. In the
political, economic, and social sphere, some prominent ones include
Marxism, progressivism, and liberalism, as well as conservatism and
libertarianism. Other ideologies in the intellectual and political sphere
include postmodernism as well as positivism. Usually, scholars critique these different ideologies in terms of each other, e.g., they give
a Marxist critique of liberalism, or a liberal critique of Marxism as
described above. Then there are ideologies that are generally, or should
be, discredited, such as various forms of Nazism or racial supremacy.
Following the Golden Rule in the university as the basis for examining
ideologies would save lives.

As a rule, dangerous ideologies depart radically from the Golden Rule and the motto. Nazism, with its focus on the supremacy of race, is inherently contradictory to the Golden Rule both ethically and factually since the Golden Rule rejects the idea that one group of humans is inherently better than another and would also demand the factual basis for this claim, which does not exist. In contrast, many people have more difficulty in seeing how Marxism and communism contradict the Golden Rule. Indeed, communism has had many followers who not only opposed Nazism but genuinely fought for concepts like equality and justice. Yet communism, unlike democratic forms of mixed economies or social democracies, leads to categories and theories that oppose common humanity, truth, and justice. Adopting the categories of worker and bourgeois, communism led to the demonization of the latter.[1] The result in the Ukraine was that Stalin ordered all the kulaks (peasant landowners) killed "as a class," which accounted for three million dead and thereby starved a quarter of the rest of the population to death. He also sent tens of millions to the gulags (Siberian work camps), resulting in countless deaths. Or in Cambodia, Pol Pot ordered the killing of all people with eyeglasses, among other groups, as potential members of the bourgeoisie.

While some argue Stalin and Pol Pot are an aberration, these despots' views are consistent with the dictatorship of the proletariat and the proclaimed necessity of eliminating enemies of the revolution. In fact, universally, communist leaders have had no qualms killing thousands if not millions to achieve their goals.[2] Mao caused the death of approximately 75 million of his comrades during his reign. He is ascribed to have said that it would have been acceptable had three hundred million of his comrades died if that ensured the victory of the Chinese Communist Party. Tragically, the list of Marxist tyrants is long and depressing. But one commonality is clear. At its heart, there is no common humanity in communism, just a war of classes.

The Golden Rule's focus on examining real actions also critiques the theoretical underpinning of communism. For example, the ownership of the means of production does not make sense as the only theory for understanding or establishing justice. Rather, as became clear in Soviet-led communist systems, not just cronyism of party appa-ratchiks but wide-ranging freeloading and lack of motivation led to widespread fraud and theft that ultimately imploded the system. The Chinese Communist Party learned these lessons and has a semi-capital-ist mercantilist system under a façade of communist-sounding talking points. In the final analysis, the theory of communist internationalism was a cover for the imposition of an overarching ideologically imperial culture. Thus, communist regimes' purported rejection of nationalism was actually a charade. Soviet communists were Russian imperialists under a new banner.[3] The Chinese Communist Party would have made the Han Chinese imperialists proud.[4] Arab socialists implemented Arab supremacy in the Arab League countries they led.[5]

The motto and the Golden Rule can also be applied to mainstream ideologies. One can, for example, consider liberalism and conserva-tism, two mainstream ideologies that inform the politics of many coun-tries today as well as the morals of many individuals. Both of these ideologies have changed over time. Initially, conservatism had fea-tures contrary to the motto and the Golden Rule as a defender of an unjust status quo. Conservatives believed in royal power rather than citizenship, in inequality before the law based on social class or on sex. Liberalism—whose early British exponents were, as Eric Nelson describes in *The Hebrew Republic*,[6] influenced by Jewish texts and concepts about equality before the law, the separation of powers, and the rejection of monopoly—could be much more easily squared with the Golden Rule and the motto. For indeed not only is the idea that nobility is inherently superior contrary to the Golden Rule, it is also contrary to fact—nobles are not a better race of humans. Similarly, the influence of the Southern wing of the Democratic Party before 1970, which wished to maintain racial inequality in the US, also was contrary to the Golden Rule.

Today both liberalism and conservatism accept equality before the law in theory. They differ on other issues such as free speech, the role and limits of government, protections given to religious freedom when they clash with other freedoms, and economic policies. The motto and the Golden Rule can be used to assess the underlying values of these two movements but also the extent to which their preferred policies will achieve their stated goals. Scholars can rightly question whether the Chicago School or Keynesian Economics has a better prescription for bringing economic prosperity. Are cooperative enterprises less efficient than owner-led ones? Is efficiency itself the best criteria? What is the impact of rent control and minimum wage? What does the data say? These are all important scholarly inquiries. Someone who upholds the motto or the Golden Rule will read the perspectives of different schools and evaluate them in relation to facts. In my field of banking, questions arise about the types of regulations that help consumers and those that hurt, a question which should be primarily practical but has become ideological. Here too the motto should guide scholars to do more than simply uphold the ideology they prefer and to examine the issue at hand.

Often, scholars in the humanities and social sciences are not explicit about the ideology and underlying axioms that underpin their research. On the one hand, there are many scholars who are openly Marxist in their approach both in the questions they ask and the values they bring to bear in the judgment of facts. Famous Marxist historians abound, such as E. P. Thompson, who wrote the classic *The Making of the English Working Class*.[7] Other scholars are known for their nationalist or conservative approach, such as Victor Davis Hanson.[8] Famous liberal historians include Peter Gay, author of *The Enlightenment: An Interpretation*.[9] Frequently, Marxist, liberal, nationalist, conservative, and other ideological historians have been in conflict with each other about how to interpret the past. Many of these ideological differences can be found in the social sciences as well. My emphasis on the motto and the Golden Rule serves not to dismiss ideologies but to ensure that we can evaluate them and that they don't predominate academic approaches to issues.

Referring to the motto and the Golden Rule offers an overarching framework for examining numerous ideologies rather than scholars just examining them in terms of each other. If during the Cold War, Marxists, liberals, and conservatives battled it out in many university disciplines, today it is hard to ignore that in the social sciences and humanities, progressive and radical scholars are so overrepresented that students are increasingly unaware that there are intelligent scholars who view the same question differently. As an experiment, on occasion I have asked college students over the last five years to define capitalism regardless of their personal opinion of it. Many do not understand that capitalism is simply a free market, private enterprise system in which the market determines the allocation of resources. The answer I sometimes get is a vague diatribe against big corporations, an unfair system of health care, labor oppression, income inequality, and a couple of times, complaints about the Electoral College thrown in for good measure. All of that could be true, but it is still not relevant to my question. Those who have taken economics courses do better on my quiz, but even some of them are confused. The bottom line is that college students are constantly being told that capitalism is bad without really understanding what it is because they are not given the full range of views on the topic. Most are under the misapprehension that Sweden practices socialism, when it is a welfare state with a robustly capitalist economy. It is a good idea to know what one opposes. As the apocryphal slogan says, if you can afford only one newspaper, read that of the opposition.

In fact, in many disciplines in the humanities and social sciences, Marxist, postmodern, or decolonial perspectives are replacing the motto as a basis for understanding the world to the exclusion of other perspectives. As mentioned above, Thrasher really has no patience for anyone who does not adopt these theories as axiomatic. His exclusionary perspective is not unique; rather it is a common perspective of those influenced by critical theory. Indeed, it is not the presence of Marxist, postmodern, or decolonial theories on campus that is the problem; it is their hegemony. Many faculty members even go as far as to justify the necessity of outlawing opposition views.

The background for this approach comes from a particular strand of critical theory, which therefore requires a brief explanation. Critical theory is essentially a Marxist analysis of social phenomena with the objective of creating a more just society as defined in Marxist terms. Critical theory, however, became its own school of thought because it also integrated concepts from psychoanalysis, sociology, and literary theory and rejected some theoretical elements of traditional Marxism.[10] Having originated in Weimar Germany at the University of Frankfurt in the 1930s, its main originators were mostly Jews exiled to the United States, notably Max Horkheimer and Theodor Adorno. Another one of them was Herbert Marcuse (a mentor of Angela Davis), who went on to have a profound influence not only in the academy but among the entire American New Left in the 1960s. Marcuse's thinking is highly complex and I cannot do it justice here. Nor should he and his students be taken to represent all of critical theory, a method that regarding our topic, anti-Zionism, informs the scholarship of scholars who advocate anti-Zionist Conspiracy Theorists like that of Angela Davis as well as that of scholars who oppose anti-Zionism such as those belonging to the Critical Theories of Antisemitism Network including the prominent sociologist, the late Robert Fine.[11] However, I will address a key point Marcuse made that is essential to our discussion: he rejected tolerance of ideas that went against his principles. In an essay called "Repressive Tolerance"[12] for a volume called *A Critique of Pure Tolerance*, Marcuse argued against tolerating views that did not advance his concept of freedom. Marcuse's view on tolerance has been the focal point for the tension in academia between advancing knowledge based on the standards of evidence and of justice or upholding various political principles as being more important than factual truth or universal applicability.

The influence of critical theory—especially Marcuse's concept of repressive tolerance—on many disciplines, especially "studies" programs like American studies, is beyond dispute. In fact, the ripple effects of Marcuse's concept of repressive tolerance are growing exponentially. The result has been a justification of snuffing out scholarly approaches and viewpoints uniquely on ideological rather than factual grounds. This is the root of cancel culture and of the silencing of opposing viewpoints. The issue is not that certain ideas are being excluded. The academy has always and must always discriminate between good and bad scholarship and must reject the latter. Unfortunately, the influence of Marcuse's strand of critical theory uses criteria that are ideological rather than factual and Golden Rule–based (that is to say universally applicable). The effect on scholarship about Israel in numerous departments is to exclude writings that are not anti-Zionist, irrespective of the facts or ethical double standards. This has only compounded the problem of the predominance in the academy of scholars who use critical theory to condemn Zionism over those who apply it to critique anti-Zionism. Nonetheless, critical theory should be taught at the universities for the influential philosophical and political theory that it is, with all of its strands represented, and not transformed into a single dogma to evaluate all scholarship.

I don't, however, want to overstate this point. Not all scholars who adhere to one or other strand of critical theory advocate rejecting contrary viewpoints. More generally it seems that a sizeable minority of scholars still feel that providing students with a wide range of scholarly approaches (whether diverse ideologically, methodologically, or in scope) is a worthy endeavor. This is the viewpoint of Jonathan Haidt, for example, who, though liberal, thinks there is value in considering ideological diversity, including conservative and Marxist perspectives, because bringing divergent views into conversation sharpens our understanding, whatever the issue. Using the motto and the Golden Rule as a framework invites these different ideological perspectives to be in conversation and also excludes those, like Nazism and communism, that have literally led to the deaths of many millions of individuals.

The danger of extreme ideologies in the academy is not an exaggeration. Intellectuals have not only embraced extreme ideologies, but they have also been agents in creating extreme regimes. Dissenters have been co-opted or forced to submit to remain in the system. The Bible provides a conceptual framework for recognizing extreme ideologies that reject the motto and Golden Rule that still has relevance today: *idolatry*. Post-1945, we moderns would view Nazi Germany and the Soviet Union alternatively as totalitarian and/or corrupt; the Bible calls all societies that reject the Golden Rule idolatrous. Idolatry might seem like a quaint word that no longer applies to the modern world, but in fact it is a theory about power. Idolatry in essence is a set of lies about power. It ascribes super authority and even superpowers to finite beings (god-kings or rulers, or groups of people), natural processes, or ideologies, often in combination. According to the Bible, once you make this error, you deny a universal humanity (especially through the deification of people or leaders); you pervert truth, since truth becomes relative; and you destroy any possibility of justice, since there is no common humanity and therefore no common principles of justice.

The rejection of idolatry is the foundation of all the other biblical laws, which are themselves foundational to justice today, such as no murder, no stealing, no perjury, and other matters of not treating your fellow as you would not want to be treated. In classic idolatrous societies throughout history, rulers were deified, and they or an elite cadre decided on the law. Yet the idolatrous god-kings of old and modern-day dictators face a fundamental paradox. All humans, including themselves, are limited by nature; they can't actually be gods. From Pharaoh to Stalin, dictators have masked the reality of their common humanity through poetry, pageants, myths, and theater, as well as secret informers and demonstrations of state brutality, all to make believe that their view of reality is true. What the Bible calls idolatry refers to authoritarian or totalitarian ideologies. Loyal followers can celebrate this via the poetry, pageantry, myths, and theater of the ideology and thus savor a taste of the god's power. Thus, long after Hitler's death, neo-Nazis and communists collect memorabilia, parade flags, march in demonstrations, and murder Jews. Stalin's followers still flock to his grave. For a more recent example, just watch China's well-staged celebration of the seventieth anniversary of the Chinese Communist Party's ascension to power. The ceremonies were all about the god-king, the idolatry of the CCP, and providing the masses with a taste of being part of the power.

Peoples and states that advance idolatrous ideologies are not only corrupt in themselves, they necessarily seek to dominate other groups; that is, they engage in imperialism. Because every idolater knows in his or her heart of hearts that there could always be a bigger, more powerful god somewhere else, idolatrous leaders and ideologies seek to destroy those other gods and god-kings and subjugate the conquered peoples under their now even more glorious god. Idolatry offers the justification: if my god is more powerful and my people more powerful, then we have the right to rule over you. Thus, all the idolatrous states of antiquity conquered neighboring territories, often brutally exiling or killing their conquests, as occurred with ancient Assyria and Babylon, and subjecting conquered peoples to slavery.

Even early idolatrous tribes did not simply engage in border disputes but rather sought to conquer others. This is true for the Mongols, who murdered 10 percent of the world population wreaking havoc all over Asia and the Middle East. Modern idolatrous states utilize the Nazi state program of Lebensraum, which justified the invasion and submission of so-called inferior peoples. Indeed, the more idolatrous the state, the more likely it is to seek to crush other peoples, whether physically or through economic burdens. This feature of idolatrous societies is one of the reasons they have always had trouble with the Jews, who in their at least theoretical commitment to the Bible have rejected the power of god-kings and the supremacy of oppressive ideologies since the ancient Pharaoh of Exodus. While totalitarian or idolatrous societies have victimized all manner of people, as Cassam and Byford have noted, Conspiracy Theories about Jews have had a disproportionate place in these regimes and among their followers. It is to this that we shall now turn.

WHATSOEVER THINGS ARE PURE

WHY JUDAISM AND ZIONISM DRIVE THEIR OPPONENTS CRAZY

Since on political matters Thrasher and Butz likely agree on nothing other than that Zionism is evil, let us further examine why this particular issue would be their sole point of commonality. In other words, why Zionism, and why the Jews? Why are Jews and their national self-determination demonized and placed at the center of a conspiracy, especially since both Thrasher and Butz's ideologies have much more formidable opponents?

Conspiratorial thinking with its irrational elements of demonization and obsessive focus on one cause for all bad stuff is a feature, not a bug, of extreme ideologies, as Cassam has argued. Totalitarian ideologies and states rationally oppose real and ideological opponents but irrationally oppose Jews and Judaism. Since totalitarianism is based on a specific worldview about humans, reality, and justice, it is clear that it would oppose groups with differing views and opposing interests—in other words, real opponents. Thus, Nazi opposition to communism, the liberal tradition, and even Christianity makes sense. Yet the Nazis went to bizarre lengths, rationally speaking, to destroy the Jews and, more to the point, attributed to the Jews malevolent power beyond any reasonable consideration.

The same is true of the Soviets. The Soviets victimized many nationalities, seeking to assimilate the Baltic countries with an influx of Russian immigrants. Stalin, himself a Georgian, wrote a book on Marxism and the nationality question that explicitly aimed to dissolve the smaller nations. He decreed the execution of a large number of Georgian nationalists during the Great Purge of the 1930s. The Soviets also established state atheism and waged a war against religion by confiscating church property, ridiculing religion in schools, and harassing believers. In 1925, the Soviets created the League of Militant Atheists. Christianity, Islam, Judaism, and other religions in the Soviet Empire faced harsh persecution, especially in the large cities. In China, the Cultural Revolution did away with much of the three great religious/philosophical traditions of China: Confucianism, Taoism, and Buddhism.

Yet like the Nazis, the Soviets went to preposterous lengths to discredit Zionism in particular. Their assessment of Zionism as a danger to communism went far beyond what strategic opposition to Jewish nationality and religion would warrant. They expended scarce resources to disseminate information about the enormous dangers of Zionism to communism. It was an appraisal that is very hard to square with the reality of postwar Israel and even with Jewish Diaspora political power—and even more so if you include Jewish support for socialism. The Soviets, like the Nazis, had a fervent and exaggerated fear of an imagined Jewish/Zionist conspiracy to destroy them. The over-the-top, counterproductive, and irrational nature of the communist and Nazi evaluations of the Jewish/Zionist threat suggest that something deeper is going on with those ideologies. The insights of a famed anthropologist may help us develop a hypothesis for this hate.

Mary Douglas's insights about pollution and taboos in many traditional societies explain Nazi and communist Conspiracy Theories. In *Purity and Danger*,[1] Douglas defines "dirt as matter out of place [...] It implies two conditions: a set of ordered relations and a contravention of that order."[2] She explains that "these pollutions, which lurk between the visible act and the invisible thought, are like witch-craft...their inherent power to harm does not depend either on external action or on any deliberate intention. They are dangerous in themselves." For both extremes, their ideologies establish a set of ordered relations that exclude Zionists from humanity, leaving Zionists as a form of dirt with the polluting power this dirt entails. In other words, Douglas understood the interplay between idolatry, which demands conformity with the cult, and the purity of those participating in the cult. Even the most ardent academic supporter of Students for Justice in Palestine at some level must comprehend that the Jews are not European colonialists with no claim to the land of Israel, even if they detest the thought. Jews are distinguished by their accomplishment of multi-millennial survival and also the influence of their Scriptures, which permeates much of the world. This becomes a blemish on far-right and far-left theories. We are reminded as well that Martin Heidegger also thought the Jews were ontologically out of place. In his view, the Jews had no place in the world. For Heidegger, they were dirt on the goodness of the German will for the world, and so Jews, like dirt, had to be removed. Yet modern ideologies, especially those that proclaim a scientific basis like Nazism and communism, cannot simply describe the Jews as pollution or taboo; instead, other rationalizations, or at least monikers, must be given. Wilhelm Marr knew that fancy-sounding names for hating other people were more effective.

Conspiracy Theories from both extremes have one common denominator, namely that Jews/Zionists are inherently evil. Both sides build their explanations out of some hint of anomaly, some sort of inexplicable detail that protrudes as conspicuously out of place or something that doesn't fit in to the presumed power structure and then is exaggerated and distorted into an all-out Conspiracy Theory. For the far right, this is usually the suspicion of the fact that Jews are overrepresented in the media, finance, government, and even university leadership, which is transformed into a conspiracy to take over America, even when these Jews are in no way united and in real terms are not that numerous.

Other lies follow suit: Jews are able to accomplish this because of their fake whiteness or because they have some sort of secret power, even though we know of other diasporic minorities that are overrepresented in certain industries. (Try googling the name Patel in the hospitality industry.)

From the far left, Jews are also out of place because they are one of very few indigenous peoples who have reclaimed their language and their land. They have the only Jewish state in a neighborhood of fifty or so Muslim-majority countries. Jews stand out because they don't fit the white European decolonial framework. Like crumbs on a clean carpet, the Jews stand out and the carpet demands a vacuuming. Israel comprises less than 0.19 percent of the square miles of the land in a region so dominated by Arabs politically that it is referred to as the Arab world. Further, Israeli Jews account for only 0.16 percent of its population. Yet that is deemed unacceptable and intolerable by those who see Jews as pollution.

The far left takes the idea that the Jews joined with Britain and that many Jews who were part of the Zionist movement moved to Ottoman Palestine, fleeing from Russia, in order to fabricate an anti-Zionist conspiracy. The Jews/Zionists are transformed into imperial agents and Europeans, rather than a Diaspora people looking for allies, as was the case of the Armenians and Greeks, for example, when fighting for their independence. Jews may claim to be non-white, and a majority come from lands otherwise defined as non-white, but some Jews look white, so the far left insists they are all Europeans. The inherent pollution that the Jews possess in these ideologies gets rationalized by conspiracies that take some little fact and distort it into a conspiracy to maintain the veneer of the "truth" and "objectivity" of these irrational and ultimately immoral ideologies.

The Conspiracy Theories also provide a rationale for erasing Jews/Zionists, or in the current lexicon, canceling them. As Douglas explains, "Purity is the enemy of change, of ambiguity and compromise."[3] To protect all this "from skepticism is to suppose that an enemy, within or without the community, is continually undoing its good effect."[4] One way to cancel this pollution, this dirt, "is the confessional rite,"[5] as Douglas writes. "The polluter becomes a doubly wicked object of reprobation."[6] As modern ideologies, Nazism and communism cannot simply express these beliefs in the impurity of Zionists; instead, Conspiracy Theories become the rationales that justify treating all people with any hint of Zionism or any Zionist association as dirt, enemies, non-human specks that must be eliminated.

As Douglas describes, confession is the major way out. The only way for a Jew to escape impurity is to join the Yevsektsiya, the Anti-Fascist Committee, or Jewish Voice for Peace and confess in a public ritual that they are not part of this pollution. There can be no crack in the walls of the extremes. For the far right, there is no confessionary ritual for Jews/Zionists themselves, just destruction. The best the Jew can hope for is the auto-da-fé. For other pale-skinned peoples of derision, confession might work. It does not matter how incomprehensible an argument against Jewish self-determination is; it must be acknowledged as totally true, incontrovertible, apparent, and only challenged by people who must be wholly evil regardless of any other aspect of their lives. There is no compromise since Zionist sovereignty is an all-evil conspiracy to hurt others. Unanimous condemnation of Jews is all that makes sense. Even a Jewish member of a student government who does not ostentatiously renounce Zionism becomes a danger for all those around and must be eliminated. Ambiguity, on the other hand, means individuals and groups are not purely good or purely evil, which must be dismissed as clearly wrong.

We see the extreme ideological origin of Butz and Thrasher's anti-Zionist Conspiracy Theories as well as their rationalizing function. Butz gives his readers a genealogy of this thought at the beginning of his book. He describes his encounters with other revisionists. He is careful, however, not to refer to neo-Nazi circles. As Lipstadt shows, in the context of the discrediting of Nazism in the postwar period, the revisionists doubled down on brandishing their supposed scientific objectivity.[7] Butz is one of the major figures to take this approach. For Butz, the uncovering of a conspiracy clearly in his own mind justifies his obsession and dislike for this heinous people, the Zionists. His conspiracy starts with a few facts, like the Jewish origins of some of the peripheral lawyers in the Nuremberg trials, and then explodes into a malevolent Conspiracy Theory from there, all described in academic language and accompanied with lots of footnotes. For Butz, the Jews become a fixation. A dirt he has to cleanse. Based on his publication history, I would conjecture that Butz spent his entire sabbatical year and then some writing *The Hoax of the Twentieth Century*. Given his previous impressive research trajectory, had he spent that year on science, he might have become a major academic figure.

Douglas takes as her source material many idolatrous cultures and, as such, her paradigm fits well with what we have described as the idolatry of both the far right and far left. Douglas reaffirms her conclusions about the concepts of purity and taboo in the preface to her 2004 edition of *Purity and Danger* but highlights one chapter and concept that she fully retracts—that happens to be about the Bible. "This is the place to confess to a major mistake,"[8] she writes. "I was way out of my depth when I wrote [about Leviticus] nearly forty years ago. I made mistakes about the Bible for which I have been very sorry ever since. Longevity is a blessing in that it gave me time to discover them."[9] I was impressed and reminded that one of my professors at Northwestern, Kenyon Poole, would always quote John Maynard Keynes in his response to a criticism about his changed views: "When the facts change, I change my mind. What do you do, sir?" Yet we have a generation of academics these days who are so devoted to their wrong-minded theories that they invent new facts and ignore or obscure real evidence. This is the opposite of true scholarship, and it is done all in the name of purity. Far-right and far-left ideologues and, even more so, regimes, rarely recant. Instead, they go to great lengths to preserve their version of the truth.

The Bible mocks this sort of idolatrous obsession with purity on many occasions, but perhaps no more bitingly so than in the story told in the Book of Esther. The Persia of those days is a paradigm of idolatry. The king has immense imperial power of 127 provinces from India to Ethiopia, and his word is immutable. (Esther 1:1) Any law he proclaims cannot be abrogated or changed under any circumstances. (Esther 1:19) Throughout the book, it is clear that the way to advancement is to tell the king what he wants to hear whether it is true or not. Indeed, rather than seek truth or good policy, courtiers spend their time trying to figure out what will find the king's favor, or lying to him in a way that will advantage that courtier.

An official by the name of Haman becomes extremely successful at manipulating the king and is made prime minister. He assumes a supremely privileged position of enormous power and wealth. (Esther 3:1) There is literally only one tiny hitch in his whole life; it is a teeny speck, practically invisible, until it is pointed out to him—a Jew named Mordechai does not kneel as Haman passes. (Esther 3:2–4) This drives Haman absolutely crazy, and he becomes obsessed with the whole Jewish people because of Mordechai. (Esther 3:5–6) This made no sense, as the Jews had no power in those days—the First Temple had been destroyed and the Jews were widely dispersed. Mordechai was not ostentatious about not bowing down. He probably stayed toward the back of the crowd, and it only became an issue because two guards could not resist telling Haman. Other Jews apparently had no problem bowing down to Haman. The Jews were pretty assimilated, taking part in a massive multi-month party the king had thrown in honor of his reign. (Esther 1:3–7) Esther, who was taken to the palace to be considered for the queen replacement reality TV–style competition, was not discernably Jewish even though she must have been taken from a Jewish neighborhood.

Despite the Jews being powerless, largely compliant, and assimilated, Haman fears them (Esther 3:6) and comes up with a *meshuganah gornisht bolbe* that he tells to the king in a way that will bring out the king's worst *dybbuks* of being undermined in some way—in other words, a Conspiracy Theory. From time immemorial, "crazy, worthless, stupid, made-up tales bring out the demons in susceptible, unthinking people," particularly idolaters who definitionally believe lies about power and authority even if it is their own. Haman is at one with the German Nazis and Soviet Communists who feared Jews way out of proportion with reality and then promulgated lies to justify their irrational hatred. Haman is skilled at this dark art of creating Conspiracy Theories. Based on his deceit, the king decrees the destruction of the Jews.

Some non-Jews are troubled by this. If it could happen to the Jews, it could happen to them too with the whim of the king. But no one stands up to defend the Jews; these non-Jews in the story remain dumbfounded and silent. (Esther 3:15) This was the Jews' first role as the canary in the coal mine.

Thankfully, the story ends happily when Esther creates an elaborate scheme to make the king realize the truth. Esther's stratagem forces the king to act like a scholar. He calls for his history books without any of his advisors around to put a spin on what is recounted or to come up with some lies. He thinks on these things in the quiet of the night, checks out the reliable reports, discerns what is honest and sorts out the real story, and ultimately recognizes that Haman is manipulating him with tall tales. (Esther 6:1–9) With the truth, darkness turns into light, oppression into joy. We need this to happen in large sections of the humanities and social sciences.

PART V

WHATSOEVER THINGS ARE HONEST 2

HOW GOOD THEORIES AND GOOD PRACTICES GET TURNED BAD

The United States is not a totalitarian country, so the question arises as to how and why anti-Zionist Conspiracy Theories have gained such a foothold in the university. I believe an example from the banking industry offers a parallel to explain how a false theory can come to be accepted as truth by so many smart faculty members who presumably are trained to know better. The corruption in the banking industry that occurred with the degeneration of a fact-based theory into a false one is a cautionary tale for today's academy.

Our story starts in the 1970s, when subprime mortgage lending was a solid and evidence-based practice that was good for would-be homeowners and good for banks. It was a proverbial win-win business deal. The developments in financing prime and subprime borrowers were well researched and based on facts, leading the Bank of America to launch the first private prime mortgage-backed security (MBS) in 1977. MBS securities worked very well since they were closely linked to the underlying data about the mortgages that were their building blocks and were initially comprised entirely of prime loans. These securities were so well structured that the AAA, AA, A, and even BBB segments all had *no* losses for decades. They provided a new and healthy way to include more people in the home ownership community by enabling financial institutions to profit while also dramatically lowering interest rates charged to consumers.

During the late 1980s and 1990s, banks and rating agencies worked to expand MBSs to new groups that did not fit into standard underwriting. But here too they made sure the evidence fit the theory. Folks who worked on commission, were self-employed, had variable income, or worked "off the books" were offered "alt-A" or various "subprime" loans with more restrictive terms than prime loans. These loans were successful because they were more conservatively underwritten than regular loans. Alt-A loans were usually for no more than 50 to 60 percent of the value of the home, and subprime loans did not exceed 40 to 50 percent of home values. For over two decades, these loans were solid. A large portion (75 to 85 percent) of them were with riskier borrowers, but these risks were offset by more conservative terms that would allow them to be put in an MBS with a AAA rating. Being rated AAA meant that these bonds enjoyed a special prestige with regulators, risk managers, and the rating agencies themselves. All of these AAA bonds would enjoy similar low rates of interest approaching those of other AAA bonds backed by much stronger collateral or more creditworthy borrowers such as sovereign developed countries. The loans worked because they fit the facts.

Then this good theory morphed into a bad theory with devastating consequences. At some point in the '90s, certain financial institutions and mortgage brokers saw a profitable opportunity and began to add weaker loans into MBSs and still call them by the same name. The initial impulses might have been virtuous—to allow non-prime borrowers to get better terms on their mortgages—but the only evidence available was from a rising market in which payment problems were solved by the house being sold to a new buyer for more than enough to pay off the mortgage. Quickly, investment bankers, mortgage bankers, house speculators, and others along the feeding chain recognized this profit potential and either went along with new weaker loans or even fanned the frenzy by adding even weaker and riskier loans to these securities, again based on conjecture. These actors further succeeded in convincing rating agencies to accept their false assertions with attestations that these new mortgage-backed securities were as solid as the old ones. They achieved this by using more and more elaborate language—what I called in an earlier chapter word bombs, or fancy jargon that made the experts feel not only that they were right but part of a special club, while also disguising their lack of factual basis. Thus, virtually the entire industry got on the bandwagon of accepting the lies about this product and its value.

An informal monopoly of information took shape regarding this massive part of the US economy, with people reinforcing this false and corrupted version of subprime mortgages at every turn, including word bombs like this: "We are today presenting our new ABC Mortgage-Backed Security, in which each tranche has been stratified with Intex data, Case-Schiller diversified, Z spread normalized and tested under SX-3 44R-generated Monte Carlo simulations. We further present a zip code geo concentration analysis and introduce a new subordinated sub tranche which will sufficiently compensate for our California earthquake risk assessment with all our estimates based on stochastic oscillators to a 99.9% confidence level using several heuristic annealing scenarios." The words made it sound like the data was being presented very conservatively when in fact it was not. Few paid attention to what the words really meant or recognized how limited the definitions really were.

The rating agencies, which are supposed to be *the* gatekeepers of standards, not only failed to do their job, which was to ask about the facts, but were scandalously early word bomb adopters. No one looked into whether the house prices had been inflated or if the developments in question were being bought by speculators who were putting no money down, or if the borrowers were presenting their real financial information. Perhaps they did not want to sound stupid because all the presentations seemed so very sophisticated. The word bombs gave everyone the mini-deified feeling of being on the elite inside and being really, really smart, and by the way there was also the appealing din of lots and lots of money rolling in over the transom. Realtors, investors, banks, and, yes, consumers who made out had every incentive to praise, extoll, acclaim, exalt, revere, and deploy the MBS machine, and as they did so they bid up house prices to amazing levels. In Merced, California, home prices tripled in a few years to over $300,000 for a typical home at a time when the local per capita income was $24,000. Homes were being refinanced at a dizzying pace as new higher appraisals fueled by MBS financing drove up values. In one unexceptional case in Merced, a home was refinanced six times over a few years with cash-out refinancing, taking the mortgage debt from $86,000 to over $350,000. The linguistic sleight of hand was insidious, as terms such as alt-A and subprime MBS were fine when applied to underlying mortgages of 40 to 60 percent financing, but they were just junk bonds when applied to optional negative amortization floating rate mortgages with teaser rates close to zero. Yet most financial market experts ignored the truth. Sunday morning hour-long informercials inducted the uninitiated. That happy noise of the money rolling in is oh so alluring. When the theory was exposed as false, 89.0 percent of subprime mortgages and 90.9 percent of alt-A mortgages that had previously been rated AAA were downgraded to "junk bonds." Amazingly, this was all done without any subsequent apologies by the rating agencies, a scandal of no accountability that I cannot go into here but deserves a book of its own.

We know how the financial markets were corrupted by these shoddy securities being falsely touted as AAA; it is not a mystery. There simply was no a priori mechanism to stop this unhinging of concepts from facts, because in the interim it made everyone look so good and made some folks so much money. In fact, those who were early critics of this new orthodoxy were retired, silenced, sidelined, or fired. These stodgy folks looking at the facts were told they just didn't "get it." Lew Ranieri (one of the founders of the mortgage securities markets) passionately warned publicly of the dangers of these fake AAA securities risking all the good that MBSs had initially brought to homebuyers.

He was scoffed at as cranky, incorrigible, and "twentieth century." Jeff Kronthal, head of mortgages at Merrill Lynch, was fired for telling the CEO and the board not to be seduced by the short-term profits of aggressively participating in the subprime market. Michael Gelband, who had warned Lehman of the risks of their subprime book of mortgages, was marginalized and left the firm. In this way, we see the informal monopoly of those who supported the bogus MBSs since, like all monopolies, they were able to cut out their critics and competition.

Those who should have had better judgment, like the government-sponsored entities of FNMA and FHLMC, also became convinced by the word bombs and thick analyses with lots of numbers, pie charts, graphs, and interactive spreadsheets. They too thought the word bombs and faux analyses were very sophisticated and smart. (It was only later that it became known that FNMA and FHLMC could not even prepare their own financial statements under generally accepted accounting principles and went the equivalent of bankrupt.) In fact, not only did FNMA and FHLMC fail to expose the issue, they added jet fuel to the fire. They were incentivized to get as large as they could using their full faith and credit call on the US government. And in what seemed like a wonderful mechanism at the time, creating even more happy noise, the more alt-A and subprime-backed AAA bonds FNMA and FHLMC bought, the better these bonds performed because of the sheer weight of the buying power of these government-sponsored entities. The other "adults in the room" were supposed to be the rating agencies described above. Of course, the music did stop and many of the participants bloodied by the carnage wondered what went wrong. The cause wasn't a mystery: the 2000s version of subprime mortgages looked nothing like the 1970s, 1980s, and early 1990s versions despite being called by the same name.

By the 2000s, the once good theory of subprime mortgage lending had become totally bad. It is now clear that an entire industry had been corrupted by some bad ideas that had become weaponized because there were strong incentives to do so. It is also clear that words and terms can be weaponized or used to obscure what should be the real debate. Securities firms debated with rating agencies about the percentage of subprime and alt-A loans that should be AAA when in fact none of the bonds should have been considered investment grade from the get-go. The whole theory that these were loans that should even go into an MBS was wrong.

While this is not a precise parallel to the current corruption of decolonial theory and how it has led to the hegemony of anti-Zionism in much of academia, it does rhyme well. The MBS example is a parable of the perils of getting involved in a dispute in which terminology is used to obfuscate faults in a theory and also create a club of smart-sounding people from which dissenters are expelled.

There is a biblical story that well illustrates how systemic failure is the result of turning away from the truth. In chapter 36 of the Book of Jeremiah, the prophet dictates a book to his disciple Baruch, who first reads it aloud at the Temple, then to some of King Jehoiakim's courtiers. Even these sycophants recognize the truth of the words of the book and thus are emboldened to bring it to King Jehoiakim himself. The king listens to the book and then dramatically slices off each column as the book is read and throws it into a fireplace. He does not explain why he does this; he simply makes the point that his word is truth and those who contradict it are definitionally liars. This defiant treatment of the truth reassures his courtiers, who lose their fear and fall into line behind the king's authority. Further, at the king's instruction they set out to find Jeremiah and Baruch to kill them.

Like King Jehoiakim, who thought he could burn the truth away, when the first reports of underlying defaults in the mortgages started appearing, the prices for the securities actually went up as the agencies and banks doubled down on their lies, dismissing those who said that the jig was up. As depicted in the book *The Big Short*,[1] the investors who correctly saw that these MBS securities were about to go bust actually faced margin calls when they least expected it. The folks who made these bets were astounded at the power of those who peddled the fake truth of the strength of these junk securities. But both the oligopoly behind the junk MBSs and King Jehoiakim faced "true ups," a time when the real truth would have to be known. In the case of the junk MBSs, once house prices stopped skyrocketing, some underlying borrowers defaulted on their mortgages and the rating agencies had to acknowledge that these securities were not AAA, and indeed were not even fit for prudent investors. King Jehoiakim had to face the wrath of the Babylonian army. Sadly, not just the MBS oligarchs and King Jehoiakim faced doom but all of those whom they ruled as well. The mortgage crisis ruined the credit and, in some cases, lives of hundreds of thousands of American families.

Today's universities and anti-Zionist Conspiracy Theories have striking parallels to the causes of the Financial Crisis of 2008 and the rise of bogus MBSs. We are seeing an increasing intellectual monopoly around lies about Zionism and Zionist Conspiracies Theories. These lies and fake theories are like the bogus MBSs that were started by bad actors who were not true to their institutional mission. The academic phenomenon also began slowly but is now exploding. Indeed, it is not that Palestinian leaders like Arafat or the bankers should not have their own interests in mind; rather, they should not promote these on false pretenses. Further, what turbocharged the flames was the willingness of followers to spread lies to advance those interests.

Scholars know that the PLO and the Soviet Union deliberately distorted theories about colonialism to recast Jews as imperialists and settler colonialists and promoted anti-Zionist Conspiracy Theories with the overt goal of delegitimizing and destroying Israel. Yasser Arafat knew Jews had an ancient history in the land of Israel, and yet he said that the Jewish Temple never existed, causing President Bill Clinton to raise an eyebrow. As recently as 1929, the Waqf historian Aref al-Aref wrote that the Al-Aqsa Mosque as "the site of Solomon's temple is beyond dispute."[2] In 2011, Palestinian National Authority president Mahmoud Abbas said, "we say that the nation of Palestine upon the land of Canaan had a 7000 year history BCE. This is the truth, which must be understood and we have to note it, in order to say: 'Netanyahu, you are incidental in history. We are the people of history. We are the owners of history.'"[3] This would put the Palestinians in the land thousands of years before the founding of what became ancient Egypt, whose inhabitants were not Arabs. And we know Arab League countries pressured nonaligned countries to adopt their stance. Both the Soviets and Arab nationalists used soft power to gain adherents (radio, news, university funding, and so forth). Some may even believe the lies out of ideological loyalty.

What is tragic is that others may have gone along with the lies because they were following their incentives. Professors and departments may have become adherents because they opposed colonialism and did not bother to look into the facts, just like bankers who wanted to see more credit available but did not bother to check if the new MBSs were good. It was easier to go along than to be subjected to angry noise for disputing the prevailing theory and actually examining the facts. The so-called adults in the room in the academy—the professors on tenure committees, the heads of various studies associations, or the American Association of University Professors charged with keeping the rules and regulations on academic discourse—have put their stamps of approval on dubious theories, which, as Puar does, "stretches the speculative into the now."

Perhaps even more tragic than the lies is the utter failure of teaching the basic analytical skill of applying principles universally. Indeed, these academics do not ask or train their students to ask basic questions about all parties. For example, they do not ask what defines settler colonialism and/or indigeneity and if and how Israelis or Palestinians fit these categories. Instead, the theory is provided prepackaged (Israel is a settler colonial apartheid state and Palestinians are indigenous), leaving students simply to repeat the answers on cue or fill in the details. Likewise, the accusations of ethnic cleansing and apartheid actually have real meaning and can and should be examined systematically. The same could be said about specific outbreaks of the conflict.

Though many critics at least claim to judge the conflict by international law, they do not ask how the law applies to both parties. Instead, the theory is already proven, Israel is guilty of war crimes, and students are drilled as to why they are compelled to understand the (spurious) connections. Yet questions abound. Are precision strikes legal? What about the blockade, the rockets, or the March of Return? Similarly, if the standard is human rights, other basic questions must be asked about the ideology and motives of all parties involved. In addition, while the collaboration between Israel and the US is condemned constantly, we hear nothing from Puar, Thrasher, Davis, or any other of the academics discussed here about Qatar, Turkey, and Iran, who provide Hamas with funds and arms. So many courses are focused almost exclusively on theories about Israel's evil that the other side is a straw man and students are taught that this is academic discipline.

The Bible again anticipated the inertia that facilitates corruption. Jeremiah (chapter 38) tells King Zedekiah the absolute truth about the power of the Babylonians, his failed military alliances, and his feckless advisors. The text indicates that Zedekiah both believed Jeremiah and found it impossible to act on the truth. It was just too difficult to get out of the web of falsehoods and fakers in which he was entrenched. Jeremiah begs him to act and gives him a plan that will spare his life, his dignity, and most importantly the lives of the people. Yet Zedekiah just can't take action. Jeremiah pleads, "The men who were your friends have seduced you and vanquished you. Now your feet are sunk in the mire." (Jeremiah 38:22) That is the case in academia as it was in MBS land; they are so sunk in the mud that they ignore the truth in front of them.

What has exacerbated the current academic crisis, as occurred in the subprime crisis, is the outlawing of opposition views. Just as securities firms fired people not singing the word bomb tune of fake MBSs, having diverse views in academia will get you fired or not accepted into a PhD program. In the academy, as in banking, the authority of experts is rarely questioned. I, for one, generally just took the word of my professors and teaching assistants and assumed a given perspective was legitimate from the point of view of academic standards, even if I was taught to consider different perspectives. Just about all investors take the word of the rating agencies when they judge a security AAA. Even after the Dodd-Frank Act forbade regulators to use rating agency opinions, *everybody* still uses them. Ideas and securities can become loonier and loonier if listeners feel any counterargument will expose them as not quite smart enough or as opponents to valued objectives such as the end of colonialism or access to credit. The incentives to conform are strong in the worlds of finance and academia. And like Zedekiah, who could not save himself even when he knew of his impending doom, it is awfully hard to admit publicly one is wrong and take action even if one knows so in one's heart.

The Bible is replete with examples of royal courts where everyone has to lie. The Book of Esther tells of the court of King Achashverosh, where courtiers were executed, or banished, if they said something that the king did not want to hear. In academia, the incentive is to become ever more extreme and vocal with respect to Zionism. With entire departments voting for BDS resolutions, students face intense pressure to loudly proclaim their denunciations of Israel. Today, being active in Palestinian causes is the required accoutrement and marker of a person's ideological bona fides on many campuses across the nation. In the Soviet Union, Jews joined "Anti-Fascist Committees" and in Iran, at the end of Jewish religious services under the observance of the regime, Jews are obliged to chant, "Death to America" and "Death to Israel."[4] The problem is more than false ideas having taken over a sector of society, in this case the academy. Those who promote these false claims will repress any dissention and, for the moment, nothing is standing in their way. The events at Northwestern in the last two decades have made this shift clear.

IF THERE BE ANY PRAISE 2

THE EROSION OF THE GOLDEN RULE ON NORTHWESTERN CAMPUSES HAS BEEN FACILITATED BY THE UNIVERSITY'S RESPONSE

As an active Northwestern alumnus, I paid some but not a lot of attention to what was happening on campus. During the 1980s, I returned to campus almost every year to do interviews and staff recruiting events for Salomon Brothers. I sought business advice every so often from Gene Lavengood, Gene Lerner, and Joe Swanson, three of my professors at Northwestern's Kellogg School of Management. It was great to be able to buy *them* lunch. I became somewhat involved in alumni events, joining a few committees. A decade ago, after serving on a New York county grand jury, I joined the advisory board for the Medill Justice Project (now the Medill Investigative Lab), which does amazing work. I was not necessarily following trends in the university on any particular topic. Nevertheless, over time I could not help but realize that the university's administration and the faculty had basically turned a blind eye to the erosion of its own standards—that is, the motto—on campus.

In the 1990s, I increasingly understood that the university and students were handling Holocaust denial in ways that at best demonstrated confusion about academic standards, and at worst outright abandon. I was vaguely aware that the tension from Butz's presence on campus had never fully dissipated. In the spring of 1991, I heard that he had written a featured opinion piece for the *Daily Northwestern* explaining why he believed the Holocaust was a hoax.[1] The editors seemed to think they were encouraging freedom of speech. The problem is that giving space to Holocaust denial in a university newspaper is not an issue of freedom of speech. As discussed previously, freedom of speech relates to the right of American citizens to criticize the state; it does not apply to nonstate organizations. The *Daily Northwestern* has no obligation to publish any view that does not meet basic journalistic standards, and the fact that its editors did not understand the meaning of freedom of speech was troubling. To make matters worse, this happened despite the editors being on record for refusing to print other stories on the correct basis that they were unsubstantiated. The *Daily Northwestern* was not welcoming opinion pieces about ancient alien settlers, or how the moon landings were faked, or how the Earth is flat in the name of free speech, yet Butz's claims were about as factual. Nor had the *Daily* ever printed an article that the mistreatment of slaves has been highly exaggerated, yet it was now publishing the equivalent nonsense about the Holocaust. Although there were twelve other essays and articles in the *Daily* that month about Arthur Butz's claims, mostly rebutting them, the whole incident was bizarre. Further, Butz welcomed the flurry of attention, so much so that he added his opinion piece to subsequent editions of his book. How had the university not explained to students the basic principles of journalistic standards and the basic contours of genuine debate? I was troubled.

Things did not improve in the 2000s. In 2003, I was startled to read that the campus had been defiled by swastikas. This was not random. In one case, it happened to two students who had a picture of an Israeli flag on their door. The other was scratched onto a staircase door.[2] One swastika apparently had "Die Jews" on it. Swastikas appeared again on campus in 2015 and 2016.[3] In 2010 and 2014, the menorah in front of the Chabad House near campus was vandalized. Each time I read of far-right action at Northwestern, I recalled the Nazi hate material I received via the intercampus mail. The university did not condone these events, but the response was tepid at best.

In early 2006, Butz made headlines again both in the Chicago media as well as in the *Daily Northwestern* when he responded to Iranian president Mahmoud Ahmadinejad's statement calling the Holocaust a myth and saying that Israel should no longer exist. Butz said, "I congratulate him on becoming the first head of state to speak out clearly on these issues and regret only that it was not a Western head of state."[4] A week later, on February 14, 2006, Butz was then given the opportunity to pen a guest column for the *Daily Northwestern*.[5] In it he commented that one of his friends was serving time in prison in Europe for promoting Holocaust denial, which, he reasoned, corroborated that his false theories must be true. Further, Butz wrote, "For many years I ignored revisionism coming from Islamic countries because I found it inept. With...Ahmadinejad, I found something else, his statements were formidable in their perspicacity."[6]

The responses to Butz's comments and his guest column were abundant and generally very critical. Yet once again, in misunderstanding the concept of free speech, the *Daily Northwestern* also published some supportive letters, such as the one from Michael Hoffman, the editor for Campaign for Radical Truth in History.[7] A quick check on the internet would have revealed that the Southern Poverty Law Center classifies this entity as a hate organization devoted to Holocaust denial.[8] Yet the organization succeeded in having its name promulgated and used a turnaround linguistic style to make Butz a victim when it wrote that criticism of Butz "is a shameful and hateful diatribe which, in the name of fighting hate, makes Butz a target of super-hate....it is a sorrowful blight on the highest aspirations of service to God." Though sixty professors in the McCormick School of Engineering wrote a public petition printed in the *Daily* asking Butz to resign, they did not question why the newspaper of their university, whose standards they were supposed to be upholding, was publicizing these views in the first place. Nor did any of these professors volunteer to teach Butz's lab class and stop forcing undergraduates to be exposed to him.

Why was Holocaust denial again getting a platform at Northwestern due to ignorance of the principle of free speech? No one was addressing this question seriously. Further, since these views received little support among the faculty and students, and Butz himself refrained from promoting his political views in class, the university's stance was that this issue did not seem to affect the overall standards of the classes at the university. In fact, the notion of what should and should not be debated according to the basic standards of evidence described by the motto was being seriously eroded in the college culture by the *Daily Northwestern.*

In the 2010s, I became increasingly disturbed by other instances of the university and its students betraying the motto, this time from the far left. In 2014, Steven Salaita, who Thrasher refers to sympathetically in several tweets and whose writings were discussed above, visited Northwestern after his failure to get tenure. Salaita's proposed tenure contract was rejected by the trustees of the University of Illinois for a professorship in the Native American Studies Department. As *Israel Denial* author Cary Nelson describes in detail, Salaita's modest credentials and the factual errors in his books made him an unlikely candidate for tenure at an institution with the standing of the University of Illinois at Urbana-Champaign. Salaita, however, charged that the non-approval of his tenure arose from Jewish donor pressure, itself a conspiratorial claim, with one of his supporters claiming that the "protesters deluged the chancellor's office with emails."[9] In fact, this claim was untrue—most emails came from non-donors/non-alumni, and only one email was from a $100,000 donor, not a substantial sum for a university with an annual budget of well over $2 billion.[10] (Qatar by itself donated more than $500,000 to the university.)

Donations were not the issue but rather the volume of anti-Zionist Conspiracy Theories in his academic writings and public statements.

As noted above, among his tweets were, "If it's 'antisemitic' to deplore colonization, land theft, and child murder, then what choice does any person of conscience have?" Or "Zionists: transforming anti-Semitism from something horrible into something honorable since 1948."

The controversy was closely followed at Northwestern. The *Daily Northwestern* covered the events of his tenure process and the subsequent lawsuit. On October 5, 2014, the paper featured a Q&A with Salaita,[11] and on October 6, 2014, Salaita spoke to a packed auditorium with a photo and article taking the top half of the *Daily*'s front page under the headline, "Salaita talks free speech after job controversy."[12] The problem with the *Daily Northwestern* coverage of Salaita was that it was uniformly positive. Here, unlike with Butz, no place was given to rebuttals when there should have been. The silence was deafening since there was no shortage of people who were arguing that Salaita's depiction of Zionism was a total distortion of the facts. So, while free speech was used as a reason for giving Butz a platform, as it was to his detractors, it was also used to give Salaita one, though this time without any rebuttal. The failure of the university to address these inconsistencies or misunderstandings about free speech, academic standards, and contours of scholarly debate was astounding.

Over the years, I also heard from time to time of speakers such as Angela Davis, Salaita, and other anti-Zionist Conspiracy Theorists addressing students and being treated as rock stars on campus, again in forums where they were the sole voices to speak and where their ideas went totally unchallenged. The university seemed to show no leadership in establishing uniform standards about which issues deserved a platform at the university and how to provide an environment that encouraged debate. I was dismayed. But nothing prepared me for the events leading up to and following the BDS-backed divestment resolution passed by the Associated Student Government (ASG) of Northwestern in February 2015.

The AGS's BDS resolution was both bizarre and disturbing in what it indicated about Northwestern's maintenance of academic standards, organizational transparency, and campus civility. That the ASG would even consider a BDS resolution was surprising. At the time, it was very rare for the ASG to spend time debating US foreign policy. The ASG generally devoted its attention to issues that could directly impact students on campus. The proponents of the resolution realized this, and as a result they narrowly tailored the resolution to be about the divestment of investment in six companies then doing defense business with Israel, and even more cleverly changed the composition of ASG specifically to get this resolution considered and passed. Of the fifty-one members of ASG, six members at the time were reserved to represent "off campus" students and were not elected by any constituency. (This problem of unelected members was subsequently fixed when the ASG was reduced to forty-one members, which coincided with the elimination of unelected off-campus representatives.) Off-campus candidates applied for appointment to ASG by filling out an application. The divestment proponents sought and were successful in getting appointments to all six seats without indicating that their agenda had anything to do with Israel or Palestine. The final vote was twenty-four in favor, twenty-two against, with three abstentions. These six off-campus ASG representatives were decisive not only in the vote but also in changing the nature of the ASG to make this resolution a priority.

These were not the only unusual features of the campaign. It was meticulously executed with the insightful and astute advice of an administrator of Multi-Cultural Student Affairs at Northwestern and a professor who were behind-the-scenes advisors/mentors to the group. Both cautioned the group not to invoke or acknowledge their names at ASG proceedings, as this was supposed to be a student-led initiative. The campaign included teach-ins, links to almost all far-left organizations, and the delegitimization and demonization in vicious terms of those who opposed the vote. Organizers accused Israel relentlessly of "pink washing" and conducting "apartheid" policies, berated it for causing harm to Palestinians, and touted it as the model of white supremacist colonial domination and oppression of people of color. They also scolded critics of the resolution as "white privileged" Jews, repeating the refrain for critics to "park their privilege" at the door. They further reprimanded Jewish advocates who disagreed for attempting to choke off all criticism of Israel. Many of the proponents of the resolution speeches and admonitions echoed the writings of Jasbir Puar. Their tactics were highly organized and well executed.

Indeed, they had the advantage of a well-prepared surprise attack on anti-BDS advocates and had the added asset of having primed their alliances for timely deployment. It turns out that the Northwestern BDS resolution was part of a larger nationwide strategy duplicated at campuses across the country with less radical student bodies. The modus operandi was always the same: BDS advocates would introduce a resolution *only* demanding selective divestment from a few compa-nies that work with Israel, as well as use whatever means they could to raise the number of pro-BDS voters. Then, if the divestment resolu-tion passed, it would be brandished as a complete victory for BDS and exaggerate the student support for the endeavor. This sort of resolution is part of a more comprehensive and longer-term strategy to actually affect investment in Israel. More about that later.

The response from the university to the BDS resolution again demon-strated that it had no understanding of the implication of this initiative for their standards as an institution. After the resolution was passed, members of the campus community waited for a reaction from the trust-ees and the administration. However, the only reaction that persisted for many months and then years was that the university "was study-ing the resolution." This was in contrast to the reaction from Loyola University of Chicago, located less than four miles from Northwestern, which immediately announced its rejection of its campus student gov-ernment's BDS resolution. Northwestern's non-reaction was frustrating to those who wanted the university to reject the notion of a boycott of the one Jewish-majority nation in the world. The trustees and the uni-versity seemed most determined in their strategy to hope the whole con-troversy would go away and not besmirch the fair name of the school.

After continued non-reaction from the university, and after speaking to a few fellow alumni, I decided to organize an effort to let the university know that the ASG resolution did not speak for most of the Northwestern community. The modest initiative of Samantha Stankowicz, myself, and one other person was to create a web form that interested parties could use to sign on to a petition to the Northwestern community and the trustees. The letter we wrote is reproduced in the appendix. Our efforts, which took place largely through Facebook, garnered about 2,700 signers, all of whom had to disclose their connection to the Northwestern community and affirm approval for their name to be published publicly. Our letter ran in the form of a paid advertisement in the *Daily Northwestern* beginning on April 29, 2015. On the following days, a paragraph summary of the letter was run with the names of as many signers that could be fit legibly on the page until all names were published, which took about two weeks.

The other person involved was a Latina undergraduate student. She was deeply upset by the ASG resolution and fully participated in the initial drafting of the wording of the letter. Just before the first advertisement with our letter was to run, she called me in tears to say that her friends had told her that "she could not be part of pro-Israel work," that signing the letter would be very bad for her and her future association with certain organizations, and end some of her friendships. She said she was still behind us but could not admit so publicly. Her discomfort was discomforting.

The response from the trustees also showed a lack of understanding of the implications of this resolution for university standards. As the petition circulated, I also reached out to four trustees of the university, and several others reached out to me through various connections. Since BDS was ostensibly about how the university invested its endowment, the trustees seemed to be the right address. Some of these trustees had called or met with the president of Northwestern, Morton Schapiro, to express their unhappiness. All of them told me that the topic had only been briefly discussed at a recent board meeting and that some were personally told to let the whole thing blow over. Northwestern had connections with all the major universities in Israel, and the administration assured them that the ASG resolution would have no impact whatsoever on those relationships.

Some trustees told me that the provost, Daniel Linzer, highlighted the concurrent sensitive negotiations with Qatar relating to the Northwestern campus there. Qatar has donated over $500 million to Northwestern, mostly for the Qatar campus but some for Evanston as well. Since Qatar also remains a primary funder of the Hamas-led Gaza government, the renewal of the relationship with Qatar and Qatar's financial commitment meant the less focus on the whole BDS issue, the better. I pushed back against the trustees I spoke with and said that the board had received a recommendation from the ASG and should take a stand one way or the other. I obviously felt that the stand should be that Israel should not be singled out as the sole country on the planet targeted for divestment by Northwestern and pointed to the Loyola statement. About half the trustees I spoke with were Jewish and involved in some way with the Jewish community, but none were willing to take a public position and most didn't contemplate a change in their giving to Northwestern. In one case, a trustee said the resolution would cause them to modify their donations away from endowed professorships to physical spaces—one said, "At least a room or a garden can't become pro-BDS in my name after I give the money." I paraphrase another director who said to me, half in jest, that being a Northwestern trustee is a very big deal...it is a lot higher status than being a board member of the Standard Club. Two of the non-Jewish trustees, who initially weren't tuned into the issue, told me that they planned to speak in more detail with President Schapiro about the resolution and the university's non-response. All of the trustees said they were very sympathetic to President Schapiro because of the pressures he was under and the criticism he was taking specifically because he is Jewish. None of them understood what this selective boycott and the atmosphere around its implementation had done to the university's standards.

Sadly, the incident surrounding the boycott has not been the most extreme case of capitulation by an administration to anti-Zionist pressure that clearly goes against basic moral and intellectual standards. An example from another institution is instructive. The Graduate Theological Union (GTU) of Berkeley, California, is a storied institution that grants master's and doctoral degrees to students from member seminaries, its own departments, and member colleges representing ten faith traditions, including Protestantism, Catholicism, Islam, and Hinduism.

Daniel Lehmann was named president of GTU in August 2018. By most accounts, his start was a resounding success. He expanded GTU's international prominence via missions with faculty members to India and South Korea. He deepened GTU's connections with UC Berkeley and the Berkeley community. He was lauded as a healer for his statements and addresses after the attacks at Poway, Sri Lanka, and Christchurch, New Zealand. He had begun planning a major initiative to add an undergraduate degree program to GTU.

Yet, he had one flaw. He admitted that he was a Zionist. Further troubling to his detractors, he had also been involved in creating a gap-year program for students to study in Israel. Lehmann did not let his personal views limit active pro-Palestine programing at GTU. Nevertheless, faculty, alumni, and some in the community began a vociferous campaign to have him removed. It was successful. The board of GTU encouraged Lehmann to quietly resign. As the anti-Israel *Israel-Palestine News* reported, "Zionist head of major theological consortium pushed out."[13] The story reported that the new administration would "support Palestine programs," giving the erroneous impression that this was not the case under Lehmann.

The forces on President Schapiro may have led him to not condemn the BDS resolution, but rather he referred interested parties to reports about the delegation of Northwestern deans he led to meet leaders of major Israeli universities. Watch his actions, not his words, was his response. Fair enough, but the slow-walking process of study lasted years. Indeed, the university's strategy was essentially one of waiting for the issue to pass. And institutionally, the strategy could be judged as a PR success for a period of time. It was only in the wake of the controversy of Thrasher receiving an appointment at Northwestern that the school issued a full-throated statement condemning BDS signed by President Schapiro and new Provost Jonathan Holloway.[14] But even this condemnation was careful to emphasize Thrasher's academic freedom to hold his pro-BDS views. In other words, the condemnation did not fully explain why BDS was a betrayal of intellectual and moral standards.

I learned two lessons from the university's non-reaction and the post-resolution behavior to the BDS resolution. The first is that the real address for challenging BDS on intellectual and moral grounds is neither the administration, of which presidents are under tremendous conflicting pressures, nor the trustees, who view their posts as largely honorary without the sense that they can impact policies. The right address is the faculty, who are permanent and tenured, which means they can theoretically stand up to any pressures.

At the same time, I also learned that while the faculty are theoretically the right address on campus for addressing intellectual and moral standards in the university, in practice they are the core of the problem. For just as tenure protects faculty and enables them to stand up in the name of truth, it also protects them to promulgate lies. Academic freedom cuts both ways. After all, if enough faculty thought like Arthur Butz, they could fill all new faculty positions with like-minded people and further subject the administration to intense scrutiny if it were to interfere, as happened in the case of Salaita discussed earlier. Would a candidate with a pro-Israel background have a chance to be accepted into, or even want to apply to, the Anthropology Department's PhD program? Thus, even if the faculty is the right address, much like the bankers during the mortgage crisis, they are not easily swayed by their own colleagues, let alone outsiders.

The second address is the student body, for they are who the BDS advocates are trying to win over. Indeed, the reason the Northwestern

BDS advocates were not all that interested in the administration or trustee response, beyond pro forma outrage, is that they never had the slightest delusion that the trustees would divest from any company associated with Israel. That was never the goal. The real aim was to pass any resolution that they could claim once again called out Israel for its purported shameful Nazi-like behavior. As we have previously noted, Puar was explicit that "[BDS] is...such a minor piece of how Palestine is going to be liberated...we need BDS as a part of organized resistance and armed resistance."[15] The BDS advocates' goal, as we have learned from other Conspiracy Theory advocates, was political. It was to convince the majority of the students who are not paying much attention to the Arab-Israeli conflict that Israel is so evil that it must have been appropriate to be singled out for protest and censure. Those who were successfully converted to the decolonial view of the world would also be better at repeating the slogans. The political objective is to get an entire generation to adopt an anti-Zionist stance automatically and without much thought.

Though the corruption of intellectual and moral standards on Zionism is bad enough in itself, it is spilling over into unrelated topics and targeting Jewish students. A striking example of this occurred in 2017 after the Trump ban on travel from various Muslim countries. The outcry was immediate across the US from all progressive organizations. In the Jewish community, feelings were intense as well, since Jews have been forced to immigrate so many times in the past. As a result, many Jewish charity and advocacy organizations felt it incumbent to issue denunciations of the new policy. Yet despite this record, Jewish groups at Northwestern were not invited to join the broad coalition of organizations that planned major protests and walkouts on February 1, 2017.

Nevertheless, despite this conspicuous exclusion, a substantial number of Jewish students did attend the rallies. At a major rally in front of the Multicultural Center, attendees were greeted by three major banners that proclaimed their dissatisfaction with and defiance of the travel ban. After the crowd assembled and the speeches began, a new banner was unfurled over those banners, which read, "If you support Israeli apartheid you support the Muslim ban." A senior lecturer in the Philosophy Department, Mark Sheldon, wrote a letter to the *Daily Northwestern*,[16] distraught because "the walkout's purpose was derailed by anti-Israel sentiment"[17] and that organizers even admitted that the unfurling was always part of the plan. He noted that the focus should have been entirely on opposing the travel ban and that a unifying opportunity was "squandered."

The response to Sheldon's letter was ferocious. He was criticized for not recognizing the "intersectional perspective" and his motives were impugned. One person wrote, "Now is not the time to arrive at a demonstration, take the fruits of their labor and then attack a core aspect of their movement."[18] Sheldon was also alleged to be "reinforce[ing] the erasure of the Palestinian people and of the continual punishment inflicted on them by Israel but [he] also deploys a common trope of colonial paternalistic thought by defining and then explaining...It is shocking and that, in the protest, amid waves of disenfranchised bodies working to end the myth of American exceptionalism, one can manage to promote Israeli exceptionalism!"[19] Sheldon's implicit motives for attending the march were alleged not to have been about Muslims but about a personal political agenda. Though Sheldon's letter did not go beyond suggesting the creation of as broad a coalition as possible for combating the travel ban, his motives were described as impure and designed to undermine other objectives. The corruption in this instance reached several levels: not only were anti-Zionist views themselves based on lies being paraded unchallenged but their advocates were making baseless and unsubstantiated connections between support for Israel and the Muslim travel ban, and even worse, falsely accusing those who did not think like them. The whole event strayed very far from the intellectual and moral standards one would expect at a university.

Unfortunately, this type of incident is all too common. Blake Flayton wrote in the *New York Times*[20] of his experiences as a very left-wing student attending rallies on topics such as fair wages and having them turn into "Free Palestine" events. He described having been called a "baby killer" and an "apartheid enabler." All of these names are bullying tactics meant to demonize opponents and stifle debate. The message is increasingly that Palestine is at the heart of all progressive issues—a truly bizarre equation. And for those who don't agree, particularly Jews, the only option is to sit down and shut up.

As BDS initiatives on campus increased, I did not at first realize it, but de facto boycott and divestment from Israel was being enabled less than two miles from Northwestern's Chicago campus at the global headquarters of Morningstar, Inc. based in part on campus BDS resolutions. There the worthy goal of responsible investing was *in practice* promoting boycotting and divesting from Israel. Morningstar, one of the most significant investment research firms and credit rating agencies in the world and the parent of Sustainalytics, was early to recognize that "the importance of environmental, social, and governance criteria is growing rapidly around the world. In response, asset managers are increasingly incorporating ESG-focused strategies.... Quantitative measures such as the Morningstar Sustainability Rating...can help investors assess ESG risk characteristics."[21] Indeed it does not make sense to be worried about climate change and to simultaneously buy stocks of companies that are not taking steps to reduce their carbon impact. As a result, companies and investment funds are making major efforts to adjust their activities and investing criteria accordingly. For example, "BlackRock in January 2020 declared its desire to augment and extend its existing ESG efforts throughout its organization. The world's largest money manager's vow could prove to be a turning point for the industry—a sign that investment firms can no longer ignore ESG risks."[22]

The goal of ESG scores is to impact company actions. Numerical scores from these products help determine which companies receive investment monies and which mutual funds are recommended. Thus, if a mutual fund has a low ESG score, it will be less likely to be recommended despite positive performance, as such assets from the mutual fund will drain away over time and the managers will either earn less or be fired. Mutual funds and other institutional investment firms that are also evaluated by their ESG scores will of course avoid investing in companies with low ESG scores causing in turn their stock prices to drop. Conceptually that is all good since it encourages companies to improve their practices in order to improve their scores. The devil is, as they say, in the details, as I will describe below. But first, more on Morningstar's place in the investment world and its modus operandi.

Morningstar has become an almost ubiquitous presence for scoring companies regarding environmental and social policies as well as governance. Investment firms and companies face a dilemma since they want to embrace ESG, but they often don't know how to apply it when considering thousands of investment opportunities. Hence, they rely on Morningstar and Sustainalytics quantitative products, which is why they are so widely embraced. In fact, one senior manager of a top investment firm told me that Morningstar/Sustainalytics products were embedded in so many products and internal analyses at his firm that it would be hard to figure out where they stop. Further, when major investment banks give client advice on ESG, more often than not their advice is to pay close attention to Morningstar. To cite just one presentation from a top investment bank: "Ignore the noise...it is important to focus your efforts on the key providers most commonly used by investors—MSCI and Sustainalytics. Understand which factors might get you screened out...monitor controversy scores...business involvement screens [are vital to] understand which controversial business involvement will get you flagged." Being "flagged" effectively means being eliminated from investment consideration.

While Morningstar's business is to provide ESG scores and to encourage transparency, ironically, they are secretive about just how their own scores are judged. The only source information is

Morningstar's confidential reports and the writings of outside advisors. Regarding the former, since most Morningstar/Sustainalytics research reports and analysis are proprietary and are provided to clients only on a confidential basis, outsiders are not permitted to evaluate them. Even clients such as the senior manager of the investment firm referred to above has little choice but to simply trust the Morningstar family of products. In fact, the above-mentioned senior manager not only did not know how the scores were computed, but he was also not familiar with some issues that drove the scores. And he had no idea anything related to Israel mattered in the score. Further, there are no objective outside evaluators of Sustainalytics reports. As to the latter, though Morningstar does disclose and feature some of its outside advisors, it is hard to determine their impact on the ratings criteria since it is impossible to know if the ratings criteria emanate from the outside advisors or if the roster of outside advisers is curated to fit the internal desires of Morningstar, though the latter is the most likely. I had the opportunity to review some information on the advisors and to read some of the underlying Sustainalytics reports from sources who have direct access to them. And while I cannot say I have done a comprehensive review because as noted above, access is restricted, I believe that Morningstar facilitates boycotts and divestment from many companies that are either Israeli or do business with Israel.

A review of the outside advisors to Morningstar will indicate that when it comes to Israel, they either believe in BDS or something close to it. Company articles spotlighting these advisors note their belief in limiting investments related to Israel, among other views. One Morningstar published article reported on an advisor's list of about one hundred companies out of many thousands that should be eliminated from investment consideration, with fifty-nine being companies doing business with Israel.[23] I could find no countervailing voices among Morningstar articles or publicly disclosed advisors.

Morningstar reports also show similar support for BDS. I was stunned to see that Morningstar uses student government BDS resolutions as part of the inputs for its quantitative ESG scoring. Indeed, the return receipts for campus BDS resolutions, such as from the Northwestern ASG, are on Morningstar reports of individual companies. This shows that its subsidiary Sustainalytics uses sources that support BDS as primary inputs. An example of one Sustainalytics recent ESG review notes, "University...students named several companies, including [the company being examined] in an approved referendum in which they demanded the university not to invest in corporations complicit in human-rights abuses in the Palestinian territories...." There was no evidence of the company's products being used illegally. And it fits squarely into the BDS narrative that allegations against Israel need not be proven and theories about Israel need not be falsifiable. But of course, this relates to Israel so even common products must be assumed to be used in devious ways by the Jews. Sustainalytics cites many profoundly anti-Zionist sources. These include Danwatch, the Electronic Intifada, Who Profits, Mondoweiss, and even on occasion, the *Iran Daily* (an official government newspaper whose policy is the destruction of Israel). Pro-Israel publications were not cited unless the publication was reporting on anti-Zionist news of some sort. According to the company reports, these anti-Zionist outlets are "revealing" some sort of bad thing Israel is doing or are "issuing a report" on Israel's evilness. When the lack of evidence is self-apparent, the reports simply note that the said BDS organization "continues to investigate the issue." There were no pro-Israel sentiments, mitigating circumstances, or explanations expressed in any cited company report I was able to review. It was as Manichean as it gets. The conspiratorial language used when referring to Israel was absent elsewhere in Sustainalytics reports where a more sober tone was generally conveyed.

Controversy scores involving Israel quickly ascend. It does not take too much involvement with Israel to cause a score of 3 or 4. (A 4 rating is very high. 5 ratings are rare.) These scores are critical because they are directly inputted into algorithms and models that determine the composition of investment portfolios. This means that a person in

Peoria who has no intention or desire to boycott Israel will still have her portfolio underweighted to Israel. Their portfolio will also be less likely to invest in mutual funds that invest in the designated companies. It is still possible for Israel investments to be funded, but the bar is higher because the Morningstar scoring is a factor. This is the quiet boycott of Israel that few recognize. JLens, an investor network that emphasizes impact investing, socially responsible investing, and corporate social responsibility via a Jewish lens was among the first to notice the anti-Israel bent of Morningstar and Morningstar's murkiness in its ratings when it comes to Israel.

Morningstar of course denies an anti-Israel or anti-Jewish bias. When I brought this issue to the attention of some investment professionals, they asked their Morningstar representatives about whether or not the Morningstar investment tools had an anti-Israel bias. They all received more or less the same response—Morningstar determined the three disputed territories in the world to focus on from "client requests." These disputed territories are Palestine, Western Sahara, and Tibet, as of the time of this writing. The representatives emphasized that this has nothing whatsoever to do with the company's preferences but with client demand. That only three territories are mentioned when there are about one hundred disputed territories in the world is in itself suspect. Further, Tibet and Western Sahara have relatively few direct investment opportunities. The Tibetan companies are all listed on Chinese exchanges and their ESG score has no impact. Sustainalytics could have swapped Tibet for the Principality of Madripoor with the same real world economic impact. Western Sahara does have some Western companies which operate in resource extraction, but it is still a comparably small market. Based on the Sustainalytics reports I was able to review, Israel and the Palestinian territories receive the overwhelming bulk of attention. Nevertheless, by including these two other disputes Morningstar can claim it does not solely target Israel.

In contrast, when Morningstar representatives are asked about creating a portfolio that is pro-Israel, their answers are evasive. One investment professional directly posed the following question: "I have a lot of Jewish clients who want to invest in Israel and want to avoid companies that are involved in BDS. Do you have a tool for that?" The answer, after many paragraphs, was "no." On the other hand, it is very easy to create a means for excluding companies involved with Israel using the Sustainalytics platform. While Morningstar denies it is pro-BDS as a matter of corporate policy, I believe its tools are certainly BDS friendly and enabling.

So, what is to be done? There is no government regulation of ESG ratings, and I do not think there should be, but rating criteria should be transparent and accessible. The danger of government-imposed standards is that they might change dramatically depending on what party is in power, which could lead not only to government allocation of investment but to dramatic changes every few years. Yet to maintain their own credibility, ESG rating providers must be crystal clear and transparent as to how ratings are determined. ESG ratings providers also must provide open architecture that would allow individuals, mutual funds, and investment firms to input their own values when it comes to controversy scores. This means providing more information to the public without charge and hiring outside auditing firms to certify that ESG rating providers are producing unbiased ratings. Calls for outside evaluation of credit rating agencies from both inside and outside the financial sector have increased since the mortgage crisis revealed how woefully short their standards and procedures had become. Even more recently the SEC sued Morningstar on February 16, 2021, alleging that Morningstar "permitted analysts to make undisclosed adjustments to key stresses in the model that it used in determining the rating."[24] Morningstar responded that it vigorously disputes the charges and believes that by making the charges the SEC is, among other contentions, violating the independence of rating agencies.[25]

It is hard to avoid wondering why academics allege that there is "compulsory Zionism" in the academy or elsewhere. Anthropology departments are full of anti-Zionist faculty and de facto boycotts in the business world are even substantiated by anti-Zionist activities on campus with little outcry. If the Jews really were so smart, powerful, and controlling, they would certainly reallocate their resources. After spending considerable time reading Morningstar/Sustainalytics reports, I was reminded of the small black smear of tar that was quietly applied to the signs of Jewishly owned shops in Sveksna. A discrete signal was sufficient. Due to the algorithmic nature of modern portfolio investing, Morningstar ESG ratings go further, resulting in some investors' portfolios spurning Israel-related investments without being given a choice. That would seem to be a good definition of compulsory anti-Zionism.

The corruption of intellectual and moral standards at Northwestern even affects Palestinians who don't toe the party line. In February 2016, the Northwestern Hillel planned to host Bassem Eid, the founder of Palestinian Human Rights Monitoring Group. Eid's previous two events in the Chicago area were disrupted by Students for Justice in Palestine (SJP) activists who were "shouting at him, insulting him in Arabic and English...Eid's organization monitors human rights violations by both Israel and the Palestinian National Authority."[26] Speakers who relate to Israel in any way other than as a pariah state to be dismantled, even if Arab, draw criticism and disruption on campus, as does any attempt to discuss Palestinian politics critically. In this case it is ironic, though not surprising, that the far left and far right don't accept the testimony of the members of the victim group if they don't confirm their already held prejudices.

About three months after Eid's attempted visit, Students for Justice in Palestine invited Rasmea Odeh to speak on campus. Odeh was convicted of participating in the murder of two Israeli college students. She claims that she was tortured to make a confession. She was freed in a prisoner swap in 1979 and entered the United States. She agreed to a plea deal in the US for lying on her naturalization papers. Her penalty was that her citizenship was revoked and she was to be deported. There is no controversy over her active involvement in the Popular Front for the Liberation of Palestine (PFLP), which had conducted multiple terrorist attacks. The contrast between Eid's reception and Odeh's could not be any stronger. Odeh's speech was not impaired in any way. Instead, there was a silent protest/vigil outside the building in which she spoke, which was in memory of the two college students murdered by the PFLP. The reaction of SJP was that the vigil by Jewish students was "reactionary" and they were "disrespectful." It should be noted that President Schapiro, to his great credit, also stood silently as part of the vigil, an act for which he was harshly criticized by SJP as well.[27]

The corruption of moral and intellectual standards can also be seen in debates about anti-Semitism at Northwestern. In Jewish Voice for Peace's 2017 *On Antisemitism*,[28] anti-Jewish sentiment is defined very narrowly. According to JVP, Zionism is depicted as a central form of anti-Semitism, as it causes harm to those Jews who are part of the Palestinian coalition. Jews who are in favor of Jewish national self-determination are in contrast the cause of their own misery and therefore not the victims of anti-Semitism. This is an identical construct to the far right's view that Jews/Zionists cause Jewish hatred to befall other Jews. Most on the far right allege that if any Jews died in the Holocaust, it was other Jews, specifically Zionist Jews, who were responsible for this happening (we recall Heidegger's view of the concentration camps as places of self-destruction).

SJP at Northwestern takes the party line. One example among many is its very harsh critique of an opinion piece authored by a Jewish student, Zach Kessel. Kessel's column on January 13, 2020, written in the aftermath of the shooting and murder at a kosher supermarket in Jersey City, New Jersey, faults both the left and the right for not denouncing anti-Semitism to their respective adherents.[29] Israel is barely mentioned except for his quoting Linda Sarsour's statement "that Israel is 'based on the idea that Jews are supreme to everyone else,'"[30] which he wrote as an example of a failure on the left. In short, Kessel argued that anti-Semitism should not be used as a "political tool."

The response to the column was filled with demonizing rhetoric meant to shut Kessel down rather than address his views in a meaningful way. SJP called the column "filled with blatant lies," and stated that "anti-Semitism within its own piece [is] harmful not only to the Jewish community." Kessel's approach is "not genuine in tackling anti-Semitism...Instead of locating anti-Semitism within a larger logic of white supremacy, Kessel vilifies Representative Talib, a non-Jewish person of color...We must be stringent in what we consider anti-Semitic."[31] Further, the letter is filled with word bombs such as "we must denounce Zionism as a settler colonial project steeped in white supremacist ideology."[32] The problem is not only in the bullying tone used against Kessel; it is much deeper. JVP's definition of anti-Semitism is at odds with any understanding of discrimination applied to any other group on either intellectual or moral grounds.

The corruption of intellectual and moral standards is now entrenched. As we have learned from author Mary Douglas, "Purity is the enemy of change, of ambiguity and compromise."[33] To protect all this "from skepticism is to suppose that an enemy, within or without the community, is continually undoing its good effect."[34] One way to cancel this pollution, this dirt, "is the confessional rite,"[35] where "the polluter becomes a doubly wicked object of reprobation."[36] The only way for a Jew to escape that situation of impurity is to join the Yevsektsiya, the Anti-Fascist Committee, or JVP and confess in a public ritual that they are not part of this pollution. For the far right, there is no confessional rite for Jews/Zionists themselves, just destruction, but confession is necessary for the far left. It does not matter how incomprehensible an argument against Jewish self-determination is; it must be acknowledged as totally true and obviously apparent to all fair-minded people. There is no compromise since Zionism is a conspiracy to hurt others. Even a Jewish member of a student government who does not ostentatiously renounce Zionism becomes a danger for all those around them and must be eliminated.

Sadly, there are more examples of this logic in universities today. Rose Ritch, vice president of the USC student government, felt forced to resign over harassment that included an effort "to impeach her Zionist ass." Her resignation made the formal impeachment resolution moot.[37]

Another example of the supremacy of purity comes from the 2020 congressional campaign of Georgette Gómez, who was a serious contender for the seat of the Fifty-Third Congressional District in California. She is a queer Latina progressive whose positions and identity check all the boxes of the political action committee Justice Democrats, except for one—she has admitted to being in favor of a two-state solution, in favor of granting aid to both Israel and the Palestinian National Authority, and has said she disagrees with this particular stance of Justice Democrats. In response, sixty progressive delegates to the Democratic National Convention wrote to Justice Democrats urging that it revoke its endorsement of Gómez. While Justice Democrats did not do so, they did stop spending money on her behalf and went radio silent on her candidacy.[38] The anti-Israel website Mondoweiss made this point explicit in an article authored by several organizations, "How Liberal Zionism Hurts Us More."[39] The article explained that one can agree with progressives on everything else, but if one is not a loud anti-Zionist, it is "undeniable" that the errant progressive is "culpable" with a process that harms everyone everywhere who cares about progressive values. The article states that Gómez is either a hypocrite, does not understand anything about the history of Israel, or is repeating propaganda lines.[40] For the writers of this article, not being opposed to the state of Israel is a crime, but to impersonate a progressive and still support a two-state solution is indeed to be a false-faced infiltrator—a most traitorous position. For the far left, not being loudly anti-Zionist is now as much of a crime as being a Zionist.

In the wake of the 2020 protests against police brutality against Blacks, a student group called NU Community Not Cops (NUCNC) organized nightly demonstrations on campus and in the surrounding town of Evanston to advocate for the abolition of the Northwestern University Police Department. At first the administration tried to ignore or downplay the controversy as it had successfully done with respect to the ASG BDS resolution. The October demonstrations persisted, and on one particular evening there was some vandalizing: the spray-painting of some local businesses, a smashed grocery store window, and a controversial ending of the evening at President Schapiro's home. The mayor of Evanston issued a statement supporting peaceful protests but condemning the destruction of property. The demonstration at President Schapiro's home included chants of "Piggy Morty" and "F—k you, Morty" among others.[41] In response, President Schapiro wrote an email to the Northwestern community stating in part:

> Many gathered outside my home this weekend into the early hours of the morning, chanting "f— you Morty" and "piggy Morty"... The latter comes dangerously close to a longstanding trope against observant Jews like myself. Whether it was done out of ignorance or out of anti-Semitism, it is completely unacceptable, and I ask them to consider how their parents and siblings would feel if a group came to their homes in the middle of the night to wake up their families with such vile and personal attacks.[42]

The response from NUCNC was swift and unapologetic:

> We do not apologize to Morton Schapiro. False claims of anti-Semitism have been used throughout Northwestern's history to shut down student activists, especially Palestinian activists, and to divide coalitions by falsely claiming that anti-Zionism is anti-Semitism. Because of the pervasive myths of colonialism and white supremacy, we find ourselves having to repeat: anti-Zionism is not anti-Semitism. We continue to stand in solidarity with Palestinian liberation by our shared virtue of abolition.[43]

The group also suggested that the pig connotation of Jews was a fourteenth-century relic and no longer very relevant.[44] The response was disturbing on several counts, demonstrating a doctrinal, not fact-based approach. Indeed, even a perfunctory Google search of "Jews and pigs" shows that this anti-Jewish trope is not limited to fourteenth-century depictions of Jews in the form of gargoyles sucking from the teats of pigs. In fact, pig images are common anti-Jewish tropes. The rock musician Roger Waters regularly depicts images of the Star of David on large pig balloons at his concerts. Many neo-Nazi illustrations depict Jews and pigs together.

Further, contrary to the accusation in the response, Northwestern doesn't have any history of using Zionism to shut down activists (though as noted, Northwestern did have a long history of a "Jewish quota" in its admissions policy). Schapiro did not even raise the issue of Zionism, so there is no external reason why NUCNC felt it was "having to repeat: anti-Zionism is not anti-Semitism." It would seem to be a non sequitur to the conversation, though it was a central accusation against Schapiro. However, this insertion was not entirely surprising since the issue of anti-Zionism was actually a common trope of NUCNC unconnected to Schapiro's statement.[45] NUCNC made it clear: you cannot share progressive values with them unless you are against Israel.[46] In their view, opposing Zionism is inextricably linked to the Northwestern University Police Department issue. Finally, the NUCNC also felt empowered to define anti-Semitism in ways that most Jews would not identify with.

All of these statements and positions were left totally unchallenged by faculty and other students. Instead, forty-two present Jewish students and fifty Jewish graduates signed a letter to the *Daily Northwestern* in which they endorsed the NUCNC protesters and affirmed their alignment with NUCNC, stating that they "refuse to let debates over Israel-Palestine derail the necessary work of student organizers demanding the abolition of NUPD."[47] One current student who signed the letter confided that they disagreed with the letter's statement on Israel but signed it anyway to ally with the protesters. Not to have signed would have derailed that person's participation in certain progressive campus organizations. Blake Flayton reported an Instagram note he received: "I don't even identify as a Zionist, but Jewish students like me [at Northwestern] are being completely gaslit by an organization we overwhelmingly supported." Another message he received said, "I am a little worried for myself and my fellow [Northwestern] Jewish students right now."[48] The atmosphere had moved from a failure to denounce the lack of intellectual and moral standards on Zionism to the open and flagrant bullying of those who did not instantaneously fall into political line.

In the wake of the May 2021 Gaza-Israel conflict, the ASG once again was called to action. Much had changed in six years. This time, a resolution was introduced, debated, and passed by a 20-2 margin in less than two days. The resolution made explicit references to "Zionist settler-colonialism," that "since 1948 [there] has been an ongoing Nakba, or disaster, that has fractured Palestinian society" and that "Palestinian and Muslim students...have been silenced and left out for far too long in this discourse."[49] This reference made it clear that all of Israel was a settler colony and therefore illegitimate. Indeed, while carefully written so as not to openly call for Israel's destruction, a fair reading of the resolution is that Israel does not have the right to exist. The 2021 resolution also reaffirmed the 2015 BDS resolution. Further, a discussion of the conflict in terms of basic principles of international law, which does put limits on both state and non-state actors no matter how one views them, was also absent. The discourse was Manichean, and impatience was displayed in the meeting with any attempt to amend the definition of anti-Semitism in the resolution, let alone discuss whether Israel was in fact a settler colonial state.

Also, in the wake of the Gaza conflict on June 7, 2021, NUCNC tweeted that "we stand in solidarity with @SJPNU and Palestine in the midst of state-sanctioned genocide by the hands of Israel...Black liberation and Palestinian liberation are intertwined. FROM THE RIVER TO THE SEA PALESTINE WILL BE FREE."

The banality of opposition to Israel incorporating the widespread dissemination of Conspiracy Theories at Northwestern is disheartening. The intensity, ferociousness, and demonizing characterizations of anyone who steps out of line to defend Jewish self-determination in any way is a given because Zionism is defined as a central evil in the world. Anyone associated with Zionism must have ulterior and mendacious motives for anything they do. Jewish members of the community may not safely bring speakers on campus, and if they protest in the mildest way, they are castigated. Students who want to be progressive but still pro-Israel are banished. The call I received from the Latina student who worked with me on the draft of the anti-BDS petition telling me how she was bullied over her willingness to express a negative view on the ASG resolution was demoralizing to this Northwestern alum.

Other trends in the university show that theory is now trumping facts, with serious consequences for intellectual and moral standards. One indicator is ideological uniformity. An article in *Econ Journal Watch* analyzed a range of academic departments across forty major universities and determined that politically liberal professors outnumbered politically conservative professors by a ratio of 12 to 1.[50] This creates an amen chorus that enables departments to drift further from academic rigor and toward doctrine, as well as idolatrous polarization and demonization.

In a study titled "Lethal Mass Partisanship,"[51] Nathan Kalmoe and Lilliana Mason demonstrate just how much we have begun to hate each other. About 60 percent of the members of both parties think that the opposing party is a serious threat to the US and its people. The survey, conducted in 2017, showed that 18 percent of Democrats and 13 percent of Republicans said they would approve of violence if their party's candidate lost, while 12 percent of Republicans and 11 percent of Democrats think it is at times acceptable to send threatening messages to public officials. On January 6, 2021, the US found that this survey was prophetic with the storming of the US Capitol. This study further revealed that 15 percent of Republicans and 20 percent of Democrats say the country would be better off if large numbers of the opposing party "just died."

In another article, "The Partisan Mind: Is Extreme Political Partisanship Related to Cognitive Inflexibility?"[52] three University of Cambridge faculty members surveyed seven hundred Americans and found that extreme partisanship was indeed closely linked with those who see the world in terms of us versus them, Manichean good and bad, without pondering any of the shades in the middle. Extreme folks on both sides have ceded part of their reasoning power to their belief system. (Tyler Cowen of George Mason University claims that as a rule of thumb, if one views an issue in terms of good versus evil, that person should assume that their IQ is lowered by ten points.[53]) Extremely partisan individuals don't need to ponder shifting information; they already know the answer. The Cambridge authors proffer Eric Hoffer's insight that any extreme movement appeals to those with the same sorts of mindsets, which Hoffer also linked to adherents' personal frustration. This fits squarely with the definition of idolatry we discussed earlier and to the commonalities of the extreme right and left. Adherents belong to one group or another. Their group, their leader, their ideology is all good and those of others are all bad. The facts no longer matter. By being part of the group, the individual gets to taste the power of the leader.

Another indicator of partisanship is a willingness to massage the facts to fit a theory or desired outcome. These days, 70 percent of scientists say that they have tried and failed to reproduce the experiments of others.[54] In 2005, John Ioannidis, professor of medicine and meta-science at Stanford University, authored an article that could have been entitled "Why the Emperor Has No Clothes" but was instead titled "Why Most Published Research Findings are False."[55] It is not so much that the research coming out of universities is a fraud (although 14 percent of researchers have said that they personally knew someone who had falsified data).[56] Rather, the desire for professional advancement, pressure to publish, the need to write something novel, and pro forma peer review enable academics who are wedded to their theories to have free rein to torture the data until it speaks. The problem is especially serious in the social sciences, where the factors are squishy and the stakes high. In the realm of psychology, a study in which results of experiments were retested found that 61 percent had null results.[57] In economics, a 2017 article in the *Economic Journal* found that "the majority of average effects...are exaggerated by a factor of at least 2 and at least one-third are exaggerated by a factor of 4 or more."[58]

I graduated from Northwestern believing that a college education would inoculate a person from believing in groundless Conspiracy Theories. After all, college allegedly taught that evidence is indispensable to proving any proposition. Hypotheses and theories were to be presented with openness, even eagerness, to let others try to disprove them, not idolize them. Contradictory evidence meant a theory was wrong, not that negative evidence is a proof that evil people and mysterious forces had successfully covered their tracks. Data was treated as sacrosanct, the academic equivalent of the "holy of holies," and could not be tampered with. Reproducibility of experiments was the gold standard.

Today, sadly, the opposite is often true. When a person graduates from college, they are so very susceptible to being conscripted to one or another theory. This is not just my intuition. In a study conducted by Professor Jay Greene, Professor Albert Cheng, and Dr. Ian Kingsbury, 1,800 Americans were asked seven parallel questions about Jews and other ethnic groups, and Israel and other countries.[59] For example, should the military prohibit a Jewish yarmulke or the parallel question, a Sikh turban? The dual loyalty question was posed with respect to Mexico and Israel. Neither group knew of the other group's questions and the statistical weightings were designed to be broadly representative of the US. Of the seven questions, four were the most similar "and which the overall sample answered roughly in the same way, subjects with college degrees were 5 percentage points more likely to apply a principle [more] harshly to Jews than to non-Jews. Among those with advanced degrees, subjects were 15 percentage points more unfavorable toward Jewish than non-Jewish examples." As the study notes, "if more-highly educated people are more hostile with respect to Jews, higher educational levels and more courses and training could increase prejudice rather than diminish it."

It is an intellectual version of antibody-dependent enhancement. ADE is the phenomenon in which some vaccines cause a person's second exposure to a disease to be worse than if they had not had the vaccine. College graduates may become so comfortable with outlandish theories unsupported by facts that crazy Conspiracy Theories like QAnon seem to be logical. The leadership of far-right groups are all college graduates and, in many cases, have advanced degrees from well-regarded universities.

THINK ON THESE THINGS

(RE)TURNING TO THE GOLDEN RULE

This book has argued that Conspiracy Theories have infiltrated Northwestern and other universities in the United States. Faculty members at Northwestern and many other universities are teaching, publishing, and presenting Conspiracy Theories. College newspapers are giving Conspiracy Theorists a voice. BDS resolutions are being passed "because that is what we are called to do," and members of the university community are demonized, bullied, silenced, marginalized, fired, or not hired if they don't salute to these Conspiracy Theories. For those who think this problem is limited to anti-Zionist Conspiracy Theories and therefore not a major worry, historical precedents point otherwise. In the words of the late Rabbi Jonathan Sacks, "The hate that begins with the Jews never ends with the Jews." None of this corruption would have been possible if faculty, the administration, and students had collectively upheld the motto and the Golden Rule.

So, is there a solution?

We can start from what we know does not work. Limiting academic freedom is a bad idea. Not only is academic freedom a core precept of Western intellectual tradition, it cuts both ways: limits on the freedom of those who are undermining the university today could be used to limit the freedom of those who will uphold it tomorrow. To have government or some outside authority oversee tenure, hiring, promotion, or academic inquiry would be another level of politicization and could lead to the further corruption of what is already a defective-enough system. Nor do trustees or administrators want to get involved.

Further, the purpose of keeping academic freedom in the hands of the faculty is because they are supposedly the experts in the field and therefore the only ones qualified to make decisions in the name of the standards and advancement of knowledge while being removed from political and economic considerations. We know that one of the first things totalitarian regimes on the right and left do is co-opt the universities. Yet we have the problem that the current tenure system and peer-review process, which are supposed to ensure academic standards, are failing. Right now, there is nothing in the system stopping corrupt faculty from hiring other corrupt faculty, or from supporting their tenure applications, or from giving a corrupt book flying colors in a peer review of the manuscript. This is already the case with anti-Zionist Conspiracy Theories. In other words, all of the current standards are only as good as their gatekeepers. And if the gatekeepers waive their role to ferret out defective scholarship, the ripple effect extends, as we have seen, to the whole system. Knowledge itself becomes corrupted. When this happens, the prophets we trust turn out to be false prophets.

The Bible anticipated this problem by arguing that no institutional framework, however well intentioned, can overcome individuals who work to subvert it. Though the biblical kings were mandated to have limited executive powers, in practice they gathered too much power to themselves and used that power corruptly. Their corruption then rippled into all areas of society. By turning lies into truth, they corrupted the courts and the priesthood. Then opportunists who claimed to be prophets arose who mimicked whatever the king wanted to hear. Ultimately, the whole society became corrupted because the people had listened to so many lies, they could not recognize truth.

Jeremiah pointed this out many times. The Book of Jeremiah (chapters 42 and 43) continues the story mentioned earlier of the useful Jew,

Ishmael ben Nethaniah, who assassinated Gedalia. The remaining people, bereft and dispirited, pled with Jeremiah to tell them the truth of whether to stay in the land of Israel. After ten days, Jeremiah returned to the people and told them the full truth. They should stay in the land. It would be tough, very tough. It would take time to rebuild, but they could do it over generations. Yet instead of taking Jeremiah at face value, the people thought that Jeremiah was lying and so they decided to go to Egypt. Not only that, they forcibly took Jeremiah with them, thinking that they were doing him a favor. The Israelites had been told before: going back to Egypt would signal a serious regression to the worst of times. But they didn't get it, because they had been lied to and were confused for so very long by the kings and false prophets who were supposed to lead them. As James Madison put it, "I go on this great republican principle that the people will...select [leaders] of virtue and wisdom. Is there no virtue among us? If there be not, we are in a wretched situation. No theoretical checks—no form of government can render us secure."[1]

Given this problem, the Bible describes the moral and intellectual qualities that are needed for judges, teachers, and leaders. When it comes to seeking judges and teachers, the Bible has a fourfold test (Exodus 18:21): they must be courageous; they must be God-fearing (not fearing what others think); they must be dedicated to truth; and they must "hate money" (i.e., hate corruption). The Bible thus combines moral qualities, courage, hating corruption, and indifference to what others think, with an intellectual one: a dedication to truth.

The biblical importance of these traits can be seen in numerous instances. Judah was willing to be a slave for life in exchange for Benjamin's freedom, showing valor and a fear of God. (Genesis, chapter 44) Moses stood up for the Israelite slave being beaten to death even though he was imperiling his own position as a prince and even his life (showing courage, fear of God, and indifference to royal riches). (Exodus 2:11–15) The same qualities were present in Princess Yehosheva, who preserved the Davidic dynasty by saving the only legitimate heir and hiding that heir from Queen Athalia. (2 Kings 11:2) They were present in Devorah, who departed from judging under her palm tree to become the military commander against the Canaanites. (Judges 4:5–9) And they were present in Esther (Esther 4:16), who bet her life on subtly getting the Persian King Achashverosh to understand that Haman's plot endangered not only the Jews but the king as well. The heroes of the Bible stood up for righteousness in the face of powers that would have predisposed them to take the easier path of compliant nonresistance. In each instance, they not only showed courage but a dedication to truth and their principles and a hatred of corruption. The commitment to intellectual and moral standards is inseparable.

Addressing the problem of corruption in the university requires recognizing—as the motto does—that intellectual and moral brilliance are not synonymous. One time, when my father was dropping me off at my dorm at Northwestern, he said that he knew there were an awful lot of smart people there, but brains alone weren't sufficient. Being, as he put it, "book smart" does not mean you understand right from wrong; it just makes you think you do. I took what my father said at the time as a sort of a personal put-down, but again, years later, I tardily realize he was right. You don't get to be a faculty member unless you are very smart, but being smart is no predictor of compassion or of any other virtue. Eight of the fifteen participants in the Wannsee Conference in 1942 who organized the "Final Solution" had doctorates. When Jews arrived at work and concentration camps, the selection of who would be put to slave labor and who would be murdered immediately was given to medical doctors. Ashley Fernandes (an MD, PhD) writes that "as a physician, you must serve the patient exclusively—not some abstracted idea of 'society.'" Physicians and health professionals in Nazi Germany decided that the good of the racial state took precedence over the good of individual persons."[2] Once the Golden Rule was set aside and doctors decided to treat society as the patient, true evil exploded. In trying to proscribe programs for identity groups, classes, and the like in ways that contravene the Golden Rule, academia is chancing a walk on this same troubled road. Yes, as Hannah Arendt argued, evil can be banal, but that banality was executed by highly educated, smart, and sophisticated individuals. They were geniuses at self-justification.

The Bible also recounts many stories where smarts and morals are in fact at odds. King David's most astute and wise advisor, Ahithophel, was also willing to give advice to David's rebelling son, and in every case the advice was ingeniously perceptive but also amoral. (2 Samuel 17) Christian theologians have compared Ahithophel to Judas Iscariot, who used his wits to betray Jesus. An even sadder example is that of King Solomon, who starts his kingship with unparalleled wisdom and moral fortitude, which impresses everyone who witnesses him speak. Yet he soon loses his moral compass. He is willing to have his brother killed to preserve his throne, which is only one of his many transgressions enumerated in the Bible. Indeed, the story of Solomon and the two mothers and the one baby is instructive for what it teaches us about Solomon. What is often overlooked is that the reason the real mother reacted by telling Solomon to spare the baby when he called for his sword was that she fully expected he would have no problem actually splitting the baby. To make matters worse, toward the end of his life, Solomon's self-conscious smartness led him to self-deification. He was so sure of his smarts that he implemented heartless policies and left a more heartless successor who caused his kingdom to descend into civil war and to split in two after he died. Smartness doesn't mean niceness or compassion, or mercy, or good judgment. As Jeremiah put it, "They are clever at doing wrong." (Jeremiah 4:22)

In my view, academia needs to return to the motto and Golden Rule with their common emphasis on facts and morals. To address the intellectual component, one must start with the fact that there is no antidote to corruption like the truth. We need to go back to Pearson's text: "Be sure you are right and then go ahead." My first suggestion is that universities should return to the basics of making sure that research studies are well founded empirically at all levels of the knowledge chain. In the social sciences and humanities, this means putting greater weight on empirical evidence and less on theories, as well as being more critical of theories. This emphasis should be reaffirmed at all stages, from undergraduate courses to tenure processes. Peer review by scholars who are known to be of a different perspective may also help to get critical assessments of the use of evidence when agreement on theory is not an incentive to push a book through. Another option would be for universities to create networks to make sure that studies and scholarship released by its professors are reviewed by several scholars in a more systematic way. Currently, the book review process for scholarship in the humanities and social sciences is somewhat ad hoc and can lead to a mutual admiration society or, to the contrary, an exclusive club rather than a process of critical appraisal based on evidence and its interpretation. Universities that join in these processes will enjoy a higher status of reliability. In the hard sciences and pure technology space, there is less need for this protection, as devices and mechanisms either work or they don't work. Still, having a process whereby experiments are replicated in different institutions would be a valuable approach. These are a few options, and I am sure there are more if scholars were to put their minds to it.

My second suggestion is that there be a mandate for a required course on the ethics of scholarship for upperclassmen and graduate students in all fields. Such courses could offer a primer on ways in which scholars have lied, misled, and falsified all in the name of ideology or personal glory. I hope this book contributes to a new genre of case studies of what should *not* be done in academia.

My third suggestion is that donations from foreign countries be limited and subject to US government scrutiny. Qatar donates over $200 million per year to US universities and is a primary supporter of the Hamas regime, which has sworn to expel if not murder all Jews "from the river to the sea." Were a private donor to donate both to the university and to any other organization designated as a terrorist group (say for example the Tamil Tigers or Aryan Nations), its funds would be severely questioned and unlikely to be accepted. Sometimes universities claim that their engagement with Qatar will lead to the country becoming more liberal and tolerant. However, neither Northwestern nor the other seventeen universities with a presence in Qatar have had a moderating influence on the regime. In short, these three concrete measures can help restore the integrity of scholarship. Much more must be done.

A focus on the motto and the Golden Rule will ensure the kind of diversity that advances rather than stifles knowledge. There are those who will rightly point out that the motto and the Golden Rule are also frameworks. In this respect, it must be acknowledged that they are also approaches to evidence. Why I think the motto and the Golden Rule remain our best framework is not only because of their universality but because they leave room for diversity while also excluding approaches that devalue facts or our common humanity. The same ancient sage, Hillel, who formulated the negative version of the Golden Rule is renowned to Talmudic scholars for his frequent disputations with his intellectual opponent, Shamai. Never once did he accuse Shamai of betraying the Golden Rule or basic foundations of truth and morality. In fact, just the opposite is true. Their disputes are considered the model of arguments "for the sake of heaven"—that is, arguments that arise when people who are sincerely seeking the truth disagree.

Indeed, there is a great deal of room for quite different perspectives among people who adopt the motto and follow the Golden Rule. And that is how it should be. The questions that scholars address are often complicated and can quite logically be approached from different perspectives, and this variety enriches scholarship and advances knowledge. Ideological scholarship and theories can and have led to horrors and do not deserve the cover of academic freedom that they sadly are receiving.

As this book draws to an end, some may feel I owe an apology to my dear alma mater. I have put Northwestern in an unflattering spotlight. The criticisms I have leveled at Northwestern could be made as well to most of the universities in America. And yes, I could have done that, but I don't think I would have been able to express how deeply I would like to see change at this particular magnificent university. Many Northwestern faculty members teach and inspire students and conduct vital and positive research to make this planet a better place. I remain very grateful for the education I received there.

In these final paragraphs, I would also like to anticipate some likely criticisms. This research project has given me the opportunity to read many criticisms of Zionism in article, letter, and book form, and despite the proliferation of these texts, there is a small menu of responses to Zionists that continually reappear. Reviewing this menu can also be instructive since, sadly, much of it consists of false accusations, bullying, and lies. Within the confines of the Golden Rule, I invite those who disagree to do so. But here are some standard anti-Zionist responses that do not fit within the parameters of the Golden Rule.

There will be some who will falsely state that I am justifying a view that Israel cannot be criticized or censured in an attempt to cover up their own distortions of history. This is an all-purpose criticism that is leveled against any defense of Zionism. Usually, and certainly in this case, it is entirely false. I am fine with criticizing Israel. I do so myself. But this cannot be confused with support for the end of the Jewish state and for the subjugation, expulsion, or extermination of the Jews who live there. A person can advocate for a one, two, three, or any other number of state solutions while still recognizing the indigeneity of Jews to the land of Israel. Whether you are a believer in the Bible or not, there are too many archaeological and other historical sources that depict the Jews in the land for at least three thousand years for it to be denied. You cannot make up stories about Israeli Jews entering history over the last two hundred years from their homeland in Europe, or about drones buzzing around Gaza gassing people, or about Jewish theft of Palestinian organs, or whatever the meme of the day is and blame it on Zionists under the guise of scholarship.

My point is simply that there will never be peace by teaching a false history. Palestinians and Israelis and their neighbors are the ones who need to be talking to each other about real issues and potential compromises. The chorus of self-styled experts from campuses around the United States and the world tying Palestinian issues to every other issue related to decolonial theory, critical theory, or any other theory of the day delays, limits, and may even destroy any chance at ultimate peace. Encouraging the shunning of one necessary party in a peace agreement is obviously not a smart idea unless the goal is to eliminate the shunned party altogether. Puar, Hermez, and other BDS leaders indicate that this is the real goal. Those who sign up for BDS should recognize they are calling for the destruction of Israel and the death of many Jews. Attempts to sugarcoat that with fancy words should be ignored.

There will be some on the far left who will contend that to contradict or argue with the views of venerable figures such as Steven Thrasher, Angela Davis, Steve Salaita, Jasbir Puar, or other scholars of oppressed peoples or classes is unacceptable under any circumstances. They will argue that these individuals have a special status, so their views have special status. I believe that this contention is wrong on three counts. First, to exempt anyone from being contradicted is a form of idolatry, which leads to bad outcomes for everyone. Even the Roman Catholic popes have only invoked the doctrine of "infallibility" once in history, and even then, only with regard to a specific theological concept. Second, every individual I discussed is brilliant, talented, and articulate and therefore more than fully capable of defending their views based on facts if they choose to do so. Not to engage with their views is a type of patronization. Third, as the reader no doubt recognizes, I believe that some of their views actually lead to oppression of minorities and of people of color whose plight has been studiously ignored because of false theories.

There will be some people on either extreme who will resort to critiques and bashing without addressing anything I have written. That is also a standard tactic. It will probably be the usual word bombs of contending that this is a Jewish or Zionist or white supremacist obfuscation of facts to further the baby killing, organ stealing, maiming, scheming, xenophobic, homophobic, racist, apartheid, genocidal, dual-loyalty, bloodthirsty pro-Israel fifth column conspiracy. Such people will likely further claim that this book is filled with falsehoods, is complicit in the silencing of those who disagree with Israel; and that it is therefore *literally* killing people. They will also insist that anyone who reads this book should be shunned for enabling these crimes. Dealing with evidence or truth is truly beside the point for those folks. On the far right, I have already been vilified as "jooish," among other less pleasant terms, and have appeared on neo-Nazi lists of Jewish bankers, and that was *before* making it onto the radar of IHR.

Finally, there are some who will say that this book's focus on Jews is not appropriate given the historic moment in repairing the systemic racism that people of color have faced all over the world including in the United States. The prophets admonish the people again and again that the place to find God is in the defense of the poor and oppressed. Chapter 5 of the Book of Amos, a favorite of Dr. Martin Luther King, makes clear that overcoming social injustice is not a task for the faint-hearted but rather for those who take faith seriously. There are enormous wrongs in the treatment of people of color that need to be righted. But this effort does not mean that we should ignore other grave biases in academia that are likely to cause great harm. The Hebrew prophet Amos admonishes us to focus on all manner of injustice. And we read "Justice, justice, you shall pursue." (Deuteronomy 16:20) Readers of the Bible must be active allies of those oppressed or else they are reading the Bible for entertainment and not guidance.

Both extremes are inextricably linked by their underlying intellectual frameworks, and though they may each wax and wane in different environments, over the long term they are equally frightening and dangerous to both Jews and broader society, particularly people of color. The record of both fascist and communist governments is murderous. It should also be remembered that Jews in the US do face real physical dangers. One only has to think of Charlottesville where marchers chanted, "Jews will not replace us!" Jews in the US have been murdered in pogroms my father would have recognized in Pittsburgh, Poway, Jersey City, and Monsey. In 2018, there were almost 1,879 serious anti-Jewish incidents in the US, about double the level of 2015.[3] At least one rioting insurrectionist at the US Capitol on January 6, 2021, wore a shirt emblazoned with "Camp Auschwitz." A congresswoman (and graduate of a well-regarded university) on the far right imagines "Jewish space lasers" evilly being used to cause forest fires.[4] On the far left, the term anti-Semitism has been redefined to mean that any Jew not on their side does not deserve protection. In practice, far-left rallies have become similar to those on the far right in that they no longer distinguish between "bad Zionist Jews" and "good anti-Zionist Jews." During and after the May 2021 Gaza conflict, Jews were physically attacked in New York, Los Angeles, Tucson, Skokie, and Miami by groups of protesters. No one asked for the victims' political opinions, and the accompanying verbal harassment made it clear that they were being attacked simply for being Jews. Unfounded hatred and violence toward Jews is on a steep rise.

I invite critics to play by the Golden Rule as I have tried. I have made a conscious effort to frame my criticisms respectfully, if at times with some rhetorical flourish. I have only addressed opinions that Butz, Thrasher, and others have publicly disseminated, as well as associations with individuals they publicly associate or align with. I have made no personal comments with respect to anyone cited, nor have I negatively commented on any of their scholarship outside of their views of Zionism. I have also not written them or any Northwestern faculty members off, which itself goes against the Golden Rule. In this respect, I believe this book advances the sort of discourse and dialogue that can lead to positive change and reconciliation as the Bible would profess.

The Bible explains in the simplest terms how we can avoid idolatry. In Leviticus 19:18, humanity is implored to "love your fellow as yourself." As we have noted, the ancient Jewish sage Hillel said the entire

Bible could be summed up as "don't do what is hateful to you to your fellow. The rest is commentary, go learn it." Yet clearly this doesn't happen all the time. Not everyone is loving or lovable. So, what are we to do? The Bible tells us in the preceding, less famous verse, "Don't hate your fellow in your heart; you shall rebuke/debate/criticize/engage your fellow, and don't take upon yourself sin because of them." This means that we should not hate our fellow human beings because of prejudice. We should not write off, dismiss, cancel, shun, or demonize anyone else based on our preconceived notions. This includes Butz and Thrasher. They have each made scholarly contributions in their fields of study, and those should be and are in fact rightly acknowledged. But if a reason should arise to object in other areas, we must not remain silent, or then it becomes our sin. We must engage with our fellow in the way that we would want to be engaged. Everything is on the table except for hatred. To be able to engage and discern what is open to disagreement and what are patent lies, we need to employ critical thinking skills and cognitive flexibility. We need teachers who don't have an agenda other than to teach their students to think. One point that has always stayed with me from Heidegger's *What Is Called Thinking?* was his statement that "the most thought-provoking thing in our thought-provoking time is that we are still not thinking." I would add with some irony that he was right about that then and now.

As we conclude, let us recall Professor Pearson's discussion of the Northwestern motto from the Introduction. Pearson points us back to Creation as the start of humanity's quest for knowledge. He said, "Toward this 'far-off divine event the whole creation moves,' but in the long conflict with sin and error weapons are constantly changing."[5] And so let us turn to that primordial commencement. An as yet unnamed man and woman who represent all of us live in a most wonderful place. Strangely, the last verses of the majestic, awesome, effortless creation depicted in chapter 1 of the Bible detail what humans and other creatures are allowed to eat. For the humans, all the fruits (with one famous exception) and vegetables are on the menu, while all the other creatures are allowed to eat only of the vegetables. There are no predators, no meat eaters, and no one with an urge to cause harm to any creature. This is a place to explore, to discover, to name, and to cooperate with all the other creatures. Then a resentful snake character emerges (who is depicted as at least as smart as the human characters), and he has a gripe. The humans can eat all but one proscribed fruit, but he is not allowed to eat any fruit and so he is unhappy, even bitter, with the status quo. To get what he wants, he obscures the facts and creates a false theory. He persuades the woman that if she can safely touch the forbidden fruit, God must be lying, and she can in fact safely eat it as well. Crucially, touching the fruit was never prohibited. His is the first false theory fashioned by manipulating actual facts to obscure the reality, which was pretty simple—eating this particular fruit was forbidden. The snake acts out of an evil motivation, but the woman naively accepts the theory and then so does the man. Ingesting a bad theory leads to biting the dangerous, potentially poisonous, fruit.

By analogy, the academy, which should be a Garden of Eden for exploration, naming, discovery, and cooperation, has become a predatory creator of false theories that could lead to the downfall of civil, democratic society based on the Golden Rule. I hope this book has made it clear that the Jews are just the first victims of false theories in our society. Our collective future depends on permitting facts to disprove theories instead of allowing theories to negate facts. Brothers and sisters, please, think on these things.

Not in Our Fair Name

Scott A. Shay WCAS '79 KGSM '80

In February, the Northwestern Associated Student Government Senate (ASG) passed -- by a very slim majority -- a resolution sponsored by NU Divest and endorsed by the BDS movement calling on Northwestern to divest from six companies that sell products to the State of Israel by which they claim these companies violate Palestinians' human rights.

Samantha Stankowicz (WCAS '14) and I have been circulating a letter that has been signed by Northwestern students, alumni, parents, faculty, staff and donors declaring that this resolution is not in our name and should not purport to represent the views of the Northwestern University community. At no level does this resolution improve the situation in the Middle East writ large or for the Palestinian people. Further it damages the cause of free speech at Northwestern for Northwestern students present and future.

An advertisement with the signatures that can fit on one page will be running every day in the Daily Northwestern until all the signatories are listed once. We have attempted to list only those who provided a valid connection to the university. The following is a very brief analysis of the resolution and its implications, which will make the motivations behind our letter clear.

Although some proponents of the resolution within the ASG argued that the resolution is not an indication of the ASG's support for the BDS movement and its political aims, this is hard to believe. In fact it is not only disingenuous to say the ASG resolution is not linked to the BDS movement, it is untrue. No fair reading of the links and materials used by NU Divest could lead to that conclusion. And frankly, even if it were not directly linked to the BDS movement, the ASG resolution is universally recognized as a victory for the BDS movement and is exhibited by the BDS movement as a notable trophy.

So it is useful to ask if it is appropriate for the ASG to align itself with the BDS movement. Such an alignment is extremely problematic for three reasons.

The first problem with this alignment is the BDS movement itself, which even critics of the State of Israel's policies have come out against for its ideology and tactics.

None other than Norman Finkelstein, himself a harsh critic of Israeli policies, has described, in a now famous interview with BDS activist Frank Barat, how the BDS movement is not only against a two-state solution, but is also against the state of Israel. Finkelstein has pointed out that the BDS movement disingenuously obscures this aim. Further he has criticized the movement for hypocritically appealing to international law to bolster its claims for Palestinian national rights while ignoring the fact that international law upholds Israel's right to exist. Thus while the BDS movement claims to fight for the rights of Palestinians it is actually fighting to delegitimize Israeli rights completely. It goes without saying that supporters of Israel have criticized the BDS movement for this reason for years. Thus it is clear even to critics of Israel that the BDS movement upholds an extreme anti-Israel view which does not advocate peace based on a negotiated two-state solution or represent the mainstream opinion in the US or in the Northwestern community.

In addition, critics of the BDS movement rightly notice that it seems irrationally and almost fanatically focused on delegitimizing Israel despite its mantel of human rights. Many have asked why the BDS movement against Israel has become such a cause célèbre when so many other countries are guilty of grievous human rights. Indeed if one supports the BDS movement for humanitarian and not political reasons, why support primarily or only the BDS movement against Israel? Why not call for divestment from Chinese, Russian, or even American companies if one's main concern is human rights?

Even Noam Chomsky, also a strong critic of Israeli policies, has made this last point in a much discussed article on the BDS movement in The Nation. Supporters of Israel have identified this double standard for years. The fact that the international BDS movement, which is composed of people from all over the world, not only Palestinians, has hostilely focused only on Israel despite this criticism indicates yet again that the movement is more focused on the specific political agenda of delegitimizing the State of Israel than on Palestinian or human rights more broadly. Further, many people have noted that the BDS movement hurts Palestinians

economically. The movement also does little to advance the cause of peace, which many Palestinians and Israelis as well as outside observers insist can only come through a negotiated solution.

Given BDS's well-known and extreme political stance, one has to be honest and call a spade a spade. When NU Divest called on the ASG to support divestment from certain companies they were actually calling on them to become fellow travelers with BDS, which means supporting the BDS movement's rejection of a two-state solution and of the legitimacy of the State of Israel. Thus, a student body purporting to represent the students at NU has now, through this resolution, officially adopted an extreme political position on this one global conflict – and this conflict alone.

The second problem with the alignment of the ASG and the BDS movement is the question of free speech.

The resolution de facto delegitimizes the Northwestern community members who have different views. I want to stress that I have no problem with NU Divest expressing its views. Were it to put out a press release every day saying that it supports BDS, I would defend NU Divest's free speech rights to do so, however greatly their position differs from mine. But what we protest is that NU Divest has successfully convinced the ASG to speak on behalf of every student of Northwestern and implicitly of the broader Northwestern community regarding the Israeli-Palestinian conflict.

Indeed by calling on the ASG to make a resolution and by the vote itself, the ASG no longer enables debate on an issue where there is a great deal of disagreement. This tactic is out of the BDS playbook of silencing and delegitimizing those opposed to it, including proponents of Israel whether they be on the left or right as well those who disagree with its tactics. This should be an anathema to any community of free speech such as a university. We should all be enabled and ennobled by our Northwestern affiliation to speak our minds about any issue and not told that some official body speaks on our behalf.

The third problem with this alignment is what the vote represents.

By seeking to use the student senate to ask Northwestern University to

divest from six stocks that it does not own, NU Divest has made it clear that actual efforts for peace are not a key component of its tactics. Instead their primary goal is to ensure that Northwestern is depicted as a univers that supports the BDS movement. Th problematic because it is not true.

It may also have serious financial repercussions. Using an official stude body to represent only one view on a highly contentious issue, thereby associating NU with the BDS moveme causes many alumni and donors to wonder just what is going on here. NU Divest has strangely maintained that tuition dollars flow into the endowme when in fact the endowment comes from donors and not tuition money. Further, the endowment is the source all the financial aid support received t Northwestern students.

With 3,700 undergraduates who deper on and benefit from financial aid generated by the endowment, one car rightly ask what NU Divest is trying to achieve with such a partisan resolutio which does not represent the variety c views held by the broader NU commu other than to convince donors and alumni that NU is no longer a univers committed to free speech. Indeed NU Divest's efforts and the ASG vote will likely cause less financial aid to be available to future students. As a past student who could not have attended Northwestern but for university finan assistance, I am distressed at the thou that this controversy was manufactur to serve the interests of the internatic BDS movement without considering h it will harm the Northwestern commu and its future students.

The Northwestern University commur must remain an open intellectual environment.

For this to be the case the ASG must withdraw this resolution. There shoul be no pro-Israel or pro-Palestinian resolutions or resolutions on any of these sorts of partisan political issues brought before the ASG. Instead NU Divest should feel free to express its opinions, as should all other campus organizations as independent groups. behalf of everyone who signed the let to the ASG, we call upon you to withdr this resolution.

Add your name at http://asgpetitionatnu.weebly.c

For more information, please contact asgpetitionatnu@gmail.com

ACKNOWLEDGMENTS

In the autumn of 2019, I began writing what I thought would be a 2,500-word essay on lessons that I had learned from my late father to commemorate the 75th anniversary of his liberation from Dachau. Around the same time, Professor Thrasher had begun teaching at Northwestern and I attended some alumni events where his NYU Doctoral Convocation speech was a matter of discussion. I went down the rabbit hole of listening to his speech online and then reading his many tweets. As I did so, I wanted to understand the intellectual basis of Thrasher's assertions. Thinking a bit more, I recognized that there was a parallel to Professor Butz's arguments and I dived into a second unpleasant rabbit hole of reading *The Hoax of the Twentieth Century*.

As I began connecting the experiences of my father to the writings of Butz and Thrasher, I quickly found myself at ten thousand words and was still going. It was at that point that I realized that I might be writing another book. When I told my wife, Susan, about the lessons I was connecting from my father to what I was reading, she encouraged me to keep going and to see where the journey would take me. Once again, I have abundant reasons to thank Susan for making so many things in my life possible. Words cannot come close to expressing my thanks and my gratitude to Susan.

As the essay morphed into a book, I reached out to Olga Kirschbaum-Shirazki who had been my research associate for *In Good Faith* and for *Getting Our Groove Back*. Olga was surprised that I would be writing a new book so soon after *In Good Faith* but said she would help as soon as she finished two translations. For *Conspiracy U*, Olga acted not only as research associate but also as editor. This would have been a longer and less interesting book without Olga's interventions. As events in academia and at Northwestern kept making this book more and more timely, Olga became my motivational coach whenever I was tempted to slow down even a bit. I thank Olga for making time in her busy schedule as an editor of the Tel Aviv Review of Books among her other commitments to take on the research and editing assignments for this book.

I knew that this book would touch on some sensitive topics so I approached a diverse group of my friends and associates, who have a wide variety of political perspectives, to review early manuscripts. So, I thank Harry Ballan, Alan Barnett, Jeremy Blocker, Derrick Cephas, Alicia DePaolo, Robert DePaolo, Alex Jakubowski, Doria Kahn, Noel Kirnon, Audrey Lichter, Simon Lichter, Susie Medak, Sadrach Pierre, Steve Salinger, Ron Scheinberg, Jolie Schwab, Motti Seligson, David Silber, John Tamberlane, Calanit Valfer, and Ruth Zeilicovich. I particularly want to thank Alan Zelenetz for his creative edits. I must hasten to add that while all of the reviewers gave me valuable feedback in the spirit of friendship and scholarship, some disagree with aspects of the book and their reading of the text does not indicate any endorsement of my conclusions.

I am glad to thank the whole Wicked Son team.

I am grateful to Lew Ranieri and Joe DePaolo, two of my longtime business partners, for their steadfast encouragement of my extracurricular writing activities. I also must thank my longtime assistant, Pat Burger, who manages my day with such efficiency that I feel like she squeezes a few extra minutes into each hour. Pat also carefully read through the final draft and offered typographical edits.

I end by reciting a modification of a Jewish blessing, known as the *Shehechiyanu*. I thank the Almighty for giving me the life that I have, for preserving me, and for bringing me to this point in my life that I could write and complete this book.

ENDNOTES

INTRODUCTION

1. Charles William Pearson, "Northwestern University," *The Northwestern* 20, no. 6, November 2, 1899.
2. Pearson, "Northwestern University."
3. Jeffrey Wattles, *The Golden Rule* (New York: Oxford University Press, 1996).
4. Harry J. Gensler, *Ethics and the Golden Rule* (New York: Routledge, 2013).
5. Arthur Butz, *The Hoax of the Twentieth Century* (London: Historical Review Press, 1975).
6. Andrew Valls, ed., *Race and Racism in Modern Philosophy* (Ithaca: Cornell University Press, 2005).
7. While there is some controversy over Confucius's views as described in this text, in general the Chinese philosophers distinguished between the Chinese states and those of Barbarians. Bo Mou, *History of Chinese Philosophy* (London: Routledge, 2014).
8. Kocc Barma is credited with the saying "Love women, but never lend your confidence to them." Source: "Who Needs an Oral Historian, When there's Youtube, Man?" No River Twice, July 1, 2015, https://norivertwice.wordpress.com/2015/07/01/who-needs-an-oral-historian-when-theres-youtube-man/, accessed February 26, 2021.
9. J. D. Zahniser and Amelia R. Fry, *Alice Paul: Claiming Power* (Oxford: Oxford University Press, 2019).
10. As will be discussed later in the book, this concern ranges from ideological uniformity within certain disciplines to outright manipulation of data.
11. Ben Sales, "Study: More than one in 10 Americans under 40 thinks the Jews caused the Holocaust," Jewish Telegraphic Agency, September 16, 2020, https://www.jta.org/2020/09/16/united-states/study-more-

than-one-in-10-americans-under-40-thinks-jews-caused-the-holo-
caust, accessed February 23, 2021.

1

1. Moshe Gil, *A History of Palestine, 634-1099*, trans. Ethel Broido (Cambridge: Cambridge University Press, 1997), 3. There is consider-able scholarly debate on the demographics of Byzantine Palestine as well as Arab Palestine until the Crusades. While I favor the conclu-sions of Moshe Gil, whose breadth of sources is peerless (including Christian, Muslim, and Jewish), the main point is that Jews never left the land of Israel completely.
2. Neil Chethik, "Prof Pens Disclaimer of the Holocaust," *The Daily Northwestern*, January 14, 1977.
3. Chethik, "Prof Pens Disclaimer of the Holocaust."
4. "Extracts From Mein Kampf by Adolf Hitler," Yad Vashem, https://www.yadvashem.org/docs/extracts-from-mein-kampf.html, accessed February 24, 2021.
5. Butz, *The Hoax*, 17.
6. Butz, *The Hoax*, 300.
7. Scott Shay, "Pragmatic Response," *The Daily Northwestern*, January 28, 1977.
8. Shay, "Pragmatic Response."
9. Claire Berlinski, "The Cold War's Arab Spring: How the Soviets Created Today's Middle East," *Tablet*, June 20, 2012, https://www.tabletmag.com/sections/news/articles/the-cold-wars-arab-spring, accessed February 23, 2021.
10. Ben Sales, "Study: More than one in 10 Americans under 40 thinks Jews caused the Holocaust," Jewish Telegraphic Agency, September 16, 2020, https://www.jta.org/2020/09/16/united-states/study-more-than-one-in-10-americans-under-40-thinks-jews-caused-the-holo-caust, accessed February 19, 2021. The underlying study reported on was done by the Claims Conference based on responses from 1,000 people in all fifty states. I saw the article and then went to the study itself, which is accessible at http://www.claimscon.org/study/. The link allows one to go to various parts of the study. The article summary is accurate.

2

1. Jovan Byford, *Conspiracy Theories: A Critical Introduction* (London: Palgrave McMillan, 2011) and Quassim Cassam, *Conspiracy Theories* (Cambridge: Polity Press, 2019).
2. Cassam, *Conspiracy Theories*, 2.
3. In so doing I follow Cassam's approach to distinguish between theories about genuine or possible conspiracies and theories about unlikely, even bogus, conspiracies. Cassam, *Conspiracy Theories*, 6.
4. Byford, *Conspiracy Theories*, 32–37.
5. Byford, *Conspiracy Theories*, 32–37.
6. Byford, *Conspiracy Theories*.
7. Cassam, *Conspiracy Theories*.
8. Cassam, *Conspiracy Theories*, 6.
9. Cassam, *Conspiracy Theories*, chapter 1.
10. Cassam, *Conspiracy Theories*, 8–12.
11. Cassam, *Conspiracy Theories*, 12.
12. Byford, *Conspiracy Theories*, chapter 4.
13. Byford, *Conspiracy Theories*, chapter 3.
14. Byford, *Conspiracy Theories*, 59–65.
15. Byford, *Conspiracy Theories*, chapter 3.
16. Byford, *Conspiracy Theories*, 32–37.
17. Byford, *Conspiracy Theories*, chapter 3.
18. Byford, *Conspiracy Theories*, chapter 5.
19. Byford, *Conspiracy Theories*, chapter 5 and Cassam, *Conspiracy Theories*, 39.
20. Byford, *Conspiracy Theories*, 110–118.
21. Cassam, *Conspiracy Theories*, chapter 4.
22. Cassam, *Conspiracy Theories*, chapter 4.
23. The notion that *logos, ethos*, and *pathos* are inextricable to personhood was made by Rabbi Dr. Samuel Lebens in an online lecture hosted by the Drisha Institute. I followed up in a private email exchange in December 2020, in which he elucidated the connection.
24. The Reed Sea is the proper English translation for the Hebrew Scriptural term "yam soof." However, it is most frequently rendered as the Red Sea. For a further explanation, see my book: Scott A. Shay, *In Good Faith: Questioning Religion and Atheism* (New York: Post Hill Press, 2018), 334, and the map on page 335.

3

1. Butz, *The Hoax*, 282.
2. Butz, *The Hoax*, 90.
3. Butz, *The Hoax*, 97.
4. Butz, *The Hoax*, 24–25.
5. Butz, *The Hoax*.
6. Butz, *The Hoax*, 34.
7. Butz, *The Hoax*, chapters 1 and 6.
8. Butz, *The Hoax*, 49.
9. Butz, *The Hoax*, 49–50.
10. Butz, *The Hoax*, 277.
11. Butz, *The Hoax*, 293–294.
12. Butz, *The Hoax*, 300–301.
13. Butz, *The Hoax*, 301.
14. Angela Y. Davis, *Freedom is a Constant Struggle: Ferguson, Palestine, and the Foundations of a Movement*, ed. Frank Barat (Chicago: Haymarket Books, 2016).
15. David Samuels, "American Racist," *Tablet*, June 11, 2020, https://www.tabletmag.com/sections/news/articles/kevin-macdonald-american-anti-semitism, accessed February 5, 2021.
16. Samuels, "American Racist."
17. Butz, *The Hoax*, 300.
18. Yaghoub Fazeli, "Iran's Khamenei on Quds Day: Israel Will be Eradicated," *Alarabiya News*, May 22, 2020, https://english.alarabiya.net/News/middle-east/2020/05/22/Iran-s-Khamenei-on-Quds-Day-Israel-will-be-eradicated, accessed February 24, 2021.
19. Ayatollah Ali Khamenei, *Palestine from the Perspective of Ayatollah Khamenei*, ed. Saeed Solh-Mirzai (Teheran: Islamic Revolution Publication, 2011).
20. Butz, *The Hoax*, 26.
21. Butz, *The Hoax*, 26.

4

1. Irving M. Abella and Harold Martin Troper, *None is Too Many: Canada and the Jews of Europe, 1933-1948* (Toronto: University of Toronto Press, 2012).

2. *Rafael Medoff, The Jews Should Keep Quiet: Franklin D. Roosevelt, Rabbi Stephen S. Wise, a*nd the Holocaust (Lincoln: University of Nebraska Press, 2019).

3. *Laurel Leff, Buried by the Times: The Holocaust and America's Most Imp*ortant Newspaper (Cambridge: Cambridge University Press, *2005).*

4. Butz, The H*oax, 64.*

5. Butz, The Hoax, 458.

6. "International Military Tribunal *at Nuremberg," Holoca*ust Encyclopedia, United States Holocaust Museum, https://encyclo-pedia.ushmm.org/content/en/article/international-military-tribu-nal-at-nuremberg, accessed February 10, 2021.

7. "International Military Tribunal *at Nuremberg," Holoca*ust Encyclopedia.

8. It is a basic principle of international law that states have a right to determine who enters their borders.

9. For a discussion of the case of civilians trying to cross the border in a conflict zone and the legality, according to international law, of Israel's use of lethal force, see: Eugene Kontorovich, "The New Arab Tactic *against Israel," The* National Review, May 18, 2011, https://www.nationalreview.com/2011/05/new-arab-tactic-against-israel-eugene-kontorovich/, accessed February 24, 2021.

10. Israel blockades Gaza; it does not control or occupy it. This perspective has been upheld in European courts; see Marko Milanovic, "European Court Decides that Israel Is Not *Occupying Gaza," EJIL: Talk!,* June 17, 2015, https://www.ejiltalk.org/european-court-de-cides-that-israel-is-not-occupying-gaza/, accessed February 22, 2021.

11. Associated Press, "Looters strip Gaza greenhouses," NBC News, Sept. 13, 2005, https://www.nbcnews.com/id/wbna9331863#.X0NnjugzaM8, accessed February 22, 2021.

12. Zera Nur Duz, "Gaza blockade: Egyptian Harassment Meets Readers," AA, July 24, 2020, https://www.aa.com.tr/en/middle-east/gaza-blockade-egyptian-harassment-meets-readers/1921503, accessed February 22, 2021.

13. Israel has diplomatic relations with forty-one Sub-Saharan African countries and is involved in commercial ties, agricultural projects, professional training programs, cultural and academic exchanges, and

humanitarian aid with these countries. Israeli Tech in water and energy has also been involved in Africa. Source: Alan Rosenbaum, "How Israel is Bringing Water and Energy to Africa," *The Jerusalem Post*, August 5, 2020, https://www.jpost.com/jpost-tech/how-israel-is-bringing-water-and-energy-to-africa-608412, accessed February 22, 2021.

14. Davis, *Freedom is a Constant Struggle*, 14.

15. David Horovitz, "Just in Case Anybody Forgot what Hamas's 'March of Return' is Really all About," *The Times of Israel*, March 31, 2018, https:// www.timesofisrael.com/just-in-case-anybody-forgot-what-hamass-march-of-return-is-really-all-about/, accessed February 22, 2021.

16. The question of who the American establishment consists of is a fraught one; certainly, on a basic level there are different centers of power in the US: economic (various particularly powerful industries), the military, key agencies and different departments within the government, owners of media corporations, and the universities, to name but a few. Some of these centers of power in the US have traditionally supported Israel while others have not. In any case, it is far from clear they form anything of a single "establishment" or that an establishment exists at all. Danielle Kurtzleben, "People Keep Talking About 'The Establishment.' What Is It, Anyway?," NPR, February 11, 2016, https://www.npr.org/2016/02/11/466049701/how-establishment-became-the-buzzword-of-the-2016-election, accessed February 24, 2021.

17. Deborah Lipstadt, *Antisemitism: Here and Now* (New York: Schocken Books, 2019), 90, 95, and 210.

18. Steven Salaita, *Israel's Dead Soul* (Philadelphia: Temple University Press, 2011), 64.

19. Salaita, *Israel's Dead Soul*, 77.

5

1. For an up-to-date comparative discussion of the Israel and Arab lobbies in the US see: Mitchell Bard, "The Pro-Israel and Pro-Arab Lobbies," *The Jewish Virtual Library*, https://www.jewishvirtuallibrary.org/the-pro-israel-and-pro-arab-lobbies, accessed February 24, 2021.

2. Bard, "The Pro-Israel and Pro-Arab Lobbies."

3. Howard Morley Sachar, *A History of Israel: From the Rise of Zionism to Our Time* (New York: Knopf, 2007).

4. Stanislao G. Pugliese, *The Most Ancient of Minorities: The Jews of Italy* (Westport: Greenwood Press, 2002) and John Klier, *Russia Gathers her Jews: The Origins of the "Jewish question" in Russia, 1772-1825* (Dekalb: Northern Illinois University Press, 2011).
5. Dean Phillip Bell, *Jews in the Early Modern World: Continuity and Transformation* (Lanham: Rowman & Littlefield, 2008).
6. Robert Chazan, *Reassessing Jewish Life in Medieval Europe* (Cambridge: Cambridge University Press, 2010) and Francesca Bregoli and David B. Ruderman, eds., *Connecting Histories: Jews and Their Others in Early Modern Europe* (Philadelphia: University of Pennsylvania Press, 2019).
7. S. D. Goitein, *Letters of Medieval Jewish Traders* (Princeton: Princeton University Press, 2015) and Walter Laqueur, *The Changing Face of Anti-Semitism: From Ancient Times to the Present Day* (Oxford: Oxford University Press, 2006).
8. Kevin Ingram, *Converso Non-Conformism in Early Modern Spain: Bad Blood and Faith from Alonso de Cartagena to Diego Velázquez* (London: Palgrave Macmillan, 2018) and François Soyer, *Antisemitic Conspiracy Theories in the Early Modern Iberian World: Narratives of Fear and Hatred* (Boston: Brill, 2019).
9. Jack Wertheimer, ed., *The Modern Jewish Experience: A Reader's Guide* (New York: New York University Press, 1993).
10. Victor Karady, *The Jews of Europe in the Modern Era: A Socio-Historical Outline* (Budapest: Central European University Press, 2004).
11. Karady, *The Jews of Europe in the Modern Era* and Laqueur, *The Changing Face of Anti-Semitism.*
12. Donald L. Niewyk, *Jews in Weimar Germany* (London: Routledge, 2018).
13. Houman Sarshar, *The Jews of Iran: The History, Religion and Culture of a Community in the Islamic World* (London: I.B. Tauris, 2019) and Sarah Taïeb-Carlen and Amos Carlen, trans., *The Jews of North Africa: from Dido to de Gaulle* (Lanham: University Press of America, 2010).
14. The most important book on this topic is yet to be translated into English: Shmuel Trigano, *La Fin du Judaïsme en Terres D'Islam* (Paris: Denoël, 2009). For an English excerpt see: Shmuel Trigano,

"The Hidden Face of Nationalism in Islamic Lands," *Tel Aviv Review of Books* (Autumn 2019), https://www.tarb.co.il/the-hidden-face-of-nationalism-in-islamic-lands/, accessed February 15, 2021.

15. Ben Hubbard, "Saudi Arabia's 'Um Haroun' Ignites Arab Debate," *The New York Times*, May 2, 2020, https://www.nytimes.com/2020/05/02/world/middleeast/saudi-arabia-um-haroun-jews.html, accessed February 20, 2020.

16. Hasia R. Diner, *Jews in America* (New York: Oxford University Press, 1999).

17. Diner, *Jews in America*.

18. Gary Y. Okihiro, *The Columbia Guide to Asian American History* (New York: Columbia University Press, 2001) and Jonathan H. X. Lee, *History of Asian Americans: Exploring Diverse Roots* (Santa Barbara: Greenwood, 2015).

19. The Defense Security Cooperation Agency, which is a part of the US Department of Defense, cooperates with more than two hundred countries across the world. Source: "Security Cooperation Overview," Defense Security Cooperation Agency, https://www.dsca.mil/foreign-customer-guide/security-cooperation-overview, accessed February 22, 2021.

20. Scott A. Shay, *Getting Our Groove Back: How to Energize American Jewry* (New York: Devorah Publishing, 2006).

21. The debate about Jewish whiteness must be understood in relative terms. The Jews in the US were closer to being white, that is to say passing for and experiencing the benefits of being part of the dominant cultural group in the US and the Americas, than other minorities. And certainly, some Jews assimilated so radically that they hid their origins. See for example Todd Edelman, *Leaving the Jewish Fold: Conversion and Radical Assimilation in Modern Jewish History* (Princeton: Princeton University Press, 2015). But to claim that Jews were white in the same way as people of European ancestry in the US is incorrect.

22. See for example James Baldwin's famous essay: April 9, 1967, "Negroes Are Anti-Semitic Because They're Anti-White," *The New York Times*, April 9, 1967, https://archive.nytimes.com/www.nytimes.com/books/98/03/29/specials/baldwin-antisem.html?_r=1, accessed February 22, 2021.

23. For an overview of US immigration history see: Roger Daniels, *Coming to America: A History of Immigration and Ethnicity in American Life* (New York: Harper Perennial, 2002). For the politics of different immigrant groups see: Francis M. Carroll, *America and the Making of an Independent Ireland: A History* (New York: New York University Press, 2021); Russell A. Kazal, *Becoming Old Stock: The Paradox of German-American Identity* (Princeton: Princeton University Press, 2004); Maria Laurino, *The Italian Americans: A History* (New York: W. W. Norton & Company, 2015). Each of these histories includes the ways immigrants also kept ties with their home countries and lobbied for them with the American government.

24. María Cristina García, *Havana USA: Cuban Exiles and Cuban Americans in South Florida, 1959-1994* (Berkeley: University of California Press, 1996).

25. Patricia Kollander and John O'Sullivan, *I Must be a Part of this War: A German American's Fight Against Hitler and Nazism* (New York: Fordham University Press, 2005).

26. Howard H. Allen, "Studies of Political Loyalties of Two Nationality Groups: Isolation and German Americans," *Journal of the Illinois State Historical Society* 57, no. 2 (Summer 1964).

27. Butz, *The Hoax*, 300.

28. Tim Mackintosh-Smith, *Arabs: A 3,000-year History of Peoples, Tribes and Empires* (New Haven: Yale University Press, 2019).

29. For a global history of ancient empires in the Middle East, see: Eric H. Cline and Mark W. Graham, *Ancient Empires: From Mesopotamia to the rise of Islam* (Cambridge: Cambridge University Press, 2011). For modern empires see: John Darwin, *After Tamerlane: The Global History of Empire since 1405* (New York: Bloomsbury Press, 2008).

30. Shay, *In Good Faith*.

31. The Turkic peoples have ruled several empires throughout history, see: Carter V. Findley, *The Turks in World History* (New York: Oxford University Press, 2005). Their most important Islamic empire was the Ottoman, see: Renée Worringer, *A Short History of the Ottoman Empire* (Toronto: University of Toronto Press, 2021). The Iranians have also ruled several empires from antiquity to the present. Their first Islamic empire was the Safavid Empire: Andrew J.

Newman, *Safavid Iran: Rebirth of a Persian Empire* (London: I.B. Taurus, 2012).

32. John A. G. Roberts, *A History of China,* Third Edition (London: Palgrave, 2011).

33. Robert G. Hoylan, *In God's Path: The Arab Conquests and the Creation of an Islamic Empire* (Oxford: Oxford University Press, 2015).

34. Chase F. Robinson, ed., *The New Cambridge History of Islam: Volume 1, The Formation of the Islamic World, Sixth to Eleventh Centuries* (Cambridge: Cambridge University Press, 2010).

35. Mordechai Nisan, *Minorities in the Middle East: A History of Struggle and Self-Expression* (Jefferson: McFarland, 2002).

36. Bruce Alan Masters, *The Arabs of the Ottoman Empire, 1516-1918: A Social and Cultural History* (Cambridge: Cambridge University Press, 2013).

37. Youssef M. Choueiri, *Arab Nationalism—A History: Nation and State in the Arab World* (Oxford: Blackwell, 2000).

38. Nisan, *Minorities in the Middle East.*

39. Nisan, *Minorities in the Middle East* and Mariz Tadros, *Copts at the Crossroads: The Challenges of Building Inclusive Democracy in Egypt* (Cairo: American University in Cairo Press, 2013.

40. Nisan, *Minorities in the Middle East* and Matti Moosa, *The Maronites in History* (Piscataway: Gorgias Press, 2005).

41. Nisan, *Minorities in the Middle East* and Daniel King, *The Syriac World* (New York: Routledge, 2018).

42. Nisan, *Minorities in the Middle East* and Michael M. Gunter, *The Kurds: A Modern History* (Princeton: Markus Wiener Publisher, 2017).

43. Albert Hourani, *A History of the Arab Peoples,* trans. Malise Ruthven (London: Faber, 2005) and Moshe Gil, *A History of Palestine, 634-1099,* trans. Ethel Broido (Cambridge: Cambridge University Press, 1997).

44. David Barnett and Efraim Karsh, "Azzam's Genocidal Threat," *Middle East Quarterly* (Fall 2011): 85-88, https://www.meforum.org/middle-east-quarterly/pdfs/3082.pdf, accessed June 1, 2021.

45. Trigano, *La Fin du Judaïsme en Terres d'Islam* and Trigano, "The Hidden Face of Nationalism in Islamic Lands."

46. Ada Aharoni, "The Forced Migration of Jews from Arab Countries," *Peace Review: A Journal of Social Justice* 15, no. 1 (2003): 53–60.

47. General Assembly Plenary Meeting, Item 108 The Question of Palestine, Speech by Yasser Arafat, 13 November 1974, https://unispal.un.org/DPA/DPR/unispal.nsf/0/A238EC7A3E13EED18525624A007697EC, accessed February 15, 2021.

48. Martin Gilbert, *The Routledge Atlas of Jewish History*, 8th Edition (London: Routledge, 2013), maps 8 and 29; Michael Avi-Yonah, *The Jews of Palestine: A Political History from the Bar Kokhba war to the Arab Conquest* (Oxford: Blackwell, 1976); and Alex Carmel, Peter Schafer, and Yossi Ben-Artzi, eds., *The Jewish Settlement in Palestine 634-1881* (Wiesbaden: Dr. Ludwig Reichert, 1990).

49. Gilbert, *The Routledge Atlas of Jewish History*, map 7.

50. Gilbert, *The Routledge Atlas of Jewish History*, maps 8, 9, and 13.

51. Gil, *A History*, 3.

52. Gil, *A History*, introduction.

53. Gilbert, *The Routledge Atlas of Jewish History*, maps 17 and 12.

54. Gilbert, *The Routledge Atlas of Jewish History*, map 21.

55. Gilbert, *The Routledge Atlas of Jewish History*, map 31.

56. Gilbert, *The Routledge Atlas of Jewish History*, maps 47 and 32.

57. Gilbert, *The Routledge Atlas of Jewish History*, map 47.

58. Gilbert, *The Routledge Atlas of Jewish History*, maps 47 and 48.

59. Gilbert, *The Routledge Atlas of Jewish History*, map 72, 76, 81, and 83.

60. Walter Laqueur, *The History of Zionism* (London: I.B. Tauris, 2003).

61. Simon Payaslian, *The History of Armenia: From the Origins to the Present* (New York: Palgrave Macmillan, 2007) and George A. Bournoutian, *A Concise History of the Armenian People: From Ancient Times to the Present* (Costa Mesa: Mazda Publishers, 2012).

62. Thomas W. Gallant, *Modern Greece: From the War of Independence to the Present* (London: Bloomsbury Academic, 2016).

63. Payaslian, *The History of Armenia*, chapter 5.

64. Oleh Protsyk and Benedikt Harzl, eds., *Managing Ethnic Diversity in Russia* (London: Routledge, 2013).

65. Deryck Scarr, *Gulliver's Other Islands: A New History of Fiji* (London: Hurst & Co. Publ. Ltd., 2017).

66. Seth J. Frantzman, *After ISIS: America, Iran and the Struggle for the Middle East* (New York: Gefen Publishing House, 2019).

67. Alireza Asgharzadeh, *Iran and the Challenge of Diversity: Islamic Fundamentalism, Aryanist Racism, and Democratic Struggles* (New York: Palgrave Macmillan, 2007). The execution of dissidents and political opponents continues to this day; for a recent example, see: Human Rights Watch, "Iran: Dissident Executed on Vague Charges," Human Rights Watch, December 12, 2020, https://www.hrw.org/news/2020/12/12/iran-dissident-executed-vague-charges, accessed February 23, 2021.

68. Benjamin Weinthal, "Iran Executes 'High Number' of Gays, says German Intelligence," *The Jerusalem Post*, June 9, 2020, https://www.jpost.com/middle-east/iran-executes-high-number-of-gays-says-german-intelligence-630751#:~:text=According%20to%20a%20 2008%20British,the%20country's%201979%20Islamic%20revolu-tion.&text=Hamburg's%20intelligence%20service%20appears%20 to,destruction%20of%20its%20LGBTQ%20community, accessed February 23, 2021.

69. Mehmet Gurses, David Romano, and Michael M. Gunter, eds., *The Kurds in the Middle East: Enduring Problems and New Dynamics* (New York: Lexington Books, 2020).

70. Gurses et al., *The Kurds in the Middle East.*

6

1. Deborah E. Lipstadt, *Denying the Holocaust* (New York: Penguin Books, 2016), 54.

2. Ian Greenhalgh, "Holocaust Truth Revealed: An Interview with Josef Ginsburg by Eric Thomson," *Veterans Today: Journal for the Clandestine Community*, August 28, 2016, https://files.secure.web-site/wscfus/10348600/7282753/josephginsburg-vt-kolnidre.pdf, accessed February 16, 2021.

3. Greenhalgh, "Holocaust Truth Revealed."

4. Greenhalgh, "Holocaust Truth Revealed."

5. Lipstadt, *Denying the Holocaust*, 22.

6. Anne Frank House, "The Authenticity of the Diary of Anne Frank," https://www.annefrank.org/en/anne-frank/go-in-depth/authentici-ty-diary-anne-frank/, accessed February 16, 2021.

7. Lipstadt, *Denying the Holocaust*, 235.

8. I confirmed this with Dr. Daphna Haran of the Leo Baeck School in Haifa. I received her report in an email dated September 17, 2020.
9. "Fake Holocaust," Aangirfan, July 1, 2019, http://aanirfan.blogspot. com/2019/07/fake-holocaust.html, accessed February 24, 2021 and "Why Are So Many Jews Denying the Holocaust?," Al-Anon Family Groups – Wisconsin & the Upper Peninsula of Michigan, September 6, 2020, https://www.area61afg.org/forums/topic/why-are-so-many-jews-denying-the-holocaust-4/, accessed February 24, 2021.
10. Chanda Prescod-Weinstein, "Black and Palestinian Lives Matter," in *On Anti-Semitism: Solidarity and the Struggle for Justice*, ed. Jewish Voices for Peace (Chicago: Haymarket Books, 2017).
11. Prescod-Weinstein, "Black and Palestinian Lives Matter," 35.
12. Prescod-Weinstein, "Black and Palestinian Lives Matter," 36.
13. "U.S.-Israel Strategic Cooperation: Joint Police & Law Enforcement Training," *Jewish Virtual Library*, https://www.jewishvirtuallibrary. org/joint-us-israel-police-and-law-enforcement-training, accessed February 24, 2021.
14. Prescod-Weinstein, "Black and Palestinian Lives Matter," 35.
15. According to the JVP website, it has over 200,000 online supporters and over seventy chapters in a community of over six million Jews. Since many of these online supporters are neither Jewish nor American, JVP's self-reported support conforms to the estimate above.
16. Moshe Zimmermann, *Wilhelm Marr: The Patriarch of Anti-Semitism* (New York: Oxford University Press, 1987).
17. Jordan Michael Smith, "An Unpopular Man," *The New Republic*, July 7, 2015, https://newrepublic.com/article/122257/unpopular-man-norman-finkelstein-comes-out-against-bds-movement, accessed February 22, 2021.
18. Martin Heidegger, *What is Called Thinking?*, trans. J. Glenn Gray (New York: Harper & Row, 1972).
19. Elisabeth Young-Bruehl, *Hannah Arendt: For Love of the World* (New Haven: Yale University Press, 2004).
20. Richard Wolin, *Heidegger's Children: Hannah Arendt, Karl Löwith, Hans Jonas, and Herbert Marcuse* (Princeton: Princeton University Press, 2015), 50.
21. Young-Bruehl, *Hannah Arendt*.

22. Richard Wolin, ed., *The Heidegger Controversy: A Critical Reader* (Cambridge: MIT Press, 1991), 150.
23. Suzanne Kirkbright, *Karl Jaspers, A Biography: Navigations in Truth* (New Haven: Yale University Press, 2004).
24. Andrew J. Mitchell and Peter Trawny, *Heidegger's Black Notebooks: Responses to Anti-Semitism* (New York: Columbia University Press, 2017).
25. Mitchell and Trawny, *Heidegger's Black Notebooks*, introduction, and Richard Wolin, "National Socialism, World Jewry, and the History of Being: Heidegger's Black Notebooks," *Jewish Review of Books* (Summer 2014).
26. Josh Jones, "Heidegger's 'Black Notebooks' Suggest He Was a Serious Anti-Semite, Not Just a Naive Nazi," *Open Culture*, March 13, 2015, https://www.openculture.com/2015/03/martin-heideggers-black-notebooks-reveal-the-depth-of-anti-semitism.html, accessed February 19, 2021 and Wolin, "National Socialism."
27. Zvi Y. Gitelman, *A Century of Ambivalence: the Jews of Russia and the Soviet Union, 1881 to the Present* (Bloomington: Indiana University Press, 2001), chapter 2. See also Bari Weiss, *How to Fight Anti-Semitism* (New York: Penguin Random House, 2019), which discusses the Yevsektsiya.
28. Gitelman, *A Century of Ambivalence*, chapter 5.

8

1. Magda Teter, *Blood Libel: On the Trail of an Antisemitic Myth* (Cambridge: Harvard University Press, 2020).
2. Times of Israel Staff, "Full Official Record: What the mufti said to Hitler," *The Times of Israel*, October 21, 2015, https://www.timesofisrael.com/full-official-record-what-the-mufti-said-to-hitler/, accessed February 19, 2021. The article cites the following document: official German record of the meeting between Adolf Hitler and the Grand Mufti of Jerusalem, Haj Amin al-Husseini, on November 28, 1941, at the Reich Chancellory in Berlin. (Source: Documents on German Foreign Policy 1918-1945, Series D, Vol XIII, London, 1964).
3. Klaus-Michael Mallmann and Martin Cüppers, *Nazi Palestine: The Plans for the Extermination of the Jews in Palestine*, trans. Krista Smith (New York: Enigma Books, 2010).

4. Donald M. McKale, *Nazis after Hitler: How Perpetrators of the Holocaust Cheated Justice and Truth* (Lanham: Rowman & Littlefield, 2014).
5. Lipstadt, *Denying the Holocaust.*
6. Lipstadt, *Denying the Holocaust,* 14.
7. Harry Elmer Barnes, "Zionist Fraud," *American Mercury* (Fall 1968).
8. Lipstadt, *Denying the Holocaust,* 14.
9. Austin J. App, *The Six Million Swindle: Blackmailing the German People for Hard Marks with Fabricated Corpses* (Boring: CPA Book Publisher, 1999 [1973]).
10. Richard Harwood, *Did Six Million Really Die? The Truth at Last* (Richmond: Historical Review Press, 1974). Richard Harwood was Verrall's *nom de plume.*
11. Gabe Harper, *William Pierce, the National Alliance, and the Dream of an All-White World* (St. Louis: G. Harper, 2003).
12. Lipstadt, *Denying the Holocaust,* 141.
13. Lipstadt, *Denying the Holocaust,* 203.
14. Lipstadt, *Denying the Holocaust,* 202–208.
15. Lipstadt, *Denying the Holocaust,* 143.
16. Zvi Y. Gitelman, *Jewish Nationality and Soviet Politics: The Jewish Sections of the CPSU* (Princeton: Princeton University Press, 2016).
17. Gitelman, *Jewish Nationality.*
18. Gitelman, *Jewish Nationality.*
19. Gitelman, *Jewish Nationality,* conclusion and epilogue.
20. Gitelman, *A Century of Ambivalence,* chapter 5.
21. Paul Hollander, *Political Pilgrims: Travels of Western Intellectuals to the Soviet Union, China, and Cuba, 1928-1978* (Lanham: University Press of America, 1990).
22. Ellen Schrecker, *No Ivory Tower: McCarthyism and the Universities* (Oxford: Oxford University Press, 1986), Van Gosse, *Rethinking the New Left: An Interpretative History,* 1st Edition (London: Palgrave, 2005), Dan Berger, ed., *The Hidden 1970s* (New Brunswick: Rutgers University Press, 2010), and Matthew Levin, *Cold War University: Madison and the New Left in the Sixties* (Madison: University of Wisconsin Press, 2013).
23. A quick search on the *New Left Review* website of articles on Israel, Zionism, or Palestine makes their editorial perspective clear.

24. Angela Davis, *Angela Davis: An Autobiography* (New York: Random House, 1974). In her autobiography, she describes meeting Arafat and her engagement with communist countries. See also Sarah Benton, "Angela Davis Makes the Palestinian Struggle Hers," *Jews for Justice for Palestinians*, September 5, 2017, https://jfjfp.com/angela-davis-makes-the-palestinian-struggle-hers/, accessed February 8, 2021.

25. Davis, *Angela Davis*.

26. Benton, "Angela Davis Makes the Palestinian Struggle Hers."

27. Benton, "Angela Davis Makes the Palestinian Struggle Hers."

28. "Actually my most recent collection of lectures and interviews reflects an increasingly popular understanding of the need for an internationalist framework within which the ongoing work to dismantle structures of racism, hetero-patriarchy, and economic injustice inside the United States can become more enduring and more meaningful. In my own political history, Palestine has always occupied a pivotal place, precisely because of the similarities between Israel and the United States...." Source: Benton, "Angela Davis Makes the Palestinian Struggle Hers." Or "Ferguson reminds us that we have to globalize our thinking about these issues (mass incarceration, the prison industrial complex)." Source: Davis, *Freedom is a Constant Struggle*, 13. Yet in describing this intersectionality, she shows her obsessive focus on Palestine: "I think it's important to insist on the intersectionality of movements. In the abolition movement, we've been trying to find ways to talk about Palestine so that people who are attracted to a campaign to dismantle prisons in the US will also think about the need to end the occupation in Palestine. It can't be an afterthought. It has to be a part of the ongoing analysis." Source: Davis, *Freedom is a Constant Struggle*, 21.

29. Davis, *Freedom is a Constant Struggle*, 45.

30. "Precisely. That was the whole point. And also it might be important to point out that the Israeli police have been involved in the training of US police. So there is this connection between the US military and the Israeli military. And therefore it means that when we try to organize campaigns in solidarity with Palestine, when we try to challenge the Israeli state, it's not simply about focusing our struggles elsewhere, in another place. It also has to do with what happens in US communities." Davis, *Freedom is a Constant Struggle*, 14, and as

Frank Barat writes in his question to Davis, "We often talk here about the reproduction of the occupation: what's happening in Palestine is reproduced now in Europe, in the US, et cetera. It is important to make the link for people to understand how global the struggle is. But in your opinion is Ferguson an isolated incident?" Davis's response, "Absolutely not." Source: Davis, *Freedom is a Constant Struggle*, 14.

31. Angela Davis, "Angela Davis calls to unite anti-racist struggles for Israeli Apartheid Week 2020," BDS, March 16, 2020, https://bds-movement.net/news/angela-davis-calls-unite-anti-racist-struggles-for-israeli-apartheid-week-2020, accessed February 25, 2021.

32. Davis, *Freedom is a Constant Struggle*, 44.

33. Jordan Harrison, "Radical Activist Angela Davis Draws Large Crowd for Social Justice Talk," *The Daily Northwestern*, May 20, 2014, https://dailynorthwestern.com/2014/05/20/campus/radical-activist-angela-davis-draws-large-crowd-with-social-justice-talk/, accessed February 8, 2021.

34. Members include the novelist Alice Walker, who quotes the conspiracy theorist David Icke approvingly as we shall see later; Roger Waters, the leader of Pink Floyd, who in addition to promoting BDS, compares Israel to pigs and touts conspiracies about the Israel lobby; the American Democratic politician Cynthia McKinney, who has accused Israel of genocide, claimed the Israel lobby was seeking to ruin her career, and supports the Nation of Islam and The Black Panthers, both of which advocate anti-Israel conspiracy theories.

35. Davis, *Freedom is a Constant Struggle*, introduction and the interviews that make up chapters 1, 2, and 3.

36. Cary Nelson, *Israel Denial: Anti-Zionism, Anti-Semitism, and the Faculty Campaign against the Jewish State* (Bloomington: Indiana University Press, 2019), introduction.

37. For more information, see their website: www.bdsmovement.net.

38. Davis, "Angela Davis calls to unite anti-racist struggles."

39. Nelson, *Israel Denial,* introduction.

40. Despite calling out and listing pro-Israel advocates on campus, SJP and JVP vociferously contend that anti-Zionists should not be listed. Although this contention seems self-paradoxical, in the spirit of the Golden Rule, I did not do an exhaustive search of anti-Zionist Northwestern faculty members. Rather, the individuals noted

in this and the following endnotes made a point of conspicuously authoring or adding their names to publicly disseminated statements, messages, tweets, and so forth. All of the individuals noted can be connected to the relevant categories at the time of this writing using simple Google search terms, such as the category and "Northwestern University." I did not conduct an in-depth search or start with names of particular faculty members as search terms (other than for the four Northwestern faculty members highlighted in the text.) Doubtlessly, more names would have appeared with more vigorous searching. But I did not want to pick up any names of individuals who did not go out of their way to publicly declare their anti-Zionist beliefs. I also did not put the names of these other faculty members in the text itself of this book, but rather in these endnotes. I did not feel that I could make the statements in the text without demonstrating the sources behind them, hence these endnotes and the reason for this explanation. A simple examination of the petitions for boycotts reveals the following names with regard to cultural boycotts: Alexander Weheliye, Joshua Chambers-Letson, Nitasha Tamar Sharma, Jorge Coronado, and Ricardo Sanchez.

41. A simple examination of the petitions for boycotts reveals the following names with regard to academic boycotts: Ada Aparicio, Chris Kuzawa, E. Patrick Johnson, Emrah Yidiz, Erica Weltzma, Helen Thompson, Jessica Winegar, Katherine Hoffman, Marquis Bey, Robert Launay, Shalini Shankar, and Thomas McDade.

42. While there has been no faculty call for Northwestern to boycott Israel economically, all faculty who supported the 2015 Associated Student Government call for Northwestern to divest from Israel certainly supported this position.

43. Signatories to this boycott include: Jessica Winegar, Joshua Chambers-Letson, Marquis Bey, Ricardo Sanchez, and Claudia Garcia Rojas. Other scholars participated in a panel in support of Salaita: Martha Biondi and Doug Kiel.

44. Signatories to this boycott include: Brett Gadsen, E. Patrick Johnson, and Martha Biondi.

45. Signatories to this boycott include: Elizabeth Shakman Hurd and Rebecca Johnson.

46. Signatories to such boycotts include: John D. Marquez and Hannah Feldman.

47. Northwestern faculty who are known to promote anti-Zionist content on their Twitter, Facebook pages and/or in media articles include: Jessica Winegar, Adia Benton, Alexander Weheliye, Banor Hess, Elizabeth Shakman Hurd, Sepehr Vakil, Wendy Pearlman, Jack Doppelt, Martha Biondi, Shirin Vossoughi, and Shalini Shankar.

48. No faculty-signed petitions have circulated against anti-Zionist scholars/speakers. As indicated in notes 219 and 220, Northwestern faculty have come out in support of anti-Zionist speakers such as Steven Salaita and Angela Davis, who gave talks at Northwestern on a number of occasions.

49. The approach of faculty at Northwestern's Crown Family Center for Jewish and Israel Studies Department cannot be accused of uncritically supporting Zionism; in fact, as with most American Jewish studies departments, the emphasis is on the European Diaspora.

50. Lara Deeb and Jessica Winegar, *Anthropology's Politics: Disciplining the Middle East* (Stanford: Stanford University Press, 2015).

51. Jadaliyya interview with Lara Deeb and Jessica Winegar, "New Texts Out Now: Lara Deeb and Jessica Winegar, Anthropology's Politics: Disciplining the Middle East," *Jadaliyya*, January 6, 2016, https://www.jadaliyya.com/Details/32836/New-Texts-Out-Now-Lara-Deeb-and-Jessica-Winegar,-Anthropology%E2%80%99s-Politics-Disciplining-the-Middle-East, accessed February 8, 2021.

52. Jadaliyya interview with Lara Deeb and Jessica Winegar, "New Texts Out Now."

53. Jadaliyya interview with Lara Deeb and Jessica Winegar, "New Texts Out Now."

54. Jadaliyya interview with Lara Deeb and Jessica Winegar, "New Texts Out Now."

55. Jadaliyya interview with Lara Deeb and Jessica Winegar, "New Texts Out Now."

56. Jadaliyya interview with Lara Deeb and Jessica Winegar, "New Texts Out Now."

57. Jessica Winegar, "How academia in the US self-censors on Israel and Palestine," *TRTWorld*, November 22, 2016, https://www.trtworld.

com/opinion/how-academia-in-the-us-self-censors-on-israel-and-palestine-3818, accessed February 8, 2021.

58. None of the anthropologists who signed to call for a BDS vote at the AAA were sanctioned even though BDS promotes many conspiracies about Israel.

59. Jeff Martin, "AAA Votes Down Academic Boycott Resolution: Other Actions Planned," American Anthropological Association, June 7, 2016. https://www.americananthro.org/StayInformed/NewsDetail.aspx?ItemNumber=14768, accessed April 19, 2021.

60. Martin, "AAA Votes Down Academic Boycott Resolution: Other Actions Planned."

61. Elizabeth Redden, "Big Night for Boycott Movement," Inside Higher Ed, November 23, 2015, https://www.insidehighered.com/news/2015/11/23/anthropologists-overwhelmingly-vote-boycott-israeli-universities, accessed February 27, 2.

62. Deeb and Jessica Winegar, *Anthropology's Politics*, 18.

63. Deeb and Jessica Winegar, *Anthropology's Politics*, 106.

64. Deeb and Jessica Winegar, *Anthropology's Politics*,106.

65. Deeb and Jessica Winegar, *Anthropology's Politics*, x.

66. Winegar, "How academia in the US."

67. Winegar, "How academia in the US."

68. Sami Hermez and Mayssoun Soukarieh, "Boycotts against Israel and the Question of Academic Freedom in American Universities in the Arab World," *AAUP Journal of Academic Freedom* 4 (September, 2013), https://www.aaup.org/JAF4/boycotts-against-israel-and-question-academic-freedom-american-universities-arab-world#.YCFRgbAzbIU, accessed February 8, 2021.

69. Diana Allan and Curtis Brown, "The Mavi Marmara: At the Frontlines of Web 2.0.," *Journal of Palestine Studies* 40 (November 2010).

70. Gérard Huber, *Contre-Expertise D'une Mise en Scène* (Paris: Ed. Raphaël, 2003).

71. James Fallows, "Who Shot Mohammed al-Dura," *The Atlantic* (June 2003), https://www.theatlantic.com/magazine/archive/2003/06/who-shot-mohammed-al-dura/302735/, accessed February 9, 2021.

72. Sami Hermez, "Judging Hassan Nasrallah," *The Electronic Intifada*, March 27, 2007, https://electronicintifada.net/content/judging-hassan-nasrallah/6831, accessed February 9, 2021.

73. Badih Chayban, "Nasrallah alleges 'Christian Zionist' Plot," *The Daily Star Lebanon*, Oct. 23, 2002, https://www.dailystar.com. lb/News/Lebanon-News/2002/Oct-23/21779-nasrallah-alleges-christian-zionist-plot.ashx, accessed February 9, 2021.

74. Jeffrey Goldberg, "In the Party of God," *The New Yorker,* October 14, 2002, https://www.newyorker.com/magazine/2002/10/14/in-the-party-of-god, accessed February 9, 2021.

75. "Hizbullah Leader Hassan Nasrallah: Implementing Khomeini's Fatwa against Salman Rushdie Would Have Prevented Current Insults to Prophet Muhammad; The Great French Philosopher Roger Garaudy Proved that the Holocaust Is a Myth," MEMRI, February 3, 2006, https://www.memri.org/tv/hizbullah-leader-has-san-nasrallah-implementing-khomeinis-fatwa-against-salman-rush-die-would-have, accessed February 25, 2021.

76. Ben Sales, "Northwestern Neuroscientist who Wrote Anti-Semitic and Racist Tweets Dies by Suicide," Jewish Telegraphic Agency, February 4, 2021, https://www.jta.org/2021/02/04/united-states/northwestern-neuroscientist-who-wrote-anti-semitic-and-rac-ist-tweets-dies-by-suicide, accessed February 25, 2021.

77. Cary Nelson, *Israel Denial.*

78. Jasbir K. Puar, *The Right to Maim: Debility, Capacity, Disability* (Durham: Duke University Press, 2017).

79. William A. Jacobson, "Vassar Faculty-Sponsored Anti-Israel Event Erupts in Controversy," *Legal Insurrection*, February 8, 2016, https://legalinsurrection.com/2016/02/vassar-faculty-sponsored-anti-isra-el-event-erupts-in-controversy/, accessed February 9, 2021. The article contains a transcript of Puar's talk.

80. Jacobson, "Vassar Faculty-Sponsored Anti-Israel Event."

81. Puar, *The Right to Maim*, 297.

82. There is controversy about the number of civilian casualties in the Israeli Palestinian conflict since distinguishing between combatants and non-combatants is not easy. According to B'tselem, the number of non-combatant Palestinians for the period from 19 January 2009 to January 31, 2021 is 2,192 and of non-combatant Israelis 728. B'tselem, *Fatalities since Operation Cast Lead*, B'tselem, January 31, 2021, https://www.btselem.org/statistics/fatalities/after-cast-lead/by-date-of-event, accessed February 25, 2021. Compare this to the

3,025 civilian casualties in Afghanistan for 2020 alone. Fraidoon Poya, "'Disturbing spike' in Afghan civilian casualties after peace talks began: UN report," UN News, February 23, 2021, https://news.un.org/en/story/2021/02/1085442#:~:text=In%20their%20annual%20Afghanistan%20Protection,per%20cent%20less%20than%20in, accessed February 25, 2021.

83. Nelson, *Israel Denial*, 203.
84. Jacobson, "Vassar Faculty-Sponsored Anti-Israel Event."
85. Nelson, *Israel Denial*. See also the websites for the above-mentioned associations.
86. Included are Angela Y. Davis, Cornel West, Robyn D. G. Kelley, and Johanna Fernández, among others.
87. The BDS website, for example, neither endorses nor condemns violent resistance, nor is violence mentioned where relevant such as during the Great March of Return, when Palestinian protesters threw fire kites, bombs, and grenades.
88. For a translation of the Hamas Charter, see: Federation of American Scientists, The Charter of Allah: The Platform of the Islamic Resistance Movement, trans. Raphael Israeli, https://fas.org/irp/world/para/docs/880818.htm, accessed February 23, 2021.
89. BDS Movement, "What is BDS," https://bdsmovement.net/what-is-bds, accessed February 23, 2021.
90. See: Barry J. Balleck, *Hate Groups and Extremist Organizations in America: An Encyclopedia* (Santa Barbara: ABC-CLIO, 2019).
91. Kate Sullivan, "3 Founding Board Members of Women's March Leaving after Allegations of Anti-Semitism," CNN, September 16, 2019, https://edition.cnn.com/2019/09/16/politics/womens-march-board-members-leaving/index.html, accessed February 23, 2021.
92. Benjamin Kerstein, "Outrage Greets Pro-BDS Petition to University of California Blaming Israel for Teaching Methods That Killed George Floyd," *The Algemeiner*, June 4, 2020, https://www.algemeiner.com/2020/06/04/outrage-greets-pro-bds-petition-to-university-of-california-blaming-israel-for-us-police-brutality/, accessed February 9, 2021.
93. Georgina Lee, "Did Israeli Secret Service Teach Floyd Police to Kneel on Neck?," *Channel 4 News*, , June 26, 2020, https://www.channel4.

com/news/factcheck/factcheck-did-israeli-secret-service-teach-floyd-police-to-kneel-on-neck, accessed April 20, 2021.

94. Kerstein, "Outrage Greets Pro-BDS Petition."
95. Benjamin Kerstein, "Accusations That Israel to Blame for US Police Brutality Are Untrue and Antisemitic, Expert Says," *The Algemeiner*, June 10, 2020, https://www.algemeiner.com/2020/06/10/accusations-that-israel-to-blame-for-us-police-brutality-are-untrue-and-antisemitic-expert-says/, accessed February 9, 2021.
96. Lee, "Did Israeli Secret Service Teach Floyd Police to Kneel on Neck?"
97. See Twitter Jessica Winegar or @jessica_winegar.
98. "Alice Walker: By The Book," *The New York Times*, December 13, 2018, https://www.nytimes.com/2018/12/13/books/review/alice-walker-by-the-book.html, accessed February 9, 2021.
99. Alexandra Alter, "Alice Walker, Answering Backlash, Praises Anti-Semitic Author as 'Brave,'" *The New York Times*, December 21, 2018, https://www.nytimes.com/2018/12/21/arts/alice-walker-david-icke-times.html, accessed February 9, 2021.
100. Bret Stephens, "A Despicable Cartoon in The Times," *The New York Times*, April 28, 2019, https://www.nytimes.com/2019/04/28/opinion/cartoon-nytimes.html, accessed February 9, 2021.

<u>2</u>

1. Soviets referred to both Zionism and Nazism as fascism and claimed that both were racist and imperialistic, thus cementing three key links that would be mainstays of far-left anti-Zionist criticism.
2. Jeffrey Herf, "Convergence: The Classic Case. Nazi Germany, Anti-Semitism and Anti-Zionism during World War II," in *Anti-Semitism and Anti-Zionism in Historical Perspective: Convergence and Divergence*, ed. Jeffrey Herf (New York: Routledge, 2007) and Lipstadt, *Denying the Holocaust*, chapter 1.
3. Lipstadt, *Denying the Holocaust*, chapter 1.
4. Allen Hall, "Revealed: The Middle East's secret army of Nazis," *The Scotsman*, February 20, 2015, https://www.scotsman.com/news/world/revealed-middle-easts-secret-army-nazis-1512181, accessed February 25, 2021. Also, Chern Chen, "Former Nazi Officers in the Near East: German Military Advisors in Syria, 1949–56," *The International History Review* 40, no. 4 (2019).

5. Editors, "Nazis in Cairo," *Patterns in Prejudice* 1, no. 3 (1967).

6. Francis Parker Yockey, *Imperium: The Philosophy of History and Politics* (Sausalito: Noontide Press, 1969).

7. Kevin MacDonald, *Understanding Jewish Influence: A Study in Ethnic Activism* (Augusta: Washington Summit Publishers, 2004).

8. David Duke, *Jewish Supremacism: My Awakening on the Jewish Question* (Mandeville: Free Speech Press, 2003).

9. Tamir Bar-On, "Richard B. Spencer and the Alt Right," in *Key Thinkers of the Radical Right: Behind the New Threat to Liberal Democracy*, ed. Mark Sedgwick (Oxford: Oxford University Press, 2019).

10. Contrary to the claims of those on the far left who argue that the far right admires Zionism, *The Right Stuff, The Daily Shoah, The Daily Stormer,* and *Occidental Dissent,* or the website of the *Institute for Historical Review*, all vilify Zionism.

11. Michael Collins Piper, "Jared Taylor and 'Zionist-Friendly Nationalism,'" *Renegade Tribune*, July 6, 2016, http://www.renegadetribune.com/jared-taylor-zionist-friendly-nationalism/, accessed February 22, 2021. Despite the obvious rejection of Zionism by neo-Nazis and the far right, it is standard in American progressive and far-left circles to claim the far right embraces Zionism. This is now a standard accusation. See for example: David A. Love, "Right-wing Zionism, white supremacy and the BDS," September 29, 2017, AlJazeera, https://www.aljazeera.com/opinions/2017/9/29/right-wing-zionism-white-supremacy-and-the-bds. Love has written for the *Guardian*, Huffpost, *The Nation,* and commented on CNN, among other mainstream progressive and liberal outlets. He is the former executive director of the Witness to Innocence organization, which helps death row exonerees.

12. While the use of the term "far right" often includes right-wing populists, in a report on the far right and Israel, Hannah Rose correctly notes that what she calls the extreme right, or neo-Nazi parties, is not pro-Israel and therefore was excluded from her study. Hannah Rose, "The New Philosemitism: Exploring a Changing Relationship Between Jews and the Far-Right," *International Center for the Study of Radicalisation* (London: International Center for the Study of Radicalisation, 2020), https://icsr.info/wp-content/uploads/2020/11/ICSR-Report-The-New-Philosemitism-Exploring-a-Changing-Relationship-Between-Jews-

and-the-Far-Right.pdf, accessed February 22, 2020. In contrast, those opposed to Zionism rarely make this distinction.

13. Countless articles in the progressive and far-left press make this claim. Most do not distinguish between the populist right and the far right. See for example: Ramzy Baroud and Romana Rubeo, "An Unlikely Union: Israel and the European Far Right," AlJazeera, July 17, 2018, https://www.aljazeera.com/opinions/2018/7/17/an-unlikely-union-is-rael-and-the-european-far-right, accessed February 22, 2021.

14. Rose, "The New Philosemitism."

15. "Le Pen visits Wilders in The Hague," DW, November 13, 2013, https://www.dw.com/en/le-pen-visits-wilders-in-the-hague/a-17223970, accessed February 22, 2021.

16. Emily Schultheis, "Teaching the Holocaust in Germany as a Resurgent Far Right Questions It," The Atlantic, April 10, 2019, https://www.theatlantic.com/international/archive/2019/04/germany-far-right-ho-locaust-education-survivors/586357/, accessed February 22, 2021.

17. Gideon Resnick, "David Duke: Donald Trump Is Too Zionist for Me," Daily Beast, April 14, 2017, https://www.thedailybeast.com/david-duke-donald-trump-is-too-zionist-for-me, accessed February 9, 2021.

18. Victor Morton, "David Duke praises Rep. Ilhan Omar," AP, March 7, 2019, https://apnews.com/article/a97b8b2d48c-163c5965c2574ccbbe3d3, accessed February 9, 2021.

19. Alex Swoyer, "David Duke Endorses Tulsi Gabbard 2020 Presidential Campaign," AP, February 5, 2019, https://apnews.com/article/1b9996bdd9fa14e48e457ab6e39c00e1, accessed February 9, 2021.

20. Andrew Anglin, "Operation: Kikebart (AKA #NoHydeNoPeace)," Daily Stormer, November 20, 2015, https://dailystormer.su/opera-tion-kikebart-aka-nohydenopeace/ , accessed February 9, 2021.

21. Taly Krupkin and Ben Samuels, "'Alt-lite' Trump Supporters Blast ADL Over Inclusion on 'Hate List,'" Haaretz, July 20, 2017, https://www.haaretz.com/us-news/alt-lite-trump-supporters-blast-adl-over-inclusion-on-hate-list-1.5431907, accessed February 9, 2021.

22. Are white nationalists turning on Trump?" Southern Poverty Law Center, November 27, 2018, https://www.splcenter.org/hatewatch/2018/11/27/are-white-nationalists-turning-trump?fbclid=IwAR3Yj-

subwGPahJ8Ko8zl0rZm_zJQZMA_IgmmO8B4Ap8xvqBUDe_lIU-WQpWQ, accessed February 25, 2021.

23. Ruhollah Khomeini, *The Imam versus Zionism* (Tehran: Ministry of Islamic Guidance, Islamic Republic of Iran, 1984).

24. Christine Hauser, "Holocaust Conference in Iran Provokes Outrage," *The New York Times*, December 12, 2006, https://www.nytimes.com/2006/12/12/world/middleeast/13holocaustcnd.html, accessed February 9, 2021 and Yaakov Lapin, "White supremacist holds rally in Syria," Ynetnews.com, November 27, 2005, https://www.ynetnews.com/articles/0,7340,L-3175767,00.html, accessed February 9, 2021.

25. TOI staff, "Saudis Remove Anti-Semitism and Anti-Zionism from Textbooks — Monitoring Group," *The Times of Israel*, December 17, 2020, https://www.timesofisrael.com/anti-semitism-and-anti-zionsim-leaving-saudi-textbooks-monitoring-group/, accessed February 16, 2021 and Neil J. Kressel, *"The Sons of Pigs and Apes": Muslim Antisemitism and the Conspiracy of Silence* (Washington: Potomac Books, 2012).

26. TOI staff, "Saudis Remove Anti-Semitism and Anti-Zionism."

27. TOI staff, "Saudis Remove Anti-Semitism and Anti-Zionism."

28. "International Recognition of Israel," Jewish Virtual Library, https://www.jewishvirtuallibrary.org/international-recognition-of-israel, accessed February 23, 2021.

29. "United Nations General Assembly Resolution 3379," Wikipedia, https://en.wikipedia.org/wiki/United_Nations_General_Assembly_Resolution_3379#Voting_record_for_Resolution_3379, accessed February 23, 2021.

30. Pierre Birnbaum, "The French Radical Right: From Anti-Semitic Zionism to Anti-Semitic Anti-Zionism," in *Anti-Semitism and Anti-Zionism*.

31. Naomi Blank, "Redefining the Jewish Question from Lenin to Gorbachev: Terminology or Ideology?" in *Jews and Jewish Life in Russia and the Soviet Union*, ed. Yaacov Ro'i (Ilford: Frank Cass, 1995).

32. Joseph Heller, *The United States, the Soviet Union and the Arab-Israeli Conflict, 1948-67: Superpower Rivalry* (Manchester: Manchester University Press, 2010) and Walter Laqueur, *The Struggle*

for the Middle East: The Soviet Union and the Middle East, 1958-68 (London: Routledge, 2017).

33. Stephen H. Norwood, *Antisemitism and the American Far Left* (Cambridge: Cambridge University Press, 2013).

34. Perusing the Communist Party USA's website shows the party's continued opposition to Israel as a Jewish state and to Zionism, and their support for Palestinian national self-determination is clear.

35. The Democratic Socialists of America have not only voted to adopt BDS but to promote BDS organizing. Democratic Socialists of America, "Democratic Socialists of America commit to National BDS Organizing," BDS, August 13, 2019, https://bdsmovement.net/news/democratic-socialists-america-commit-national-bds-organizing, accessed February 4, 2021.

36. Palestinian Boycott, Divestment and Sanctions National Committee (BNC), "Socialist International of 140 Global Political Parties Adopts BDS, Calls for Military Embargo on Israel," BDS, July 5, 2018, https://bdsmovement.net/news/socialist-international-140-global-political-parties-adopts-bds-calls-military-embargo-israel, accessed February 4, 2021.

37. "Theodore Herzl on Africa," The Jewish Virtual Library, https://www.jewishvirtuallibrary.org/theodor-herzl-on-africa, accessed February 25, 2021.

38. Quotation taken from Haim Yacobi, *Israel and Africa: A Genealogy of Moral Geography* (New York: Routledge, 2017).

39. Yacobi, *Israel and Africa* and Anita Shapira, *Ben-Gurion: Father of Modern Israel*, trans. Anthony Berris (New Haven: Yale University Press, 2014).

40. Yacobi, *Israel and Africa*.

41. Robin D. G. Kelley, *Hammer and Hoe: Alabama Communists During the Great Depression* (Chapel Hill: University of North Carolina Press, 2015) and Erik S. McDuffie, *Sojourning for Freedom: Black Women, American Communism, and the Making of Black Left Feminism* (Durham: Duke University Press, 2011).

42. As Angela Davis writes, Black radicals adopted a Palestinian perspective. Benton, "Angela Davis Makes the Palestinian Struggle Hers."

43. Greg Thomas, "The Black Panther Party – For Palestine," *Simodoun*, 30 September 2016, https://samidoun.net/2016/09/the-black-panther-party-for-palestine-by-greg-thomas/, accessed February 26, 2021.

44. The Black Congressional Caucus backs Israel's right to exist as a Jewish and democratic state and further views it as such. Nevertheless, it has been critical of Israeli policies. See, for example, a recent statement about African migrants that makes its position clear. "Congressional Black Caucus Urges Israel Not To Deport African Migrants," Jewish Telegraphic Agency, February 27, 2018, https://forward.com/tag/congressional-black-caucus/, accessed February 26, 2021. Black churches, especially evangelical ones, largely support Israel. See: Roger Baumann, "Political Engagement Meets the Prosperity Gospel: African American Christian Zionism and Black Church Politics," *Sociology of Religion* 77, no. 4, (Winter 2016).

45. "Martin Luther King on Anti-Zionism," *The Jewish Virtual Library*, https://www.jewishvirtuallibrary.org/martin-luther-king-on-anti-zionism, February 26, 2021.

10

1. Gensler, *Ethics and the Golden Rule* and Wattles, *The Golden Rule*.
2. Hadassa Ben-Itto, *The Lie that Wouldn't Die: The Protocols of the Elders of Zion* (Southgate: Vallentine Mitchell, 2018).
3. Ellen Schrecker, *Many are the Crimes: McCarthyism in America* (Princeton: Princeton University Press, 1999).
4. Selemani Murekezi, *The Truth about Rwandan Genocide and How I Survived It: Rwandan Genocide* (Scotts Valley: CreateSpace, 2010); Linda Melvern, *Conspiracy to Murder: The Rwandan Genocide* (London: Verso, 2006); and Christopher C. Taylor, *Sacrifice as Terror: The Rwandan Genocide of 1994* (New York: Routledge, 2020).
5. Martin A. Lee and Bruce Shlain *Acid Dreams: The Complete Social History of LSD: The CIA, the Sixties, and Beyond* (New York: Grove/Atlantic, 2007).
6. Allan M. Brandt, *The Cigarette Century: The Rise, Fall, and Deadly Persistence of the Product that Defined America* (New York: Basic Books, 2009).
7. Saul Friedländer, *The Years of Persecution: Nazi Germany and the Jews 1939-45*, vol. 1 (London: Phoenix, 2007).
8. Francis R. Nicosia and David Scrase, eds., *Jewish Life in Nazi Germany: Dilemmas and Responses* (New York: Berghahn Books, 2010).
9. Cassam, *Conspiracy Theories*, 5.

11

1. See: Peter Singer, *Marx: A Very Short Introduction*, Second Edition (Oxford: Oxford University Press, 2018).
2. Walter D. Mignolo, *The Darker Side of Western Modernity: Global Futures, Decolonial Options* (Durham: Duke University Press, 2011). In this landmark book, Mignolo both describes the "darker side" of Western history, particularly its history of colonialism, and also how to approach the history of the world from a decolonial perspective.
3. Mignolo, *The Darker Side*.
4. Mignolo, *The Darker Side*.
5. "There are Christian atheists and Jewish atheists, you read the Bible in a Christian way," Sacks said in response. "Christianity has an adversarial way of reading what it calls the Old Testament — it has to because it says 'We've gone one better, we have a New Testament.'" Jewish Telegraphic Agency, "UK chief rabbi: Richard Dawkins' Bible slam anti-Semitic," September 16, 2012, https://www.timesofisrael.com/uk-chief-rabbi-richard-dawkins-bible-slam-anti-semitic/, accessed February 19, 2021.
6. Decolonial theory was developed to critique Western modernity and it is used primarily to critique Western colonialism. There have been recent studies examining Chinese imperialism, though these are much more balanced. Take, for example, the study on Chinese intervention in Africa whose title poses a question: Giles Mohan et al., *Chinese Migrants and African Development: New Imperialists or Agents of Change?* (London: Zed Books, 2014) compared to books by the same publisher on European or American involvement in Africa.
7. Newman, *Safavid Iran* and Payaslian, *History of Armenia*.
8. A classic example of this is Ira M. Lapidus, *History of Islamic Societies* (Cambridge: Cambridge University Press, 2014), which is a standard textbook on Islamic societies and presents Islamic imperialism is benign terms.
9. Newman, *Safavid Iran* and Payaslian, *History of Armenia*.
10. For Turkey see: Umut Uzer, *An Intellectual History of Turkish Nationalism: Between Turkish Ethnicity and Islamic Identity* (Salt Lake City: The University of Utah Press, 2016); Michael Axworthy, *Revolutionary Iran: A history of the Islamic Republic* (London: Penguin Books, 2019) or Maryam Panah, *The Islamic Republic and*

The World: Global Dimensions of the Iranian Revolution (London: Pluto Press, 2007). Significantly, the post-Ottoman Turkish state, the Chinese state after Mao, and the Iran state after Khomeini use the term republic to describe themselves, a typically anti-imperial term.

11. Nisan, *Minorities in the Middle East.*

12. See the following Uyghur testimonies recounted on the Amnesty International website: https://www.amnesty.org/en/latest/news/2020/02/china-uyghurs-living-abroad-tell-of-campaign-of-intimidation/; Gardner Bovingdon, *The Uyghurs: Strangers in their Own Land* (New York: Columbia University Press, 2020).

13. Many observers are concerned that the debt African countries are currently accruing to pay for infrastructure projects will result in debt traps that will then lead to Chinese control over natural resources. Wade Shepard, "What China Is Really Up To In Africa," *Forbes*, October 3, 2019, https://www.forbes.com/sites/wadeshepard/2019/10/03/what-china-is-really-up-to-in-africa/?sh=-5cafc74f5930, accessed February 23, 2021.

14. The concept of peoples or ethnic groups far predates modern nationalism, but the idea of modern national self-determination of nation-states run by democratically elected governments ruling over citizens is a modern articulation of this idea that began in Europe. Thus, all movements for national self-determination today are influenced at least in part by this modern articulation, which began in Europe. Yonah Alexander and Robert A. Friedlander, eds., *Self-Determination: National, Regional, and Global Dimensions* (London: Routledge, 2019).

15. Muriel E. Chamberlain, *Longman Companion to the Formation of the European Empires, 1488 to 1920* (London: Routledge, 2014) and James R. Lehning, *European Colonialism since 1700* (Cambridge: Cambridge University Press, 2013).

16. A brief survey of books on decolonialism or postcolonial theory that include Palestine is indicative of this view.

17. Berlinski, "The Cold War's Arab Spring."

18. The first editions are Eric J. Hobsbawm, *The Invention of Tradition* (Cambridge: Cambridge University Press, 1983) and Benedict Anderson, *Imagined Communities: Reflections on the Origin and*

Spread of Nationalism (London: Verso Editions, 1983). Both books have been revised and updated.

19. Christopher Lloyd GoGwilt, *The Invention of the West: Joseph Conrad and the Double-Mapping of Europe and Empire* (Stanford: Stanford University Press, 1998) and David Hamilton Murdoch, *The American West: The Invention of a Myth* (Reno: University of Nevada Press, 2003).

20. Niels Peter Lemche, *Canaanites and Their Land: The Tradition of the Canaanites* (London: Continuum International Pub. Group, 1991), Keith W. Whitelam, *The Invention of Ancient Israel: The Silencing of Palestinian History* (London: Routledge, 1997), and Thomas L. Thompson, *The Mythic Past: Biblical Archaeology and the Myth of Israel* (New York: Basic Books, 1999).

21. Adam H. Becker, *Revival and Awakening: American Evangelical Missionaries in Iran and the Origins of Assyrian Nationalism* (Chicago: The University of Chicago Press, 2015).

22. This can be seen with the rise of courses and scholarship on global religions within the American academy and the respect with which their texts are treated.

23. Alan T. Levenson, "Was the Documentary Hypothesis Tainted by Wellhausen's Antisemitism?," TheTorah.com, https://www.thetorah.com/article/was-the-documentary-hypothesis-tainted-by-wellhausens-antisemitism, accessed February 26, 2021.

24. While there has been an effort in recent years to hire more faculty specialized in Middle Eastern and Sephardic Jewish history, this generalization remains true.

25. For a link to the video and other material on the "invisible gorilla," see http://www.theinvisiblegorilla.com/, accessed February 22, 2021.

26. Christopher Chabris and Daniel Simons, *The Invisible Gorilla* (New York: Crown Publishers, 2010).

27. Human Rights Watch, "Saudi Arabia: Clarify Status of Uyghur Detainees," *Human Rights Watch*, November 23, 2020, https://www.hrw.org/news/2020/11/23/saudi-arabia-clarify-status-uyghur-detainees, accessed February 22, 2021.

28. Far-left news outlets like *Democracy Now!* consistently report on Saudi human rights abuses due to the Saudi-US alliance. In contrast,

their reporting on Iranian human rights abuses is far more limited. The alliance with the US makes Saudi Arabia white by proxy.

29. Storay Karimi, "Refile - Afghanistan Probes Report Iranian Border Guards Forced Migrants into River, Many Drowned," Reuters, May 3, 2020, https://www.reuters.com/article/afghanistan-iran-migrants/refile-afghanistan-probes-report-iranian-border-guards-forced-migrants-into-river-many-drowned-idUSL4N2CL05G?edition-redirect=in, accessed February 9, 2021.

30. Jessica Donati and Ehsanullah Amiri, "The Last Sikhs and Hindus in Afghanistan Plead for U.S. Help," *The Wall Street Journal*, April 18, 2020, https://www.wsj.com/articles/the-last-sikhs-and-hindus-in-afghanistan-plead-for-u-s-help-11587218401, accessed February 9, 2021.

31. Hershel Shanks and Susan F. Singer, "Digging at Temple Mount Verges on the Unholy," December 24, 1999, *Los Angeles Times*, https://www.latimes.com/archives/la-xpm-1999-dec-24-me-47187-story.html, accessed February 26, 2021.

32. Butz, *The Hoax*, 14.

33. Butz, *The Hoax*, 116.

34. Butz, *The Hoax*, 295.

35. Butz, *The Hoax*, 294.

36. Butz, *The Hoax*, 58.

37. Butz, *The Hoax*, 73.

38. Butz, *The Hoax*, 414.

39. Butz, *The Hoax*, 163.

40. See for example Butz, *The Hoax*, 21, 56, 59, 66, 120, 136, 163, and many other mentions.

41. Butz, *The Hoax*, 234.

42. Compare Butz's views to those of David Duke, *Jewish Supremacism*.

43. Butz, *The Hoax*, chapter 6.

12

1. Stalin, for example, used the term "class enemies" to demonize members of the bourgeoisie and especially the kulaks. Other examples of communist class terror are documented in Nicolas Werth, Karel Bartošek, Jean-Louis Panné, Jean-Louis Margolin, Andrzej Paczkowski, and Stéphane Courtois, *The Black Book of Communism: Crimes, Terror,*

Repression, ed. Mark Kramer, trans. Jonathan Murphy (Cambridge: Harvard University Press, 1999).

2. Werth et al., *The Black Book of Communism*.

3. Gerhard Simon, *Nationalism and Policy towards the Nationalities in the Soviet Union*, trans. Karen Forster and Oswald Forster (New York: Routledge, 2019).

4. The practice of Sinicization is especially strong in Tibet and the Muslim provinces. See: Jane Ardley, *The Tibetan Independence Movement: Political, Religious and Gandhian Perspectives* (London: Routledge, 2002) and Jean A. Berlie, *Islam in China: Hui and Uyghurs Between Modernization and Sinicization* (Bangkok: White Lotus Press, 2004).

5. Choueiri, *Arab Nationalism*.

6. Eric Nelson, *The Hebrew Republic: Jewish Sources and the Transformation of European Political Thought* (Cambridge: Harvard University Press, 2010).

7. Edward Palmer Thompson, *The Making of the English Working Class* (London: Penguin Books, 2013). The book was first published in 1963.

8. Victor Davis Hanson, *The Second World Wars: How the First Global Conflict Was Fought and Won* (New York: Basic Books, 2017).

9. Peter Gay, *The Enlightenment: An Interpretation* (New York: AA Knopf, 1966).

10. Stephen Eric Bronner, *Critical Theory: A Very Short Introduction* (Oxford: Oxford University Press, 2019).

11. For critical theorists who not only reject anti-Semitism and anti-Zionism but use the methods of critical theory to analyze both, see: Critical Theories of Antisemitism Network, https://criticaltheoriesofantisemitism.net/, accessed April 25, 2021. Although the organization of these scholars is defunct, their writings on anti-Semitism and anti-Zionism are important contributions to the field and show the different strands among critical theorists on Israel and Jews. See for example: Jack Jacobs, *The Frankfurt School, Jewish Lives, and Antisemitism* (Cambridge University Press, 2014), Robert Fine and Philip Spencer, *Antisemitism and the Left: On the Return of the Jewish Question* (with Philip Spencer, Manchester: MUP, 2017) and Lars Fisher, 'Marxism's Other Jewish Questions,' in *Jews and Leftist*

Politics. Judaism, Israel, Antisemitism, and Gender, eds. Jack Jacobs (New York: Cambridge University Press, 2017), 67–83.

12. Herbert Marcuse, "Repressive Tolerance," in Robert Paul Wolff, Barrington Moore Jr., and Herbert Marcuse, *A Critique of Pure Tolerance* (Boston: Beacon Press, 1965).

13

1. Mary Douglas, *Purity and Danger: An Analysis of Concepts of Pollution and Taboo* (London: Routledge, 2006).
2. Douglas, *Purity and Danger*, 44.
3. Douglas, *Purity and Danger*, 200.
4. Douglas, *Purity and Danger*, 215.
5. Douglas, *Purity and Danger*, 169.
6. Douglas, *Purity and Danger*, 172.
7. Lipstadt, *Denying the Holocaust*, chapter 7.
8. Douglas, *Purity and Danger*, xxi.
9. Douglas, *Purity and Danger*, xvi.

14

1. Michael Lewis, *The Big Short* (New York: W.W. Norton, 2010).
2. *A Brief Guide to the Haram al-Sharif* was the official publication of the Waqf that controlled the Al-Aqsa Mosque.
3. Elad Benari, *Abbas: Palestinians Own History*, Arutz Sheva, May 25, 2011, https://www.israelnationalnews.com/News/News.aspx/144470, accessed February 28, 2021. The full video can be seen here: "Abbas claims a fictitious 9000 year-old Palestinian history in Israel," Official Palestinian Authority TV, May 14, 2011, Palestinian Media Watch, https://palwatch.org/page/2766, accessed February 28, 2021.
4. I was told this story by an informant who attended a service at which the synagogue members were aware that they were being watched by PAVA (the domestic security office) agents perhaps due to the informant's attendance. I do not know if this chant is sounded at the end of services not subject to surveillance.

15

1. Arthur Butz, "A Short Introduction to the Study of Holocaust Revisionism," *The Daily Northwestern*, May 13, 1991.
2. Sarah Dreier, "Swastikas, hate words send shock waves through NU," *The Daily Northwestern*, February 18, 2003, https://dailynorthwestern.com/2003/02/18/archive-manual/swastikas-hate-words-send-shock-waves-through-nu/, accessed February 5, 2021.
3. Tyler Pager, "More Swastikas, Racist Graffiti Found in Library," *The Daily Northwestern*, April 16, 2015, https://dailynorthwestern.com/2015/04/16/campus/more-swastikas-racist-graffiti-found-in-library/, accessed February 5, 2021, and Brian L. Cox, "Ex-NU students plead guilty to lesser charges," *Chicago Tribune*, November 21, 2016, https://www.chicagotribune.com/news/breaking/ct-northwestern-chapel-vandalism-met-20161121-story.html, accessed February 5, 2021.
4. Jasett Chatham, "Butz's Denial of Holocaust Irritates NU," *The Daily Northwestern*, February 6, 2006, https://dailynorthwestern.com/2006/02/06/archive-manual/butzs-denial-of-holocaust-irritates-nu/, accessed February 5, 2021.
5. Editors, "Only fair to give Butz a forum," *The Daily Northwestern*, February 15, 2006, https://dailynorthwestern.com/2006/02/15/archive-manual/only-fair-to-give-butz-a-forum/, accessed February 5, 2021.
6. Arthur Butz, "Iran has the US's Number," *The Daily Northwestern*, February 14, 2006.
7. Michael Hoffman, "Advertisement was hateful," *The Daily Northwestern*, February 15, 2006.
8. "Active Holocaust Denial Groups," *Southern Poverty Law Center*, https://www.splcenter.org/fighting-hate/intelligence-report/2015/active-holocaust-denial-groups, accessed February 27, 2021.
9. Nelson, *Israel Denial*, 152.
10. Nelson, *Israel Denial*, 152.
11. Lydia Ramsey, "Q&A with Steven Salaita," *The Daily Northwestern*, October 6, 2014, https://dailynorthwestern.com/2014/10/06/campus/qa-with-steven-salaita/, accessed February 7, 2021.
12. Jason Mast, "Steven Salaita Talks Academic Freedom after U. of I. Controversy," *The Daily Northwestern*, October 7, 2014, https://dailynorthwestern.com/?s=Salaita+talks+free+speech+, accessed February 7, 2021.

13. If Americans Knew Staff, "Zionist Head of Major Theological Consortium Has Been Pushed Out," Israel-Palestine News, March, 21, 2020, https://israelpalestinenews.org/zionist-head-of-major-theological-consortium-has-been-pushed-out/, accessed February 19, 2021. I had the privilege of meeting Rabbi Lehmann shortly before his formal inauguration ceremony. He told me he had not made any attempts to influence anyone else on his pro-Israel views, nor had he made any attempt to limit any pro-Palestinian events at GTU. I had met him as the West Coast book launch of *In Good Faith*, which took place at GTU. Rabbi Lehmann introduced the evening's event.

14. Morton Schapiro and Jonathan Holloway, "Statement Regarding Steven Thrasher by President, Provost," *Northwestern Now*, May 24, 2019, https://news.northwestern.edu/stories/2019/05/steven-thrasher/, accessed February 7, 2021.

15. William A. Jacobson, "Vassar Faculty-Sponsored Anti-Israel Event Erupts in Controversy," *Legal Insurrection*, February 8, 2016, https://legalinsurrection.com/?s=Vassar+faculty-sponsored+anti-Israel+&image.x=0&image.y=0, accessed February 7, 2021.

16. Mark Sheldon, "Letter to the Editor: The Walkout's Purpose was Derailed by Anti-Israel Sentiment," *The Daily Northwestern*, February 2, 2017, https://dailynorthwestern.com/2017/02/02/opinion/letter-to-the-editor-the-walkouts-purpose-was-derailed-by-anti-israel-sentiment/ /, accessed February 7, 2021.

17. Sheldon, "Letter to the Editor."

18. Ajay Nadig, "Letter to the Editor: Response to Letter by Philosophy Lecturer Mark Sheldon," *The Daily Northwestern*, February 5, 2017, https://dailynorthwestern.com/2017/02/05/opinion/letter-to-the-editor-response-to-letter-by-philosophy-lecturer-mark-sheldon/, accessed February 7, 2021.

19. Omar Shanti, "Letter to the Editor: Muslims Can think for Themselves," *The Daily Northwestern*, February 6, 2017, https://dailynorthwestern.com/2017/02/06/opinion/letter-to-the-editor-muslims-can-think-for-themselves/, accessed February 7, 2021.

20. Blake Flayton, "On the Frontlines of Progressive Anti-Semitism," *The New York Times*, November 14, 2019, https://www.nytimes.com/2019/11/14/opinion/college-israel-anti-semitism.html, accessed February 7, 2021.

21. Morningstar Manager Research, "The Morningstar ESG Commitment Level: Our First Assessment of 100-Plus Strategies and 40 Asset Managers," November 17, 2020, 1-3, https://www.morningstar.com/content/dam/marketing/shared/pdfs/Research/ESG_Commitment_Level_White_Paper_2020.pdf, accessed April 20, 2021.

22. Morningstar Manager Research, "The Morningstar ESG Commitment Level."

23. Morningstar Advisor Insight, "Investing for Social Justice From the Bottom: Advisor Rachel Robasciotti Listens to Groups on the Ground to Make an Impact," August 24, 2020, https://www.morningstar.com/articles/998577/investing-for-social-justice-from-the-bottom-up, accessed April 20, 2021.

24. U.S. Securities and Exchange Commission, "SEC Charges Ratings Agency with Disclosure And Internal Controls Failures Relating To Undisclosed Model Adjustments," February 16, 2021, https://www.sec.gov/news/press-release/2021-29#:~:text=The%20SEC's%20complaint%2C%20filed%20today,relief%2C%20disgorgement%20with%20prejudgment%20interest%2C, accessed April 20, 2021.

25. Morningstar, Morningstar Credit Ratings, LLC Position Paper: SEC v. Morningstar Credit Ratings, LLC, February 21, 2021, https://www.morningstar.com/content/dam/marketing/shared/pdfs/legal/credit-rating-sec-litigation-position-paper.pdf, accessed April 20, 2021.

26. Madeline Fox, "Harassment concerns prompt Palestinian activist to leave Northwestern without speaking at Event," *The Daily Northwestern*, February 23, 2016, https://dailynorthwestern.com/?s=Harassment+concerns+prompt+Palestinian+, accessed February 7, 2021.

27. Catherine Kim, "Organizer Rasmea Odeh speaks at Northwestern for SJP's Israeli Apartheid Week," *The Daily Northwestern*, May 16, 2017, https://dailynorthwestern.com/?s=Organizer+Rasmea+Odeh+-speaks+at+Northwestern+for+SJP, accessed February 7, 2021 and Aimee Levitt, "Jewish Students Mustered A Rare Unity To Protest This Palestinian Activist," *Forward* May 16, 2017, https://forward.com/news/372112/jewish-students-mustered-a-rare-unity-to-protest-this-palestinian-activist/, accessed February 7, 2021.

28. Jewish Voice for Peace, *On Anti-Semitism: Solidarity and the Struggle for Justice* (Chicago: Haymarket Books, 2017).

29. Zach Kessel, "Kessel: Anti-Semitism is a Problem, Not a Political Tool," *The Daily Northwestern*, January 13, 2020, https://dailynorthwestern.com/2020/01/13/opinion/kessel-anti-semitism-is-a-problem-not-a-political-tool/, accessed February 7, 2021.

30. Kessel, "Kessel: Anti-Semitism is a Problem."

31. Students for Justice in Palestine, "Letter to the Editor: Kessel Misses the Mark on Anti-Semitism," *The Daily Northwestern*, January 28, 2020, https://dailynorthwestern.com/2020/01/28/opinion/letter-to-the-editor-kessel-misses-the-mark-on-anti-semitism/, accessed February 7, 2021.

32. Students for Justice in Palestine, "Letter to the Editor: Kessel Misses the Mark."

33. Douglas, *Purity and Danger*, 200.

34. Douglas, *Purity and Danger*, 215.

35. Douglas, *Purity and Danger*, 169.

36. Douglas, *Purity and Danger*, 172.

37. Christian Schneider, "Panel Warns of Growing Threat of Antisemitism on College Campuses," *The College Fix*, September 28, 2020, https://www.thecollegefix.com/?s=panel+warns+of+, accessed February 7, 2021.

38. Matthew Kassel, "Justice Dems Boosted this Candidate until She Disagreed with Them on Israel," Jewish Insider, October 26, 2020, https://jewishinsider.com/2020/10/justice-dems-was-boosting-georgette-gomez/, accessed February 7, 2021.

39. The Palestinian Youth Movement – San Diego, Jewish Voice for Peace – San Diego, Unión del barrio – San Diego, and Center for Interdisciplinary Environmental Justice, "How Liberal Zionism Hurts us More," *Mondoweiss*, October 7, 2020, https://mondoweiss.net/2020/10/how-liberal-zionism-hurt-us-more/, accessed February 7, 2021.

40. The Palestinian Youth Movement et al., "How liberal Zionism Hurts us More."

41. Elyssa Cherney, "Jewish Groups Allege an 'Alarming Increase in Anti-Semitism and Anti-Zionism' at University of Illinois' Urbana-Champaign Campus," *Chicago Tribune*, October 23, 2020, https://www.chicagotribune.com/news/breaking/ct-university-of-illinois-ur-

bana-champaign-anti-semitism-complaint-20201024-qz53rtyb35h-h3ct2hvxbrsmofq-story.html, accessed February 7, 2021.

42. Morton Schapiro, email to the NU Community, Oct. 19, 2020.

43. NUCNC, Press Release, October 19, 2020.

44. NUCNC, Press Release, October 19, 2020.

45. Emily Sakai, "NUCNC partners with NU Dissenters to discuss militarism at NU," *The Daily Northwestern*, November 8, 2020, https://dailynorthwestern.com/2020/11/08/campus/events-campus/nucnc-partners-with-nu-dissenters-to-discuss-militarism-at-nu/, accessed February 23, 2021.

46. Over the course of the October protests, NUCNC issued at least two "Instagram stories" that relate to anti-Zionism while during the same time not mentioning any other conflict in the world outside of the US. The stories have passed their duration and are thus no longer on the Instagram account, though there are several pictures of Angela Davis and, as the *Daily Northwestern* article cited above makes clear, NUCNC links Black and Palestinian political struggles.

47. "Guest Column: Jewish students, faculty and alumni respond to Morton Schapiro," *The Daily Northwestern*, October 21, 2020, https://dailynorthwestern.com/2020/10/21/opinion/lte-jewish-students-faculty-and-alumni-respond-to-morton-schapiro/, accessed October, 22, 2020.

48. Blake Flayton, "The Hate That Can't be Contained," *Tablet*, November 25, 2020, https://www.tabletmag.com/sections/news/articles/hate-cant-be-contained, accessed February 5, 2021.

49. Emma Rosenbaum and Yunkyo Kim, "In ASG Session Attended by over 200, Senate Passes Resolution Supporting Palestinian Human Rights," *The Daily Northwestern*, May 27, 2021, https://dailynorthwestern.com/2021/05/27/campus/in-asg-session-attended-by-over-200-senate-passes-resolution-supporting-palestinian-human-rights/, accessed June 1, 2021.

50. Mitchell Langbert, Anthony J. Quain, and Daniel B. Klein, "Faculty Voter Registration in Economics, History, Journalism, Law, and Psychology," *Econ Journal Watch* 13, no. 3 (September, 2016), https://econjwatch.org/articles/faculty-voter-registration-in-economics-history-journalism-communications-law-and-psychology, accessed February 7, 2021.

51. Nathan P. Kalmoe and Lilliana Mason, "Lethal Mass Partisanship: Prevalence, Correlates, & Electoral Contingencies," NCAPSA American Politics Meeting, January 2019, https://www.dannyhayes. org/uploads/6/9/8/5/69858539/kalmoe___mason_ncapsa_2019_-_lethal_partisanship_-_final_lmedit.pdf, accessed February 23, 2021.

52. Leor Zmigrod, Peter Jason Rentfrow, and Trevor W. Robbins, "The Partisan Mind: Is Extreme Political Partisanship Related to Cognitive Inflexibility?" *Journal of Experimental Psychology: General 149*, no. 3.

53. Tyler Cowen, "Be Suspicious of Simple Stories," *TEDx Mid Atlantic*, November 2009, transcript, https://www.ted.com/talks/tyler_cowen_be_suspicious_of_simple_stories/transcript?language=en, accessed February 23, 2021.

54. Charlotte Stoddart, "Is there a reproducibility crisis in science?" *Nature*: Nature Video, May 25, 2016, https://www.nature.com/articles/d41586-019-00067-3#:~:text=Reproducibility%20is%20a%20hot%20topic,to%20reproduce%20another%20group's%20experiments, accessed February 23, 2021.

55. John P. A. Ioannidis, "Why Most Published Research Findings Are False," *PLOS MEDICINE*, August 30, 2005, https://journals.plos.org/plosmedicine/article?id=10.1371/journal.pmed.0020124, accessed February 23, 2021.

56. Daniele Fanelli, "How Many Scientists Fabricate and Falsify Research? A Systematic Review and Meta-Analysis of Survey Data," *PLOS ONE* 4, no. 5 (May 29, 2009), https://journals.plos.org/plosone/article?id=10.1371/journal.pone.0005738, accessed February 7, 2021.

57. Christopher Allen and David M. A. Mehler, "Open Science Challenges, Benefits and Tips in Early Career and Beyond," *PLOS ONE* 17, no. 12 (May 1, 2019), https://journals.plos.org/plosbiology/article?id=10.1371/journal.pbio.3000246, accessed February 7, 2021.

58. John P. A. Ioannidis, T. D. Stanley, Hristos Doucouliagos, "The Power of Bias in Economics Research," *The Economic Journal* 127, no. 605 (October 2017).

59. Jay P. Greene, Albert Cheng, and Ian Kingsbury, "Are Educated People More Anti-Semitic?" *Tablet*, March 30, 2021, https://www.tabletmag.com/sections/news/articles/are-educated-people-more-anti-semitic-jay-greene-albert-cheng-ian-kingsbury, accessed April 20, 2021.

<u>16</u>

1. Philip Kurland and Ralph Lerner, eds. "James Madison at the Virginia Ratifying Convention, June 20, 1778," *The Founders' Constitution, Vol 1*, Chapter 13, Document 36 (Chicago: University of Chicago Press, 2001).
2. Ashley Fernandes, "Why Did So Many Doctors Become Nazis?," *Tablet*, December 10, 2020, https://www.tabletmag.com/sections/history/articles/fernandes-doctors-who-became-nazis, accessed February 5, 2021.
3. "Audit of Anti-Semitic Incidents: Year in Review 2018," ADL, https://www.adl.org/audit2018, accessed February 23, 2021.
4. Ben Sales, "GOP Congresswoman Blamed Deadly Forest Fire on Jewish Space Laser," *The Jerusalem Post*, January 29, 2021, https://www.jpost.com/american-politics/marjorie-taylor-greene-blamed-deadly-forest-fire-on-rothschild-inc-657130, accessed January 27, 2021.
5. Pearson, "Northwestern University."